Making a
Success of Marriage

BOOKS BY DAVID YOUNT

Growing in Faith: A Guide for the Reluctant Christian

Breaking Through God's Silence: A Guide to Effective Prayer

Spiritual Simplicity: Simplify Your Life and Refresh Your Spirit

Ten Thoughts to Take into Eternity: Living Wisely in Light of the Afterlife

Be Strong and Courageous: Letters to My Children about Being Christian

What Are We to Do? Living the Sermon on the Mount

Faith under Fire: Religion's Role in the American Dream

The Future of Christian Faith in America

Celebrating the Rest of Your Life: A Baby Boomer's Guide to Spirituality

How the Quakers Invented America

Growing in Faith: A Guide for the New Millennium

A Journey through America's Spiritual Utopias: From the Cloister to the Communes

Celebrating the Single Life: Making a Success of Life on Your Own

SYNDICATED COLUMN

Amazing Grace
(Scripps Howard News Service)

TELEVISION HOST

Amazing Grace
(Comcast)

Making a Success of Marriage

Planning for Happily Ever After

David Yount

ROWMAN & LITTLEFIELD PUBLISHERS, INC.
Lanham • Boulder • New York • Toronto • Plymouth, UK

Published by Rowman & Littlefield Publishers, Inc.
A wholly owned subsidiary of The Rowman & Littlefield Publishing Group, Inc.
4501 Forbes Boulevard, Suite 200, Lanham, Maryland 20706
http://www.rowmanlittlefield.com

Estover Road, Plymouth PL6 7PY, United Kingdom

British Library Cataloguing in Publication Information Available

Library of Congress Cataloging-in-Publication Data

Yount, David.
  Making a success of marriage : planning for happily ever after / David Yount.
      p. cm.
  Includes bibliographical references and index.
  ISBN 978-1-4422-0009-8 (cloth : alk. paper) — ISBN 978-1-4422-0011-1 (electronic)
  1. Marriage. 2. Marital quality. 3. Marriage counseling. I. Title.
  HQ734.Y855 2010
  646.7'8—dc22   2009027626

Printed in the United States of America

For Rebecca
Love is eternal.

And for my Reader
Marriage is, for most of us, life's greatest adventure: to commit ourselves to loving a stranger for richer, for poorer, in sickness and in health, forsaking all others, until death do us part.

It would help immeasurably to possess a map to guide us through this adventure. This is such a map.

Contents

Preface

Whatever Happened to Marriage?

*J*ust as the U.S. population topped 300 million, demographers revealed that, for the first time in history, fewer than half of the nation's households are headed by married couples. Today, the typical American adult is unmarried, either living a solitary life or residing with unrelated persons.

So don't be fooled by those smiling couples you see in newspaper wedding announcements. Marriage, long in decline, is now a minority institution and shows no signs of revival. It's a cause for concern, and not just for sentimental reasons.

In recent decades, wedlock has fallen victim to a near 50 percent divorce rate. Second and third marriages contracted after divorce suffer an even bleaker success rate. Moreover, failure breeds failure, as children of divorce carry their experience of dysfunctional family life into their own adult years. Little wonder that many young Americans shy from making the mistakes of their parents.

But is marriage itself a mistake? To be sure, contemporary Americans retain their capacity to love and their desire to be loved. And no one would argue that sexual attraction has waned in the twenty-first century. What *has* happened is that those men and women who eventually do decide to wed, do so much later than ever in history and with more fragile commitment.

Part of the reason is economic. Today, men and women alike typically carry heavy burdens of personal debt through their twenties into their thirties and beyond. Theoretically, two can live as cheaply as one, but not if both are burdened by payments for college expenses and auto loans.

Accordingly, an American woman contemplating marriage realizes that she will probably have to continue working outside the home, indefinitely postponing a family while her biological clock keeps ticking down. She may decide it is more to her advantage to postpone marriage, keep her salary, and maintain professional freedom.

Taking that option will not necessarily deny her romance and a sex life, which she can find outside marriage in contemporary America if her religious scruples permit. Reliable contraception has long since removed the fear of unsought pregnancy.

Moreover, the traditional stigma attached to unmarried couples living together has been largely replaced by tolerance, if not open approval. Many baby boomer parents even encourage their children to enter into what used to be called "trial" marriage—as though the experience of living together physically could guarantee subsequent wedlock to be lasting.

We know it doesn't. The great majority of cohabiting couples never marry their partner. Most break up within five years of living together, and those who eventually do decide to wed suffer a worse-than-average divorce rate. Should they have a child—either while still living together or after marriage—they are even more vulnerable to breakup than the old-fashioned couples who postpone setting up households until after they wed.

The French, celebrated for amour, have already outdistanced Americans in dispensing of wedlock, with marriage rates 45 percent less than ours. Close to half of all births in France are to unmarried persons.

If marriage is in steep decline, how is it that our nation's population is growing? It is due to immigration and the tendency of newly arrived Americans to desire larger families. Also to the burgeoning numbers of births to unwed men and women. The Centers for Disease Control and Prevention report that nearly 36 percent of all births in America are to unmarried mothers, the highest in history. Georgia Supreme Court Chief Justice Leah Ward Sears laments that she "must work within a system designed only to pick up the pieces after families have fallen apart or failed to come together."

I am old enough to remember a time when men and women barely out of their teens eagerly sought a lifelong partner to marry. During the summer following the graduation of my college class, there was a rush of my classmates to the altar, and I was employed many times over as best man or usher. Recently, my college classmates celebrated their fiftieth annual reunion, and sure enough, most of the old couples are still married to each other.

But nostalgia is insufficient to revive the married state as the way in which Americans aspire to live. Marriage has been around since people began inhabiting the earth, and long before couples were drawn to each other by love and romance. With notable exceptions, affection as a basis for choosing a mate is a fairly recent development in human history.

The reason all societies hallow and regulate marriage is because it is acknowledged to be the cornerstone of civilized life. Gay American couples illustrate this fact when they demand the right to marry. Marriage is the voluntary acceptance of mutual responsibility. In traditional marriage, that responsibility extends to the children of the couple. Civilized society cannot endure without couples assuming responsibility for each other and for their offspring.

Imagine a society composed of single persons who hook up temporarily and at random, spawning children for whom they feel little affection and no commitment. That would be a society resembling an overgrown singles bar—a long retreat to savagery.

Of course, the single life is not automatically a self-centered and socially uninvolved one. It is a worthy alternative to marriage and can yield great satisfaction. In my book, *Celebrating the Single Life*, I suggested strategies to ensure that living alone does not translate into living apart from life.

In any case, a man or woman is not likely to embrace marriage as a purely civic duty, but rather because it promises exclusive and mutual devotion and assistance, an unparalleled richness of affection and candor, and the possibility of converting love into new life.

There is nothing wrong with marriage, and everything right with it. What we need to fix are the expectations that couples bring to it and the strength of their commitment. Marriage can be revived, but only by one courageous couple at a time.

In this book I have confined my examples of marital success to husbands and wives, but rest assured, the principles apply equally to all committed couples.

Introduction

Against All Odds

Will it change my life altogether?
O tell me the truth about love.

W. H. Auden

"*D*on't marry him!" was the advice all my wife's friends gave her when we were dating. Had I been merely Becky's friend, instead of her suitor, I would have offered her the same counsel. I was about as ineligible a bachelor as possible: already into my forties, in debt and in a going-nowhere job, a divorced single parent of three little daughters whose mother left them completely to my care but lurked close enough to intrude on our lives. To further prejudice my marital prospects, each of the girls suffered learning disabilities, requiring special education and psychiatric counseling. I was pretty much of a mess myself, a chronic insomniac prone to self-pity and distraction.

Luckily, Becky didn't listen to her friends, and here we are together thirty years later determined to live happily ever after.

Not that it's been easy for her. When I met Becky she had just emerged from a brutal marriage and divorce and had barely two dimes to rub together. She also realized that, although she would inherit full-time responsibility for my three daughters, I could not give her children of our own. On top of all that, she had to continue working to keep the family afloat financially.

She sounds like a saint, doesn't she? Well, if saints can be sexy and smart, sophisticated and successful, then a saint she is, but she wears her halo lightly. I just thank God she's my wife and that we're still together. The best part of the marriage vows, I believe, is that bit about "till death do us part." That's the best life insurance anyone could ask for. It's not for sale. Rather, it's an

1

enduring love gift between a man and a woman that rests less on romance than on mutual respect, trust, friendship, and affection.

Although Becky and I got our first marriages wrong, we have gotten this one right. We picked ourselves up, dusted ourselves off, and started all over again. Failure isn't at all bad if couples can learn from it.

This year some 2.3 million Americans couples will wed, most of them for the first time. Marriage has been called the triumph of hope over experience. But as an institution, wedlock has been in trouble for a long time. Nearly half of first marriages end in divorce, twice the failure rate of the 1960s. For those who wed again, the survival rate only worsens. Fully three in five subsequent marriages will fail. The costs are horrendous—not just broken hearts, but shattered spirits, shrinking budgets, and neglected children.

I can't pretend to be Cupid with a quiver full of magic arrows that guarantee love will last, but there's a lot of practical wisdom about marriage out there that my wife and I have absorbed over the years, and I'd like to share it with you.

In one of Becky's novels she suggests two tests that reveal whether a marriage will survive: Can the couple vacation together without constant quarreling? And: Can they survive hanging wallpaper together? I'm happy to say that as a couple we pass the first test, and relieved that we have never attempted the second.

Life itself may be a predicament, but marriage is a challenge, a contract, and a commitment. By rights, it should also be a lifelong celebration. At best, two of God's creatures can discover that by joining forces they can solve life's largest predicament, or at least learn to laugh at it together, loving all the while.

First, let us confront the naysayers.

"I don't believe in marriage," the regal actress Katherine Hepburn complained to anyone who would listen. "It's bloody impractical to love, honor, and obey. If it weren't, you wouldn't have to sign a contract."[1] Bawdy actress Mae West agreed, wisecracking that "marriage is a great institution, but I ain't ready for an institution yet."[2]

I can't vouch for Mae, but I'm inclined to believe that the late, great Hepburn protested too much against wedlock. There was really only one marriage she didn't believe in—the one that kept her celebrated costar Spencer Tracy from becoming her own husband. Tracy was already a married man when she met him on the set of their first film. "I'm afraid I am a little too tall for you," she observed of the five-foot-nine actor on their introduction. "Don't worry," he replied. "I'll cut you down to size."[3]

Shortly thereafter, Tracy left his wife to become Hepburn's constant companion until, in failing health, he died in 1967. They never married, because the actor was a Catholic. Whether or not Hepburn truly believed in marriage, Tracy clearly did not believe in divorce. The actress survived, sharp-witted and single, to the age of ninety-six. She was an exception in a nation that continues to wed despite the dire statistics of divorce.

Nevertheless, marriage in the new millennium is no longer the central institution under which American households are organized and children are produced and raised. The most common living arrangement today is a household of unmarried adults with no children. Nearly two-thirds of American households have no offspring at home.[4]

What became of the traditional family? It has suffered from almost a 50 percent divorce rate plus a more than sixfold increase in the percentage of births to unmarried mothers. Those Americans who marry do so later than ever in our nation's history and typically only after a trial run.[5]

Social revolutions, like wars, leave victims in their wake. With the advantage of hindsight, it is now clear that a major victim of the sexual revolution of the 1960s was the institution of marriage. Given the availability of reliable contraception and a hip mantra—"If it feels good, do it"—holy wedlock fast became an optional lifestyle to be shunned or postponed by couples.

Desire and romance persist, but personal commitment has long since yielded to casual sex and cohabitation. In 1960 only one couple in a hundred was living together out of wedlock, but by the end of the century one in ten American men and women aged eighteen to twenty-nine were cohabiting.[6]

Today marriage is an afterthought for close to half of the couples who eventually do decide to wed after living together. The bad news is that marriages of couples who have cohabited are twice as likely to end in divorce. Moreover, instead of strengthening the cohabitors' casual living arrangement, the birth of a child makes breaking up even more likely.[7]

Like many Americans I was raised in a religious tradition that considers marriage to be a sacrament—a sure call on God's grace to enable men and women to keep their vows "for better, for worse, in sickness and in health, till death do us part." Cohabiting couples often wish for lifelong romance, but until they commit to one another, their love is fragile and untested.

In Britain the government has considered reviving common-law marriage to render the practice of sex without commitment more respectable. English commentator Melanie Phillips balks at the proposal, arguing that "the rights of marriage can follow only from accepting its responsibilities."[8] A century ago the playwright Henrik Ibsen expressed the same sentiment. "Marriage," he said, "is a thing you've got to give your whole mind to."[9]

People of faith believe that marriage mirrors the love that binds God to humankind. Although the history of religion portrays the Creator's commitment to his creatures, it also acknowledges his progeny's reluctance to return the favor. Samuel Johnson offered this appreciation: "Marriage is the best state for man in general, and every man is a worse man in proportion as he is unfit for the married state."[10]

There is a line from one of Shakespeare's sonnets that many couples include in their wedding ceremonies: "Love is not love which alters when it alteration finds."[11] People change. Husbands and wives are not the same persons they were when they took their vows to have and hold each another till death separates them. When the young Abraham Lincoln took Mary Todd to be his wife, he could not predict her fragile hold on sanity, nor could he reckon on the depths of depression to which he would be prone. Yet he inscribed Mary's wedding band, "Love is eternal."[12]

Strictly speaking, marriage is a contract, but few couples in the Western world approach wedlock as purely a business proposition. Unlike commercial negotiations, love rests on deep devotion and emotion. When spouses negotiate with each other, they do so not as competitors but as equals, friends, and supporters. They trust each other, seeking mutual satisfaction rather than personal advantage.

Whereas success in business consists of getting what you want, love is about getting what you *need*—even when partners don't completely grasp at the outset of their life together just what that need might be.

Ironically, commercial negotiations have two advantages over lovers' quarrels. The former are guided by law, and they often employ mediators or arbitrators. Whereas, when couples collide, the spouses typically lack both guidelines and referees to steer them to agreement. Few of them consult marriage counselors. Those who do often wait too long to seek a professional perspective.

Making married love last relies on respecting differences, accepting apologies, letting go of the past, treading softly on the spouse's vulnerabilities, and leaving the door open to reconciliation after disputes. Outsiders instantly recognize good marriages by how intimate couples are. They spend time together, preferring each other's company to that of others. They share their interests, hopes, fears, and dreams. A good marriage is complementary, unafraid of differences, each spouse helping the other to grow as a distinct individual, even when that places an apparent distance between them. Devoted spouses touch each other physically and emotionally, and not just in the bedroom.

People who look at love from the standpoint of consumers rather than producers are inevitably disappointed. For love is, above all, the gift of oneself. True love knows no fear. A fervent lover runs the risk of appearing foolish and suffering real loss, notably of independent action. The lover not only lowers the drawbridge to his heart, but also leaves his armor behind, riding forth fully vulnerable to Cupid's arrows.

As readers of the Bible realize, once a lover is disarmed, his beloved may turn out to be an enemy. (Ask Samson about Delilah!) Still, to truly love, husbands and wives must overcome their self-protective fear of confrontation and commitment, foolishness, and loss of freedom. As Tennyson insisted, "'Tis better to have loved and lost/Than never to have loved at all."[13]

True love is disciplined. Whatever overlay of passion it may carry, married love is based on a simple, yet profound, comradeship, sensible and generous. But it is not so self-giving as to preclude self-respect. Just as you can't get blood out of a turnip, you can't get love out of a codependent, insecure, clinging spouse. Love requires a certain emptying of self to the other, but there must be a strong self to share with one's spouse.

Lamentably, some marriages fail because one spouse has grown while the other has shrunk. Ovid offered the simplest antidote: "To be loved," he said, "be lovable."[14] After a lifetime of acting in romantic roles, Charlton Heston concluded that lovemaking requires more enthusiasm than expertise. It is the one activity in life, the late actor affirmed, in which amateurs outshine the pros.[15]

No love, however authentic, is risk free. Even the love of God carries the risk that the Creator will demand more than we care to offer. It is easier in every instance to say, in effect: "Love me, but don't stay the night"—which may account for the fact that couples settle for "relationships" or engage lawyers to craft prenuptial "agreements" rather than make a simple but wholehearted commitment to love.

Clearly, for many couples that kind of lifelong commitment needs time to mature. After a decade of marriage, author Erica Jong and her husband, in the presence of their closest friends, finally elected to burn their prenuptial agreement. Jong predicts that, over time, such small conflagrations will become domestic rituals as courageous couples learn to trust one another rather than weighing the possibility of divorce even before they are wed.

Jong and her husband had reason to be shy of marriage. She had gone through three husbands before meeting Ken. He was twice divorced and had survived another long live-in relationship. Their wedding invitation was stamped in red: "A Triumph of Hope over Experience" over the line "Erica and Ken are astonished to announce their marriage."

The prenuptial agreement was her idea—to protect her money and to acknowledge that her judgment about men had been faulty and might be yet again. Ken, who is, of all things, a divorce lawyer, reluctantly went along with her. Today Jong acknowledges: "If you join your life with someone else's, you become a hostage to fortune in such a way that no legal document can protect you. Marriage is primal stuff—two people confronting their own mortality. It is not for the faint of heart." She predicts that priests, rabbis, and ministers will be asked to devise new vows, asking spouses: "Do you love one another enough to burn the prenup?"[16]

There is another contract that married couples happily burn—the mortgage papers on the homes they have shared long enough to pay off the loan. That's yet another kind of freedom, and it attests to having lived together long enough to come to trust one another. The seriousness of marriage is reflected by the fact that, when couples take on debts, both have to sign.

With marital breakup so common, it's little wonder that children of divorced parents are reluctant to make that commitment when they reach adulthood. Lacking trust and hope, some settle for cohabitation or serial relationships. Others question whether they can *afford* to get married.

David Blankenhorn, head of the Institute for American Values in New York, instead challenges young couples: "Can you afford *not* to get married?"[17] Financial cooperation and economies of scale, he notes, make married life more affordable than single living—one apartment and auto to share, along with a single set of furniture and appliances, and so on. But marriage also boasts the advantages of partnership—permanence, trust, sharing, mutual dependency, and an offsetting of individual weaknesses.

Marriage also changes attitudes, as demonstrated in my own exurban Virginia neighborhood. It took all of fifteen years for all of the eight townhouses in our row to be owned by the couples who live in them rather than be occupied by transient renters. The transformation has been dramatic. Now lawns are trimmed, yards are landscaped, flowers grow, homes are cared for. And we're all more neighborly, because we know we're going to be here together for a while.

Just like marriage!

Despite disincentives, each year some 2.3 million American couples pledge their troth "till death do us part," on average investing more than $30,000 in the wedding ceremony, reception, and honeymoon alone.[18] That's just the *average* outlay of all marriages, from elopements (where the only costs are the license and the justice of the peace's fee), to the rarified multimillion-dollar nuptials of celebrities.

The wedding industry in the United States extracts $50 billion a year from love-struck couples and their well-wishers. According to the *Washington Post*, the average American engagement now extends for sixteen months, during which time couples shop for $4 billion worth of furniture, $3 billion worth of housewares, and $400 million worth of tableware.[19]

It is a substantial investment of money, but nothing approaching the personal investment of love, trust, and self that yields dividends in a lasting marriage.

Marriage is a creative art, but it is in some respects also a science—a behavioral science governed by rules that anyone with sufficient motivation can follow. We can debate whether marriages are made in heaven, but I believe that God is a patron of committed love, and that good people can make good marriages.

Marriage is the ultimate do-it-yourself lifetime adventure. Whether you are already married or only contemplating wedlock, it's worth the effort to get it right.

A Fine Romance

Putting It Together for a Lifetime

> There is no more lovely, friendly, and charming relationship,
> communion, or company than a good marriage.
>
> Martin Luther

*M*any years ago, when I was dean of a Virginia college across the Potomac from Washington, D.C., I hosted groups of married couples for Marriage Encounters weekends. Some of the spouses were old enough to be mistaken for parents of our undergraduates.

When students and faculty inquired what these "oldsters" were studying, I answered that they were brushing up on their lives together—not unlike a 50,000-mile service checkup on the family automobile to keep it in running order.

Not least among the attractions of a Marriage Encounter was that spouses enjoyed a few days together free of domestic duties and the demands of their children. Yet another attraction was that, unlike much of marriage counseling, it was not a desperate measure. Perhaps best of all, participants looked forward to the opportunity to compare their own wedded lives with the experiences of other couples. Most spouses returned home relieved to have learned that the challenges and blessings of wedlock are remarkably similar from couple to couple.

Marriage Encounters has since become a worldwide nonprofit movement that boasts of millions of graduates and promises to "help married couples turn a good (or even ho-hum or boring) marriage into a *great* marriage."

According to their prospectus, a Marriage Encounter weekend helps couples

- Rediscover the spark that was there on their wedding day
- Rediscover the best friend they had when they were first married
- Learn how to keep their marriage vibrant and alive

If this strikes you as too good to be true, consider that participants are not desperately trying to save dysfunctional marriages, but merely aiming to recapture the intimacy, trust, friendship, and romance that brought them together in the first place.

What the Encounters teach best is *communication*—the courage to replace silent grudges with talking and sharing. Often that is all that is needed to live happily ever after.

MARRIAGE IS NO MYSTERY

Arguably, marriage owes more to art than to science, but the good news for commitment-shy and divorce-prone America is that there are proven formulas for marital success. We know a great deal about marriage—how it works, how much satisfaction it can bring a couple, and how spouses can contribute to its failure.

Good marriages have common characteristics that are apparent to sociologists and demographers alike. Rest assured, there are divorce-resistant recipes for courageous couples who are determined to live happily ever.

These recipes are deceptively simple to state but demanding in practice. Happy marriages share these ingredients: mutual kindness, respect and reverence, plus the appreciation of one's spouse as an exciting and trustworthy person and a sympathetic lover. Spouses in successful marriages respond to their partner's emotional needs, share household tasks, and cooperate in the raising of children. Sharing a common faith and investing in romance only improve odds for a happy marriage.

Over the years, surveys by the National Marriage Project, George Gallup Jr., and the National Opinion Research Center have consistently reported that when a couple agrees on values, friendship, communication, sexual satisfaction, mutual respect, and religious faith, they pronounce their marriage to be happy and permanent. If they had to do it all over again, these couples agree they would marry the same person.

In his analysis of Gallup and NORAC surveys, sociologist Andrew M. Greeley notes that "sex and character combine to be the most powerful influences on marital happiness," but cautions that "it is not the frequency of sex that shapes marital happiness, but its quality and its openness."[1]

Joint church attendance is less an indicator of marital happiness than wishing for the same things and agreeing on the same values. Some 90 percent of couples who pray together report "very great" sexual satisfaction. Couples who agree on both religious faith and family finances double their chances to live happily ever after.[2]

MARRIAGES IN DISARRAY

The same surveys consistently reveal that marital unhappiness doesn't necessarily lead to infidelity or divorce. Moreover, most couples in unhappy marriages acknowledge that their conflicts are not of long-standing but of relatively recent origin.

Discontented husbands and wives echo remarkably similar complaints, among them that their spouse is dull, unattractive, ill mannered, has poor personal hygiene, or resists helping with domestic tasks.[3] Clearly, none of these complaints is unfixable.

To be sure, it takes more than a little time to reach a state of mutual misery in wedlock. Spouses over the age of fifty are more than three times likelier than younger couples to complain that their marriages have bottomed out.[4]

In descending order of frequency the mutual complaints in troubled marriages are: too little trust and respect, resistance to compromise, lack of kindness and common values, boorish behavior, infrequent lovemaking, and physical violence prompted by excessive drinking.[5]

Fortunately, only one in twenty couples reports their own marriage to be in such dire straits. Indeed, one in five seriously unhappy couples believes that they will actually fall in love with each other again within the next five years.[6]

Happy couples report sexual satisfaction no matter how long they have been married. But what of romance? Does it last? In the Gallup surveys, 47 percent of couples in their initial year of marriage reported that they were still falling in love with each other. Alas, by the second year of wedlock romance slips to 35 percent as a motivator, then to 13 percent in the third year.

Although the glow may dim, love can survive. Researchers report marital contentment to be cyclical. At any one moment fewer than one-fifth of American couples are in the "falling-in-love" phase, while more than half report themselves "settling down" into wedlock. Even more intriguing is that at any stage one in four married couples young and old consider that they are "beginning again"—reviving the romance of their earliest years together.[7]

Predictably, spouses' perceptions of each other alter as romantic passion yields to comfortable contentment. Whereas nine of ten newlyweds find each other exciting, that perception holds for only a little over half of couples once the marriage matures. There is yet another critical factor in new romance: Close to half of newlyweds regard their partner as "godlike," that is, worthy of worship and adoration. Within a couple of years of wedlock that perception fades by half as spouses slip from their pedestals.[8] Love may not be utterly blind, but it clearly favors rose-colored glasses.

CAN ROMANCE SURVIVE MARRIAGE?

I confess to being *uxorious*. Don't bother to look up the definition. It means being extremely affectionate toward one's wife, or even submissive to her. I plead guilty to the former definition; Becky would swiftly disabuse you of the latter. In her estimation, I am a high-maintenance husband. Still, she loves to be loved, respected, and revered. Doesn't everybody?

Anyone who has read my books and columns will recognize that, although my instincts are religious, I am anything but conventionally pious. I allow that if I did not love God fearlessly, I might shy from worshipping my wife. But I can testify from experience that God's presence in a marriage perpetuates romance. Revealingly, my favorite book of all time, G. K. Chesterton's *Orthodoxy*, is subtitled "The Romance of Religion."

Andrew Greeley, a celibate priest as well as sociologist, concurs that the presence of God in a marriage resurrects the paradise depicted in Genesis, wherein the first man and woman walked in the company of the Creator who loved them.

At the outset I part company with anyone who suspects the original sin in Eden to have been sexual. When God is invited into a loving marriage, so is lovemaking. Fully half of all husbands and wives at any stage in marriage who regard their spouse as godlike and who make love frequently report that they have never stopped falling in love with each other.[9]

Surveys also confirm that romantic love is not just typical of newlyweds. Many marriages continue to be passionate simply because romance is in the character of both spouses. Predictably, lovemaking declines in frequency with age, but of those couples who report still being in love, 40 percent report frequent lovemaking even after the age of fifty-five.[10]

Nearly half of romantically inclined couples over the age of fifty-five report greater sexual satisfaction than earlier in the marriage. By contrast, only one-fifth of *young* couples consider themselves to be skilled lovers.[11] Are the starry-eyed senior citizens kidding themselves? If so, their delusion is mutual and satisfying.

To be sure, consistent passion in marriage is not typical, even when one of the spouses is passionate in character. Rather, most lasting marriages are affectionate, responsible, and busy, and only intermittently intimate. Still, about one-sixth of couples sustain a romantic intimacy throughout wedlock.[12] Theirs are lifelong love affairs, filled with wonder because husband and wife persist in discovering each other to be wonderful.

BURDENS ON INTIMACY

Many lasting marriages are not lifelong passionate love affairs, but affectionate working relationships. They satisfy, but fall short of intimacy and playfulness. Part of the problem, surveys suggest, can be traced to our lingering Puritan heritage. Granted, marriage is not "all about" sex, but it *is* about intimacy, and any spouses can learn to be vulnerable to each other in order to become one flesh and one spirit.

For people of faith, a sense of God's presence in the marriage is a strong motive for increased intimacy. Husbands who think of God as a loving father and friend are more than twice as likely to give themselves in abandon to their wives. For women, freedom from inhibitions increases from 32 percent to 54 percent as the marriage matures. The warmer and more tender a couple's image of God, the more likely they are to achieve intimacy with each other.[13]

A chronic financial shortage can put worrisome burdens on a marriage, but having more money than necessary buys only a little more contentment—about 7 percent according to surveys. A college education also has a strengthening effect on marital happiness, but again only about 7 percent more. By contrast, mutual trust (90 percent) and respect (68 percent) are already strong in American marriages at *every* financial and educational level.

Children and in-laws can be either blessings or burdens on a marriage, but when spouses agree on how to deal with them, elders and dependents do not hamper their trust, respect, or intimacy. Spouses, after all, are married to each other, not to their parents or their children. Religiously mixed marriages are not necessarily conflict-ridden, but they are more vulnerable to disagreements over managing children and parents.[14]

FIDELITY AND RECONCILIATION

Sexual infidelity is the stock-in-trade of Hollywood melodrama, but in real life husbands and wives are overwhelmingly faithful to each other. Nine of every ten spouses in America have had only one sexual partner during the course of their marriage—their own husband or wife. Where married couples admit to multiple sex partners, those liaisons were made typically before or between marriages, not while they were married. While divorce has increased exponentially in America, infidelity within marriage remains a comparative rarity. Moreover, three-fifths of couples reject the notion that children take the fun out of marriage. Fully half of couples reject the idea that fun ever leaves a marriage for *any* reason.[15]

Fidelity tends to persist even when a marriage runs into serious difficulties. Between three-fifths and two-thirds of American marriages are, by the spouses' own estimation, very happy or very content. At any point in time, only one marriage in ten is experiencing what the couple admits to being serious problems, while another one in four is only falling somewhat short of the couple's mutual expectations.[16]

Ironically, happily married couples have been brainwashed by Hollywood to believe that most other peoples' marriages are troubled. Two-thirds of happy couples believe they are more faithful to each other than they assume other couples to be. Appallingly, only one couple in four "strongly agrees" that most married couples in America are faithful to each other.[17]

How to account for this misperception? I suspect it stems from news and entertainment media depictions of casual sex, philandering, spousal abuse, divorce, and serial marriage. Obviously, we can't peer into the living rooms or bedrooms of other real married people, so it's tempting to believe that married life for most other couples resembles a television soap opera.

Although more than a third of couples readily admit they have considered divorce in the past, close to two-thirds of them now say that divorce is not at all likely. Reconciliation, incidentally, tends to take place most among couples married more than twenty-five years who no longer have children at home. The possibility of such reunion rests on a troubled couple's ability to agree to disagree—in short, to compromise with each other.

Fully 78 percent of husbands and wives who admit their spouse is open to compromise succeed in reconciliation. Even when compromise is impossible on a number of issues, their willingness to disagree openly without rancor promotes reconciliation. Just talking to each other more often, rather than giving one's spouse the silent treatment, helps to heal a troubled marriage.[18]

IMPEDIMENTS TO RECONCILIATION

Discontented couples who make love less often than weekly are only half as likely to reconcile as those who continue to make love more frequently. Even bickering couples tend to work things out in bed.[19]

It has been argued that living together before marriage is a practical way for a couple to test their compatibility. But when cohabiting couples decide to marry, then encounter problems, only 39 percent of them successfully reconcile (compared with 65 percent for spouses who did not live together before marriage). Apparently, the experience of postponing commitment makes formerly unwed couples more likely to abandon the marriage when it develops problems. But here again, frequent prayer by both spouses is the most powerful motivator for reunion. If prayer is not a part of their lives, troubled couples require a combination of frequent sex (two to three times a week) and frequent conversation to motivate reconciliation.[20]

Of course, reconciliation does not solve all the problems that conspire to wreck a marriage. Many husbands reconcile by accepting a situation they feel to be less than ideal.[21]

In both happy and difficult marriages, both spouses agree that wives on the whole work harder at holding the marriage together. Husbands young and old are more likely than their wives (80 percent versus 73 percent) to regard their spouse as their best friend, possibly because women are more adept at making friends than men.[22] One in four wives complains that her husband cares more about his career than about her. But in an economy where most wives share the burden of breadwinning with their spouse, one in five husbands complains that his wife is wedded to her work.[23]

Few of the foundations of a happy marriage are weakened as the couple grows older together. Physical passion tends to wane, but only in frequency of lovemaking, not in its quality.

THE PERSISTENCE OF PASSION

Passion is not just for newlyweds with firm young bodies. The brain, after all, is the most important sex organ, and the longer a loving couple enjoy each other's company, the more memories there will be to spark renewed passion. Surveys indicate that 42 percent of husbands and wives in their sixties report "very great satisfaction" from their sex lives together, as do one in five couples in their seventies. One-fifth of couples over sixty still enjoy intercourse every week.[24]

People over sixty report finding their spouse to be physically attractive as often as younger people do theirs. Moreover, people in their sixties are more likely to consider their spouse a romantic and skilled lover (55 percent) than couples under that age.

It is true that sexual *satisfaction* in most marriages declines over the age of sixty, but that may be explained by the fact that, on the whole, lovemaking becomes less frequent, ecstatic, imaginative, and playful over time. Still, those couples over the age of sixty who are dedicated to keeping passionate love alive (about one in four) report being as satisfied sexually as younger husbands and wives.[25]

Analyzing the surveys, Greeley predicts that "the older lovers for whom passion and play have not stopped after a long life together of cherishing one another will have the last laugh. They are entitled to that laugh, and they can afford to have it."[26]

When married couples of all ages were asked to describe their emotions before and after lovemaking, overwhelming majorities reported physical satisfaction, delight in pleasing their spouse, deep love, pride, ecstasy, and a desire for more of the same. Fully half of couples report an easing or healing of strains in their life together. Nearly as many feel joy.[27]

HOW THE SEXUAL REVOLUTION AFFECTED MARRIAGE

There is a widespread impression that the sexual "revolution" of the 1960s turned sexual morality upside down, devaluing marriage. Granted, easy access to contraception made extramarital sex safer, and the prevailing "If it feels good, do it" mantra also offered this corollary: "If it no longer feels good, end it"—effectively squeezing the shame out of divorce. Today traditional sexual taboos no longer affect films and television, and pornography clogs the Internet. However, the prevalence of sexually transmitted diseases has had a dampening effect on unhappy spouses seeking satisfaction by straying.

It is now clear that the sexual revolution did not revolutionize marriage as an institution. Considering the frequency and ease of divorce, it may be statistically more hazardous to enter wedlock now than before, but—once wed—spouses today are not only routinely faithful to each other but also happy with each other.

Although men and women today have more commonly enjoyed a number of *pre*marital partners, it does not follow that they will seek even one *extra*marital partner. The contemporary tolerance for premarital sex does not at all carry over to adultery, which continues to be overwhelmingly condemned by both sexes and by religious and secular society alike.

Indeed, since the 1970s, just as the National Marriage Project's annual survey reveals increasingly tolerant attitudes toward premarital sex, it also reported increasing *dis*approval of extramarital sex. More than nine of every ten Americans say adultery is always or almost always wrong. This dramatic statistic suggests that even many adulterers disapprove of their own philandering.[28]

What really has changed since the sexual revolution, and how does it affect contemporary marriage? Clearly, reliable contraception has made it possible for women before and during marriage to control their fertility and compete in the job market. But the Pill has not made women promiscuous. Even as early as 1990 a majority of American women under the age of thirty reported having had no more than one sexual partner in their lives to date. If married, that sole partner was their husband.

In the intervening years, sexual activity among teenagers has become common, with three out of five having intercourse by the twelfth grade. Moreover, 51 percent of girls and 44.6 percent of boys admit to being repeatedly sexually active at that early age. But there is no reason to believe that promiscuity is a habit they will take into marriage.[29]

More worrisome is that living together before marriage has increased exponentially, as American men and women are committing to marriage later than ever. Statistically, the marriage bond is weaker among those couples who postpone commitment in favor of cohabitation. Should they decide to tie the knot, that knot is more likely to unravel in divorce.[30]

Of course, couples who find themselves in such a relationship need not fall victim to such dire statistics. What counts is their commitment to each other, strengthening the ties that bind.

MARITAL PRESSURES ON WOMEN

Despite their increased freedom of choice in deciding to marry, have children, and pursue a career, American women began to report a decline in morale as early as the mid-1970s. A decade later slightly fewer than one in three women claimed to be very happy.

Part of the reason may be traced to the fact that, as divorce has become more prevalent, it has punished women more severely than men. Whereas half of divorced men remarry, only one in three divorced women finds a new life partner.[31]

During marriage there is still an erosion of morale among women who work. The problem appears unrelated to job satisfaction or marital contentment, but to the pressure of meeting two competing sets of expectations—the family and the workplace. Working women are happy with both marriage and their jobs, but not with the combined pressure. As the second generation of feminists acknowledged, "You can have it all, but you can't have it all at the same time."

The increased practice of living together before marriage has also been less rewarding to women than to men. Cohabiting men are twice as likely to report contentment in relationships without commitment. Indeed, nearly a third of women over the age of thirty-five expressly regret their premarital sexual affairs; slightly more than half of women *under* thirty-five already express the same regrets. In sharp contrast, fewer than one man in five acknowledges regretting his premarital alliances. On balance, the sexual revolution has probably favored men over women, to the detriment of marriage.[32]

Another legacy from the sexual revolution of the 1960s is the rampant increase of sexually transmitted diseases. The Centers for Disease Control reports the nation's highest incidence of gonorrhea and chlamydia among American girls fifteen to nineteen. Nearly half of all sexually transmitted diseases are suffered by fifteen- to twenty-four-year-olds.[33]

The premarital and extramarital sexual marketplace in America today has become a danger zone for both men and women, boys and girls. Fidelity and exclusivity—the traditional cornerstones of marriage—more than ever safeguard the physical and emotional health of husbands, wives, and their children.

PROSPECTS FOR RESTORING MARRIAGE

I introduced this chapter with the words of the reformer Martin Luther, formerly a celibate priest, who became an enthusiastic convert to wedlock at the age of forty-two. For all the battering it has taken in recent decades, marriage remains the safest, most secure, and satisfying relationship to which a man and woman can aspire. Despite the erosion of wedlock, "America is still the most marrying of western nations."[34]

More than ever, wedlock requires courage, clear-sightedness, and commitment as its foundations. Passion may fade over time, but—given the attention of both spouses—romance can be a lifelong possession. Indeed, love can deepen, and man and wife can grow as a couple in ways not open to them as mere individuals. They can become God's greatest creation—no longer just you and me, but a miraculous *us*!

If you are already married or know the person with whom you wish to live happily ever after, you can skip the next chapter. But if you have not as yet found your soul mate, we'll need to talk next about courtship.

STEPS IN THE RIGHT DIRECTION

Conduct an Inventory

1. Make an inventory of your life to date. A major allure of marriage is that it pairs you with someone who thinks you're wonderful and who

tells you so. Of course, you know better what you're like. Take a look at your strengths and weaknesses. If you occasionally have difficulty living with yourself now, so will your spouse later. You may have to do some changing. Identify those changes.

2. Ask yourself whether you can happily spend a lifetime with your spouse just the way he or she is right now. If, once married, you expect to alter your spouse's habits and attitudes, you are likely to be sorely disappointed. Identify any quirks in yourself and your spouse that could cause conflict later. Talk them out now. Beware of each other's facile promises to reform.

3. Make an inventory of other persons in your life who have a claim on your time and affection. To be successful, marriage demands that you and your spouse be each other's first priority. That means that parents, friends, and even children must be subordinated to your spouse in their claims on your attention. Can you balance these claims?

• 2 •

Deciding to Marry

Finding the Love of Your Life

To be together with someone in a way that makes life a little less
bleak and solitary and lonesome.

John D. MacDonald[1]

I'd like to reveal that my wife and I were introduced to each other in
church or at a tea party, but it isn't true. Still, neither did we connect in a
singles bar or across a crowded room. We first set eyes on each other in a
Washington, D.C., office building where we worked for different employers.
Only recently separated from our previous spouses, neither of us was on the
prowl for a new entanglement.

Space was so tight in the building that Becky was consigned to the crook
of a corridor, through which a stream of chattering coworkers passed to get
from one part of the building to the other. Sphinx-like, she became adept at
ignoring all distractions, especially human ones. Accordingly, my clumsy attempts at charm were repulsed. Early on, in an attempt to engage in friendly
conversation, I asked why she didn't hang a picture or two on the wall to
make her surroundings more pleasant. "I *work* here; I don't have time to hang
pictures!" she replied in a flinty voice, eyes narrowed.

At the time we met I was the single custodial parent of three little daughters, all under the age of ten. Wagering on their charm, I invited them one
day to see where Daddy worked, and introduced them to the sphinx. Sure
enough, my tactics worked. Becky could not ignore the tykes, especially when
one of the girls shyly shared a stuffed animal with her.

In a matter of months we were married, and none too soon, because
our courtship was exhausting. I lived in the suburbs with the girls. Becky
lived in the city nearly forty miles away. The only way to be together was

to drive home in rush hour each evening after work, collect the kids from the sitter, prepare dinner, then drive Becky back into the city, with the girls bundled in sleeping bags in the car's hatch. On a rare weekend date without the children, Becky prepared a gourmet dinner for me at her apartment. I fell asleep at the table.

We were married on a sunny Sunday in October in the parish church of Washington National Cathedral by the rector, who shortly became bishop of Maryland. He deftly completed the brief ceremony during the halftime of a Washington Redskins game, returning to the rectory TV screen in time for the second-half kickoff. Aside from best man and matron of honor, our only witnesses were my daughters, whom Becky subsequently adopted. There was no honeymoon, but there was happiness. And, together under the same roof, we finally got a full night's sleep every night.

CONNECTING

Our courtship antedated the era of online dating. Had I been restricted to finding a spouse via the Internet, I suspect I would still be a bachelor. Consider this: Exhausted DWM, mid-40s, ISO bright, attractive, professional S/DWF who will raise my three little daughters, whose natural mother is still lurking about. Humorless, in debt, and feeling sorry for myself. No time for sunsets, walks on the beach, or roasting marshmallows in the fireplace.

If the Internet wouldn't have helped me much, it does for 40 million other Americans. That's how many consult online dating sites every month at the moment. According to columnist David Brooks, writing in the *New York Times*, spouse searchers have adapted to courtship in cyberspace. Consistent with traditional courtship, online daters typically do not rush into intimacy, but check each other out, exchanging e-mail messages for weeks or even months, then progressing to phone calls for a few more weeks.

"Only then will there be a face-to-face meeting, almost always at some public place early in the evening, and the first date will often be tentative and Dutch," Brooks reports.[2] Intimate relationships develop gradually. Granted, cyberspace is cold, and surfing for love is not unlike playing the commodities market. But it also makes it easier to shed an unwelcome suitor before he becomes a stalker.

And it is easier to find someone with similar interests and values through online dating. In fact, it's possible to scan literally millions of potential soul mates in a single evening, sorting for compatible age, education, income, height and weight, religion, politics, ethnicity, and other characteristics. Online dating sets to rest the old proposition that opposites attract. Granted, no one wants to endure a life in the company of a carbon copy of him- or herself. Nevertheless, solid and satisfying marriages are strengthened by similarities, not by differences.

Sites specialize to suit prospective suitors. JDate caters to Jews. EHarmony requires its members to complete detailed, introspective questionnaires. Not surprisingly, it is especially popular with women. Even self-absorption can be a shared value. The Vanity Date website preens that "we have a vision of creating the largest database of the world's most good-looking, rich, and superficial people."

Alas, in cyberdating, it does help to be physically attractive. The photo on the member's home page draws the most attention—twice as much as a prospective spouse's income. But smiles help a lot. So do the self-descriptive essays, although many subscribers assure prospects that they are at once wealthy, brilliant, self-confident, and sexy. David Brooks quotes examples:

> I am a vivacious, intelligent, warm-hearted, attractive, cool chick, with a sharp, witty, and effervescent personality.
> I am a slender, radiantly beautiful woman on fire with passion and enthusiasm for life. I am articulate, intelligent, and routinely given the accolade of being brilliant.

Clearly, cybercourting is not for wallflowers.

FINDING MR./MS. RIGHT

There are no warranties in the online marriage market. Men and women alike lie about their age, job, income, marital status, and whether they have children. One in five online daters is a married man on the prowl for an affair. In cybercourtship men almost always make the first contact. "Whatever else has changed," Brooks reveals, "men are more likely to be predators looking for sex, while women try to hold back."

Carolyn Hax writes an advice column for the "under-thirty crowd" for the *Washington Post*. When a seventeen-year-old college freshman revealed that she was spending hours every evening corresponding with a cyberspace soul mate she had yet to meet, Carolyn told her to shut down the computer and get out on campus, where there are real flesh-and-blood males who don't hide behind a website.

That's good advice for a coed, but once they are in the nine-to-five workaday world, singles don't bump up against many live marriage prospects. When the handsome, affluent young lawyer who handled my divorce acknowledged that his social life consisted of evenings spent with his golden retriever, he was reduced to asking Becky and me to introduce him to eligible women.

In just the first six months of 2003, Americans invested $214.3 million in the online search for a soul mate. In August of that year alone, online dating was the preoccupation of 27 percent of all Internet users.[3]

Studies by Katelyn McKenna at New York University and others suggest that, despite the commercialism of cybercourtship, Internet relationships are no less powerful than those that begin face to face. A keyboard is a slower, less pressured means of revealing oneself to a stranger than a quick pickup line in a bar.

Hedging their bets, some online daters don divergent disguises. Before Spring Street Networks limited the number of self-descriptive profiles a single person could post, some users assumed as many as a dozen different personalities, from shy to seductive—some as respectable as Dr. Jekyll, others more like dangerous Mr. Hyde.

In recent memory it was possible for couples to retrace their relationships through the love letters they had written to each other over the years. By contrast, e-mail tends to be deleted, so there is usually no record of these romances. Instant messaging is also vastly more casual than searching for the appropriate words to express one's affection. Still, cybercourtship accommodates flirtation via the keyboard. But testing the chemistry that makes a couple know they are right for each other requires a face-to-face meeting.

Jennifer Egan offers the example of Angel, a forty-two-year-old divorced father in Boston, who discovered Carmen, a thirty-nine-year-old woman who had recently moved from Puerto Rico to Connecticut. They quickly graduated from e-mail to phone calls. Within a month, Carmen agreed to drive to Boston so they could meet.

"I did not go by the looks of her," Angel said, "because she had no photo posted on her profile. I was basically just going with what the heart said. We met at South Bay shopping center in the parking lot, right in front of Toys 'R' Us." When Angel first caught sight of Carmen, "I said: 'Wow. Damn, I'm good!'" At first almost overwhelmed by shyness, they stumbled into conversation. She stayed the night, sleeping in a separate room, and returned to Connecticut the next day. Soon she was visiting Boston every weekend, planning to move there.[4]

For every felicitous connection, there are scores that fizzle. Leslie Hill, thirty-four, a human resources manager in Silicon Valley, is not unusual. She "dated" 100 men online before meeting her second husband on Match.com. Just as it's easy to meet someone online, it's also easy to dump someone or be dumped. But good things happen. In the first six months of 2003 alone, over 140,000 Match.com members left the site because they were successful in finding the person they were seeking there.

THE BUSINESS MODEL

With Americans marrying later than ever, and with divorce creating a huge pool of older singles, there is increased pressure to find a mate to share one's life. Despite progress toward equity between the sexes, women sense that they are at a disadvantage as they age. Rachel Greenwald urges them to enter the marriage market aggressively. Her strategy is contained in a book, *Find a Husband After 35 Using What I Learned at Harvard Business School.*

Rebecca Mead explains Greenwald's premise: "Women over 35 have a harder time meeting men than they did when they were younger, while men find themselves, as their temples gray and their financial investments mature, confronted with an abundance of nubile prospects."[5]

Greenwald proposes a fifteen-step "strategic plan" for a woman to "market" herself, starting with convening focus groups of friends, associates, and even former boyfriends to tell her how to dress, wear her hair, and project herself as a "brand" distinct from other women (for example, "Witty, Easy to Talk To, Golfer.") In addition to cyberdating, she also advises women to write 100 or more friends announcing, "This year, I would like to find someone wonderful to spend my life with. Do you know any single men you could introduce me to?"[6]

Following Greenwald's counsel can be both exhausting and expensive. She advises women in search of a husband to budget between 10 percent and 20 percent of their annual income for that purpose and to spend evenings and weekends anywhere prospects might gather. She even approves of jury duty as an opportunity to meet men. At the theater she advises going to the ladies room *during* the performance so she can be free to circulate during the intermission.

Greenwald acknowledges that the rigors of the search for a spouse can get so intense that a woman may "just need a good cry." She also cautions single women that Mr. Right could have a few flaws. "Don't be so picky," she advises her women readers.[7]

"THE RULES"

Greenwald's aggressive marketing approach to marriage contrasts sharply with the tactics proposed by Ellen Fein and Sherrie Schneider, authors of *The Rules for Marriage*, which recommends a deferential attitude toward men.[8] A sampling from their forty-three rules gives the flavor of the rest:

Rule #5: Lower your expectations in the first year.
Rule #8: Be supportive.

Rule # 9: Let him win.

Rule # 13: Don't expect a lot of sympathy from your husband.

Rule # 17: Don't scream, speak softly.

Rule # 23: Do things you don't want to do.

Rule # 26: Listen to his advice and try to appreciate it.

Rule # 33: Don't expect applause for doing chores.

If this appears to resurrect the old patriarchal view of marriage, Fein and Schneider are the first to agree: "The fact is, to be happily married, a woman sometimes needs to treat her husband like a client or customer whom she wants to keep happy (let him be right). You're probably thinking, 'Why can't it be equal? Why doesn't *he* have to do all the things you're suggesting, like don't say the first mean word or make up first?' Our answer: because that's the way it is."

Feminists were furious when *The Rules* became a runaway best seller, drawing attention to the fact that the marriage of one of the authors actually failed between the writing and publication of the book.

CHOOSING MARRIAGE

A decision to marry is reasonable, but reason seldom has much to do with it. Charles Darwin carefully weighed the advantages and disadvantages of wedlock, but his heart quickly triumphed over his head. He scribbled these disjointed notes in 1837 or 1838, arguing pro and con:

This Is the Question

Marry

Children—(if it please God)—constant companion (friend in old age) who will feel interested in one, object to be beloved and played with— better than a dog anyhow—Home, and someone to take care of house— Charms of music and female chit-chat. These things good for one's health. Forced to visit and receive relations *but terrible loss of time.*

My God, it is intolerable to think of spending one's whole life, like a neuter bee, working, working and nothing after all.—No, no won't do.

Imagine living all one's day solitarily in smoky dirty London House.— Only picture to yourself a nice soft wife on a sofa with good fire, and books and music perhaps—compare this vision with the dingy reality of Grt Marlboro' St. Marry

Marry—Marry—Marry. Q.E.D.

Not Marry

No children, (no second life) no one to care for one in old age.—What is the use of working without sympathy from near and dear friends to the old except relatives.

Freedom to go where one liked—Choice of Society *and little of it*. Conversation of clever men at clubs.—

Not forced to visit relatives, and to bend in every trifle—to have the expense and anxiety of children—perhaps quarrelling.

Loss of time—cannot read in the evenings—fatness and idleness—anxiety and responsibility—less money for books etc.—if many children forced to gain one's bread.—(But then it is very bad for one's health to work too much)

Perhaps my wife won't like London; then the sentence is banishment and degradation with indolent idle fool—

Darwin concluded his argument with himself: "Cheer up—One cannot live this solitary life, with groggy old age, friendless and cold and childless staring in one's face, already beginning to wrinkle. Never mind, trust to chance—keep a sharp look out.—There is many a happy slave—."[9]

Darwin wed Emma Wedgwood on January 29, 1839. It was a happy marriage.

Kafka's Indecision

Seventy-three years later, the novelist Franz Kafka put himself through a similar exercise in deciding whether to wed Felice Bauer, to whom he was twice engaged between 1912 and 1917. In his diary Kafka noted:

Summary of all the arguments for and against my marriage:

1. Inability to endure life alone, which does not imply inability to live, quite the contrary, it is even improbable that I know how to live with anyone, but I am incapable, alone, of bearing the assault of my own life, the demands of my own person, the attacks of time and old age, the vague pressure of the desire to write, sleeplessness, the nearness of insanity—I cannot bear this all alone. I naturally add a "perhaps" to this. The connection with F [Felice] will give my existence more strength to resist.

2. Everything immediately gives me pause. Every joke in the comic paper, what I remember about Flaubert and Grillparzer, the sight of the nightshirts on my parents' beds, laid out for the night, Max's marriage. Yesterday my sister said, "All the married people (that we know) are happy, I don't understand it." This remark too gave me pause, I became afraid again.

3. I must be alone a great deal. What I accomplished was only the result of being alone.

4. I hate everything that does not relate to literature, conversations bore me (even if they relate to literature), to visit people bores me, the sorrows and joys of my relatives bore me to my soul. Conversations take the importance, the seriousness, the truth of everything I think.

5. The fear of the connection, of passing into the other. Then I'll never be alone again.

6. In the past, especially, the person I am in the company of my sisters has been entirely different from the person I am in the company of other people. Fearless, powerful, surprising, moved as I otherwise am only when I write. If through intermediation of my wife I could be like that in the presence of everyone! But then would it not be at the expense of my writing? Not that, not that.

7. Alone, I could perhaps some day really give up my job. Married, it will never be possible.

Kafka broke off their engagement twice and remained unmarried, except to his writing, throughout his life. In a letter to Felice, he sought to excuse himself: "My health is only just good enough for myself alone, not good enough for marriage, let alone fatherhood."[10]

Skilled as he was as a writer, Kafka would have failed as a cyberdater and probably as a husband.

Two Become One

Plato explained the attraction of the sexes by arguing that human nature was originally unitary, but became divided into male and female, thereafter straining to be reunited. He quotes his teacher Socrates: "So ancient is the desire of one another which is implanted in us, reuniting our original nature, seeking to make one of two, and to heal the state of man . . . and the desire and pursuit of the whole is called love."[11]

George Bernard Shaw echoed Plato, claiming that the great majority of mortals are at the mercy of what he called the Life Force that attracts them to each other. "The trap," he wrote in *Man and Superman*, "was laid in the beginning."[12]

Writing in an age of faith, Geoffrey Chaucer acknowledged that "virginity is indeed a great perfection," but argued that Christ

> Spoke to those who would live perfectly,
> And by your leave, my lords, that's not for me.
> I will bestow the flower of life, the honey,
> Upon the acts and fruits of matrimony.[13]

In his *Anatomy of Melancholy*, Robert Burton hailed wedlock as a cure for that disease, hailing marriage as "a sweet delight, an incomparable happiness, a blessed estate, a most unspeakable benefit, a sole content, on the other. . . . Be not then so wayward, so covetous, so distrustful, so curious and nice, but let's all marry."[14]

Which is what Erica Jong's daughter did after her four-times-married mother and her stepfather burned their prenuptial agreement after ten years of tentative wedlock. Despite being seven months pregnant, daughter Molly wore white and insisted on a traditional ceremony—"the sort of mega-wedding that Jewish princesses dream about," her mother explained.

> My daughter's generation has launched into marriage and childbirth as if they invented them. . . . So we had a white wedding. . . . There were 400 guests, nine bridesmaids, nine groomsmen, engraved invitations, a string quartet, two photographers, a partridge and a pear tree. But the traditional trappings could not disguise the fact that this was a very contemporary wedding. Both bio-dad and stepdad marched the pregnant bride down the aisle. The extended family included stepmothers, stepgrandmothers, half-brothers, and many of the mother of the bride's former boyfriends.

Jong muses: "Our deepest instinct tells us that joys are increased and pains diminished when we meet them two by two. . . . Like geese, like penguins, we seem to be pair-bonding creatures. It takes four wings for us to fly."[15]

The Triumph of Hope over Experience

Even Friedrich Nietzsche, who died insane, hallowed marriage, offering this advice: "You should propagate yourself not only forward, but upward! May the garden of marriage help you to do it. . . . Marriage: that I call the will of two to create the one who is more than those who created it. Reverence before one another, as before the willers of such a will—that I call marriage."[16]

In reading through dictionaries of quotations about marriage, Erica Jong notes that "pundits throughout the ages have equated the institution with slavery. Yet all the pessimistic prophets on the planet have not been able to prevent people from going off into the sunset two by two. The truth is that we do not run our lives according to opinion polls or punditry."[17]

The heroine of Daniel Defoe's *Roxanna* disagreed, objecting that "the woman was that had an estate, and would give it up to be the slave of a great man, that woman was a fool . . . that while she was thus single she was on her own, and if she gave away that power, she merited to be as miserable as it was possible that any creature should be." In the end Roxanna reconsidered her objection to marriage: "A sincere affection between a man and his wife answered all the objections that I had made about the being a slave, a servant, and the like; and where there was a mutual love there could be no bondage, but that there was but one interest, one aim, one design, and all conspired to make us both very happy."[18]

Samuel Johnson took objection to the romantic notion that certain men and women are meant for each other, preferring the virtues of arranged marriages. "I believe," he said, "marriages would in general be as happy, and often more so, if they were all made by the lord chancellor, upon a due consideration of the character and circumstances, without the parties having any choice in the matter."[19]

Anthony Trollope disagreed:

> I am inclined to believe that most men and women take their lots as they find them, marrying as the birds do by force of nature, and going on with their mates with a general, though not perhaps an undisturbed satisfaction, feeling inwardly assured that Providence, if it have not done the very best for them, has done them as well as they could do themselves with all the thought in the world. . . . So that the thing does not require quite so much thinking as people say.[20]

The novelist Ford Madox Ford was at once passionate about marriage and resigned to it:

> Whatever may be said about the relations of the sexes, there is no man who loves a woman that does not desire to come to her for the renewal of his courage, for the cutting asunder of his difficulties. . . . For every man there comes at last a time of life when the woman who sets her seal upon his imagination has set her seal for good. He will travel over no more horizons; he will never again set the knapsack over his shoulders; he will retire from those scenes. He will have gone out of the business.[21]

MARRY ME, MARRY ME, MARRY ME

It would be difficult to discern a more enthusiastic partisan for the married state than the seventeenth-century poet and churchman John Donne, who writes in "The Good Morrow":

> Let us possess our world, each hath one, and is one.
>
> My face in thine eye, thine in mine appears,
> And true plain hearts do in the faces rest,
> Where can we find two better hemispheres

Without sharp North, without declining West?
Whatever dies, was not mixed equally;
If our two loves be one, or, thou and I
Love so alike, that none do slacken, none can die.[22]

Donne notwithstanding, marriage does not simply happen spontaneously. It must be proposed.

It was Britain's Queen Victoria who proposed to Prince Albert. In her journal she recalled:

> I told him I was quite unworthy of him and kissed his dear hand. . . . I really felt it was the happiest brightest moment in my life, which made up for all I had suffered and endured. . . . How I will strive to make him feel as little as possible the great sacrifice he has made. . . . I feel the happiest of human beings.[23]

For all his brilliance as a writer, Evelyn Waugh's proposal to the nineteen-year-old Laura Herbert was less than persuasive:

> I can't advise you in my favor because I think it would be beastly for you, but think how nice it would be for me. I am restless & moody & misanthropic & lazy & have no money except what I earn and if I got ill you would starve. In fact it's a lousy proposition. On the other hand I think I could . . . reform & become quite strict about not getting drunk and I am pretty sure I should be faithful. . . . I am very clever and could probably earn a living of some sort somewhere. . . . All these are very small advantages compared with the awfulness of my character. I have always tried to be nice to you and you may have got it into your head that I am nice really, but that is all rot.[24]

Despite his efforts to dissuade her, Laura was persuaded, and became Mrs. Waugh in 1937.

It is a fair guess that few wooings have been as passionately accepted as the one recounted by James Joyce in his *Ulysses*, although it fell short of a marriage proposal:

> then I asked him with my eyes to ask again yes and then he asked me would I say yes to say yes my mountain flower and first I put my arms around him yes and drew him down to me so he could feel my breasts all perfume yes and his heart was going like mad and yes I said yes I will Yes.[25]

Speaking for myself, marriage is the greatest proposal I ever made, and its acceptance the greatest gift in my life.

GETTING MARRIED

Nothing could be more private than marriage, but no other human institution is more public, because society itself has a stake in ensuring that couples be sincere and responsible. After all, property is at stake, and often children as well.

The state licenses marriage and places restrictions on the marital bond, legally defining marriage. Although still a scandal, adultery is no longer criminal in half of the United States. But incest, polygamy, and bestiality are. Interracial marriage was once proscribed. As I write, controversy continues over the right of persons of the same sex to marry.

In any case, neither the state nor the church controls marriage. They merely witness couples freely entering into wedlock. Neither clergy nor civil magistrates "marry" a couple. The couple alone possesses that power. Their marriage is their creation, their mutual commitment, which can only be witnessed by others.

Nowhere is this more apparent than in Quaker weddings, where congregations assume the role of clergy, as ministers to one another. During a couple's engagement, a committee of Friends meets with them to assure themselves of their commitment to each other. The ceremony of commitment takes place within the Quakers' regular meeting for worship:

> No one gives away the bride, and no third person pronounces them man and wife. They give themselves to each other. Friends believe that God alone creates the union and gives it significance. Neither a bridal party nor an exchange of rings is necessary, although both have become customary today.[26]

Holding hands, the couple in turn pronounce their promises: "In the presence of God and these our friends, I take thee to be my (wife/husband), promising with Divine assistance to be unto thee a loving and faithful (husband/wife) so long as we both shall live." Everyone present signs the marriage certificate as witnesses. In Quaker homes the certificates are often framed and displayed, and passed down from generation to generation.[27]

✌⌘✌

STEPS IN THE RIGHT DIRECTION

Ponder What Qualities You Seek in a Mate

1. List your priorities. All of us have them. Must your mate be physically attractive? Possess a sense of humor? Be a brilliant conversationalist?

Be clear: Are you seeking someone like yourself? Or are you seeking someone who compensates for attributes you lack?

2. How do you plan to relate to your spouse? Do you expect to make most of the decisions that involve you both, or cede most of the decisions to your mate? Marriage is not an exercise in dominance versus submission, but a collaborative adventure requiring compromise.

3. What habits and pleasures have you enjoyed as a single person that you are willing to give up for marriage? Talk it out beforehand. Often it's just a matter of moderating behavior, like not spending every weekend watching sports on TV.

· 3 ·

Fidelity

Being True to Each Other

Ah, love, let us be true to one another!

Matthew Arnold

$\mathcal{P}$opular culture would have us believe that American men and women are promiscuous bed-hoppers, boffing like bunnies. But when *Time* magazine investigated the myth, it discovered that the average American woman has only two sex partners in her lifetime, while American men have six—in each case counting their current spouse. Whatever their previous sexual experience, men and women, once married, are faithful to each other.[1]

Economists Andrew Oswald of Warwick University and David Blanchflower of Dartmouth College have studied over 50,000 men and women in Great Britain plus tens of thousands in the United States, and have established "that greatest satisfaction comes from a monogamous relationship, but for those who sleep around, sex is literally devalued."[2]

Because of their profession, Oswald and Blanchflower were curious about quantifying the value of contentment in marriage. They calculate that a loving marriage makes a person as content as an *extra* $100,000 a year in income. Moreover, they reveal that, on average, married couples are happier than singles or divorced, and that first marriages are happier than second ones.

Blanchflower's conclusion: "The optimum number of sex partners that give the greatest happiness is one."[3]

Parents perennially advise their sons and daughters to date an array of potential partners. The idea is to make friends with the opposite sex and vanquish any notion that there is something mysterious about gender. Growing up as an only child, I was prone to consider girls exotic creatures, but over time I developed many friendships uncompromised by lust or clouded by romance.

Fortunately, I went to coed schools, where the mingling of the sexes was natural and unpressured.

In the late 1960s, however, I took a post at a prominent all-men's college in New England. There was an equally exclusive all-women's college half an hour's drive away. Deprived of the easy, everyday presence of women, the male students were inclined to be macho and immature, and on weekends could become predatory.

Walking to my campus office, I was accustomed on Monday mornings to weaving my way through a gaggle of girls who had slept overnight with the boys in their dorms and were waiting alone for a bus to take them back to their own school. One weekend, my student assistant asked if I would care for his girlfriend's pet boa constrictor while he took her to New York for an abortion. At the time, single-sex schooling seemed to guarantee that, once married, the men and women would be lifelong *strangers* to one another because their experience of each other was only sexual.

WHAT MAKES A MARRIAGE?

Marriage is like no other relationship. It is total, permanent, and exclusive. Emotionally, domestically, and financially, husband and wife are not unlike Siamese twins. Over the years I have encountered hip-but-bored couples who flirted with "open marriage," removing their wedding bands on weekends to seek brief encounters with strangers. To the best of my knowledge, they are no longer couples. Marriage cannot be compromised and still be marriage. Wed*lock* is aptly named. It literally means throwing away the key.

Catholics, who are not permitted to remarry in their faith after divorce, nevertheless can request an annulment, arguing that one or both of the spouses entered wedlock with reservations that, ipso facto, invalidated the marriage. More American Catholics get annulments than their coreligionists in all other nations combined. Two common so-called "defects" are that either husband or wife entered marriage refusing to have children, or that one or both of the spouses had no intention of remaining faithful. Most unhappy couples opt for civil divorces, but the very notion of Catholic annulments underscores how demanding, total, and exclusive the marriage bond is. Wedlock requires that a man and a woman forsake all others.[4]

Stanford University sociologist Ann Swidler acknowledges that, rather than feeling liberated by the removal of society's sanctions on divorce, many couples feel their own marriages to be threatened. Yet, speaking of their own spouses, many also feel challenged to take their commitment to the marriage all the more seriously. Precisely because they view marriage as so vulnerable to dissolution, they tighten the ties that bind them to their spouse. Ironically, the prevalence of divorce has had the effect of enriching those marriages that last.[5]

Marriage, Swidler argues, is a difficult institution to sustain, yet she acknowledges that people persist in making the commitment and making marriages work. Moreover she extols marriage precisely because wedlock is the sworn enemy of all that is cynical, exploitative, materialistic, and indifferent in our popular culture.

"A good marriage," she says, "is when you become better when you're with the other person, not because they do good things for you, but because you truly rejoice in the other person's flourishing. The ideal of marriage is ever more the one place in a society like ours, where you can fulfill the highest virtues of which we are capable: sacrifice, understanding, commitment."[6]

Acknowledging her own marriage to be a good one, she pays tribute to her husband for the many ways he has helped her, adding, "but all these laid end to end don't go halfway toward capturing what it has meant to love and be loved by him."[7] She affirms that living "happily ever after" doesn't have to be confined to fairy tales.

WHY DO VOLES FALL IN LOVE?

Human beings are among the scant 3 percent of all mammalian species that form monogamous relationships. Because the human brain is similar to a particular faithful species, the prairie vole, scientists have been investigating those sociable mouselike critters in an attempt to determine why humans are drawn to lifelong exclusive bonds.

According to the *Economist*, initial mating between vole couples demands a twenty-four-hour effort, after which they bond for life: "They prefer to spend time with each other, groom each other for hours on end and nest together. They avoid meeting other potential mates. The male becomes an aggressive guard of the female. And when their pups are born, they become affectionate and attentive parents."[8]

Oddly, these prairie voles have a close relative, the montane vole, that shares 99 percent of their genes but is promiscuous, addicted to one-night stands and lacking any interest in permanent partnerships. Based on vole studies, scientists now believe that the human predisposition to monogamy may come down to chemistry: "When prairie voles have sex, two hormones called oxytocin and vasopressin are released. If the release of these hormones is blocked, prairie-voles' sex becomes a fleeting affair. . . . Conversely, if prairie voles are given an injection of the hormones, but prevented from having sex, they will still form a preference for their chosen partner."[9]

In humans, sex stimulates the release of the same hormones, suggesting to researchers (as to poets) that human love may be an addiction. Brain scans of people in love reveal that the area involved in love is relatively small compared to that involved in ordinary friendship.[10]

Helen Fisher, a researcher at Rutgers University, proposes that love in humans comes in three "flavors"—lust, romantic love, and long-term attachment. These inclinations partially overlap, but can be distinct. So, what could be done to cure a love-besotted teenager whose ardor is unrequited? Dr. Fisher believes it might be possible to inhibit feelings of romantic love in its early stages by drugs similar to Prozac, which raises the level of serotonin in the brain. Still, once romantic love takes hold, Fisher acknowledges, it is like a locomotive. No mere chemical is likely to stop it.

As you might imagine, scientists are now toying with the notion that if chemicals can help a person get over unrequited passion, then other chemicals might help people fall in love or patch up their fragile marriages.[11] From ancient times, herbalists have sought to concoct love potions. Now it is the scientists who are contemplating playing Cupid.

However, until Cupid prevails, Marilyn Vos Savant advises that marriage will take continual mutual effort by couples themselves, working together toward the two goals of

> overcoming your own weakness, but allowing your spouse to have them. The goals may be unreachable, but if both husband and wife aim for them, they will become better people and avoid damaging their love relationship in the process. . . . People are far from perfect—even the person you marry—and if you don't learn this before the wedding, both of you surely will discover it shortly afterward."[12]

It is this lifelong challenge that prompted Clarence Day to address this plea to his wife:

> Dearest, I am getting seedy,
> Fat and fussy, kind of greedy,
> If your love is on the wane
> I can't reasonably complain,
> Yet, since legally you're mine,
> Try to be my Valentine.[13]

BEYOND MERE ROMANCE

On a recent Valentine's Day, the English columnist Minette Marrin expressed her concern that "our obsession with romantic love is directly responsible for our disastrous divorce rates, and all the troubles that follow. It is an obsession that is almost pathological, and certainly unhealthy for society as a whole. . . . The terrible problem with romantic love is that it doesn't last. While it does, there is no greater pleasure, as far as I know. It's a kind of delicious madness."[14]

Well, if prairie voles can be faithful for a lifetime to their mates and their children, so can men and women. The "delicious madness" of romance to which Marrin refers can turn into something calmer and deeper—respect, affection, comradeship, and sheer delight in each other's company. It just needs time to mature.

Witness the partnership of Lois Blumfield and Allan Berger, who have been husband and wife for more than half a century. They were wed at Temple Beth El in Rockland County, New York, December 27, 1953, when she was twenty-four and he was twenty-two. After a brief honeymoon in Lake Placid, they set up housekeeping in a tiny attic apartment in Flatbush that rented for seventy dollars a month. Not infrequently, they hit their heads on the low ceiling. In sweltering summers their plastic hangers melted into their clothes, and their only relief was to crawl out onto the roof for fresh air.

Half a century later the couple were living in a Washington, D.C., suburb. At the age of sixty-eight Allan suffered a massive heart attack, which he treated with humor, quoting Woody Allen to the effect that, "I'm not afraid of dying. I just don't want to be around when it happens." Lois nursed him back to health, but he is still burdened by diabetes.

Much earlier Lois began to have serious health problems of her own. Cancerous cells in her uterus required a hysterectomy at the age of thirty-seven, but not before she gave birth to three children. A gall bladder infection presented more complications. Then, in her forties, breast cancer forced her to undergo a radical mastectomy, which made her feel deeply insecure in their marriage. "But Allan said to me that it doesn't make any difference, and we just moved on." Her husband's prescription for dealing with the loss: "You *hallucinate* the other breast."

As young marrieds, the couple lived on Lois's teacher's salary of $2,700 a year, while Allan studied to become a psychiatrist.

Their son, Gary, also wanted to become a doctor but developed a malignant, inoperable brain tumor and had to drop out of medical school. His father recalls Gary once coming out of surgery with three limbs paralyzed. "He could only use his right hand, and had all kinds of tubes, and a respirator. Couldn't talk. And I asked him, 'How are you?' and he wrote out with his good hand, 'Okay, except for the circumstances.'" The son died at the age of twenty-five. His parents grieved for years, effectively terminating any social life except for weekly visits to the cemetery.

Their other son, Jonathan, hosted his parents' fiftieth wedding anniversary party, hailing his father as "the only man I know who can play an active game of tennis and smoke a cigar at the same time." Allan responded with humor, deeming the anniversary "a miracle," and adding, "*Truly it is.* Because I am, personally, only thirty-nine years old, and Lois is a teenager."

The Bergers credit their success in wedlock to humor and frequent arguments. "I think arguments are the spark of life," Allan says. "You argue. You work it out. And then you make nice." Applying Benjamin Franklin's wisdom to marriage, he says, "To your spouse's virtues, be a little kind, and to your partner's failures, a little blind."

As they cut their anniversary cake, Allan said of their marriage, "It looks like it's going to work out. So many of our friends have broken up. This morning, I said the same thing to Lois. 'Looks like it's gonna work out.' And she said, 'Yeah, maybe.'"[15]

THREATS TO FIDELITY

One of the allegations lodged against gay marriage is that it will lead to a resurgence of polygamy. If you can marry one person of your own sex, goes the claim, how can you be prevented from marrying more than one person of the *opposite* sex? In our divorce-driven society, serial monogamy is already a form of polygamy.

Edward Laumann of the University of Chicago has joined with colleagues to study contemporary Americans who, far from forsaking all others, actively seek multiple partners, but for sex, not marriage. Laumann and his fellow researchers resemble the cultural anthropologists of the early twentieth century who studied primitive peoples, but they are actually studying the sexual mores of contemporary Chicago neighborhoods.

What they discovered is that each neighborhood is a sexual marketplace with its own distinct rules. In most of them, marriage has been replaced by "hooking up." For example, in a large African American neighborhood the researchers call "Southtown," nearly 40 percent of the men at any one time maintain multiple long-term sexual relationships. David Brooks of the *New York Times* comments: "If men can have multiple partners, they have little incentive to limit themselves; marriage rates drop. Though they face a shortage of African-American men of equal status, Southtown's women tend not to look outside of black neighborhoods."[16]

Roughly two-thirds of non-Hispanic men in Chicago report having one-night stands. But in a largely Hispanic neighborhood the researchers call Westside, marriage and family life remain strong and sexual morality traditional. Half of the men and three out of four women believe it is wrong to have sex without love. Moreover, two-thirds of single men believe married men should work while women stay home to raise children.

I grew up in Chicago at a time when it was composed of ethnic neighborhoods that facilitated marriage and promoted family life. Today, the city's neighborhoods are increasingly defined by sexuality, and the incentives to marry are decreasing. Researchers Yoosik Youm and Anthony Paik worry that "opportunities in the sex market act as constraints in the marriage market,"[17] even though marriage correlates with happiness and children raised in marriages have clear advantages over those raised outside of wedlock.

David Brooks predicts the decline in forsaking all others will have devastating effects on the quality of life in America. "Overall," he writes, "Americans are spending less time married. They marry later and divorce at high rates, and remarry less and less. We are replacing marriage, one of our most successful institutions, with hooking up. This is a deep structural problem, and very worrying."[18]

DEALING WITH ONE'S RELATIVES

In one of Jesus's notable "hard sayings," he told his disciples that "anyone who puts his love for father or mother above his love for me does not deserve to be mine, and he who loves son or daughter more than me is not worthy of me."[19]

The marital vow to "forsake all others" follows the same reasoning. Obviously it demands sexual fidelity to one's spouse, but it also means that spouses are also preeminent in each other's lives.

You don't have to be a devotee of "Dear Abby" to realize that families intrude on marriages, sometimes coming between spouses. Even a couple's own children can slowly poison their parents' marriage by insisting that their father and mother "belong" to them rather than to each other.

It doesn't usually start this way. Family therapist Virginia Morgan Scott acknowledges, "After marriage, parents on both sides go through the process of investing in the couple and accepting the couple. . . . In-laws have a honeymoon phase, too."[20] But even in the first year of marriage a couple is typically confronted with the choice of which set of parents to join for Thanksgiving, Passover, or Christmas.

Ordinarily, in-laws don't demand that their son's or daughter's spouse actually love them, but only respect and, hopefully, like them. Nevertheless, they style themselves as the couple's *elders* and expect to be taken seriously by them, especially when they offer advice, which may be gratuitous.

After I persuaded Becky to marry me, I realized that I had better convince her parents that she wasn't making another mistake after her failed first marriage. So I screwed up my courage and set out across three states to meet them on my own. I expected them to question Becky's willingness to adopt my three daughters. Instead, they welcomed the prospect of becoming instant grandparents. But being suspicious of churches, they were less sanguine about my religious faith and trusted that I would not impose it on their daughter.

Later, when I introduced Becky to my own mother, the reception was not nearly as friendly, and my new wife was treated to gratuitous advice, which we both rejected. Happily, parental interference was minimized by the fact that both sets of parents were older and lived at a considerable distance from us.

Our situation was atypical. Barbara, thirty, of Staten Island, New York, married a man whose parents lived nearby and thrived on bickering. "My mother-in-law is very opinionated—she'll say things about my hair being too long or my eyebrows too thick. She loves me and wants me to 'look pretty,'" Barbara says. Her prospective father-in-law was even more difficult. On her wedding day, when she asked whether she could now call him by his first name, he snapped that he was still "*Mister* Black" to her. "Okay, *Mitch!*" she snapped back, and called him by his first name from then on.[21]

You and your spouse may get along swimmingly, but it's likely that you were raised in distinctive family cultures with different parental expectations. One of you was a son, the other a daughter, and parents have different expectations of girls and boys. My first wife's father expected his daughters to call him "Sir," and they always referred to him as "Daddy."

Julia Bourland warns that even when parents don't intrude physically in a couple's marriage, they can intrude mentally. She refers to these invasions as "ghosts from the past," and acknowledges that they can be stubborn. It is unlikely that you and your mate have the same childhood images of marriage, and you will be tempted to reproduce the ones you do know in your wedded life together. Long ago I hosted the young ambassador to the United States from the new African nation of Sierra Leone, who in turn introduced his wife. He pronounced their marriage to be nothing short of a miracle because, as he explained, "We come from different tribes."

Similarly, American husbands and wives bring their own peculiar family customs into their life together. Which spouse is expected to pay the bills? Are gifts opened on Christmas Day or Christmas Eve? Is the wife expected to iron hubby's shirts and handkerchiefs? As a boy, I found it odd that my friends' families brushed their teeth with toothpaste when the Younts did the "sensible" thing and used toothpowder. Each new marriage must dump the ballast of former expectations and take on new ones. Rest assured, that is not compromise; it is creative reality.

Parents are not the only persons who may make claims on your marriage. Old friends, still single or married themselves, may feel that they have "lost" you to your spouse. Some marriages accommodate regular "nights out with the boys" for husband and "nights out with the girls" for wife, but the better alternative is to make new friends *as a couple*.

ESTABLISHING BOUNDARIES

Wedlock is a crucial step into adulthood, but it's not a guarantee of the couple's maturity and autonomy. The alternative, Judith Viorst warns, is "to pay a price in our marriage for remaining, first and foremost, our parents' child."[22]

Some couples will literally move across the country to escape interfering parents, but "if we haven't established enough emotional distance, it won't matter how many miles apart we are."[23]

Early in my first marriage I asked my father-in-law to cosign a loan so we could purchase a reliable car. I made the monthly payments with interest but was uncomfortable with having to rely on his generosity. Later, when I asked him to lend us enough for a partial down payment on a house, he was close to retirement and had to turn me down. I was more relieved than disappointed.

Viorst cautions young couples not to rely on parental handouts, "especially if the money that parents give to their married children undermines their need to work, to live within their means, to be self-supporting."[24]

Family therapist W. Robert Beavers cautions against marriages in which one or both spouses are expected to show loyalty to their parents by seeming to remain children.[25] There are plenty of wives who, even after many years of marriage, are expected to phone their mothers every day.

Then there are wives like Wendy, whose husband's mother calls him every day but won't say more than a word to her if she answers the phone. Wendy's husband, Roger, is expected to come right over if Mom needs a light bulb changed. "Before we were married, Roger's mother was Roger's problem. Now she's *our* problem," Wendy complains. "I told her that she either has to acknowledge me or call her son at his office. She calls at his office."[26]

Jewish mothers are renowned for making their adult sons feel guilty for insufficient loyalty to them, but they are unfairly singled out. My former wife continues to expect her three adult daughters to include her in their vacation plans every year. A graver danger occurs when the son or daughter of a demanding parent attempts to "protect" the spouse from that parent by dealing with the parent alone. Marriage is a closely held corporation (or more precisely, an unlimited partnership). Decisions are best made by spouses together as joint agreements.

Moreover, spouses must refrain from openly taking the side of a parental in-law who disagrees with the marital partner, whatever the merits of the argument. "In other words," Viorst insists, "the marriage is the primary relationship when each of the partners has first claim on the other's love and loyalty, when each of them is, in effect, the other's home."[27]

Still, it is important to distinguish conflicts and demands from mere annoyances and inconveniences. Psychoanalyst Harvey Rich remarks that "when your soul is injured you need to fight like hell, and when it's just your sensibilities, let it go."[28] Most parents want to help their married children, but are occasionally clumsy about how to go about it appropriately. It's wise to acknowledge that, just as all marriages are made between amateurs, parents aren't professionals either. Grown children do well to listen politely to their parents' counsel, then make their own decisions with their partner. After all, we're all adults now.

MAKING THE TIME FOR LOVE

Can you conceive of Romeo checking out the other girls in Verona while romancing Juliet? Or Robert Browning on the prowl for an alternative to Elizabeth Barrett? For all the scandal and sorrow surrounding the marriage of Abelard and Heloise, each of them forsook all others. If not necessarily made in heaven, these were matches cast in concrete.

The prominent problem in marriage is not the difficulty of being unfaithful; it is the tendency to take one's spouse for granted. Let's face it: there's not a lot of time for grand amour in most married lives. Passion takes attention and effort when couples least have the time to make the investment.

Sean Elder is, for lack of a better term, a househusband. For all eleven years of his marriage he has been a successful freelance writer and editor, while his wife works out of the home as editor-in-chief of a magazine. Sean spends about half of every day to his paying profession, devoting the remaining hours to cooking, cleaning, shopping, and caring for the couple's young son and daughter, including helping them with their homework. He complains that, unlike his wife, "I am pretty much starved of adult conversation until the time she gets in," whereas by then she is sick of shop talk.[29]

This stay-at-home Dad's major disappointment is not enough sex in the marriage. He is quick to moderate his complaint:

> Despite the assertion by Dr. Phil, the daytime TV doctor, that "sexless marriages are an undeniable epidemic," that's not what I'm talking about. A sexless-marriage story would quickly devolve into a divorce story, and my wife and I have both invested too much love and energy into our marital vehicle to

sit here and watch the wheels come off. No, my wife likes sex as much as I do. She really does. She may not like it as frequently as I do. Or as urgently.[30]

The Elders' weekday evenings are short and routine, consisting of dinner, some TV news, and putting their children to bed. Both spouses are exhausted by their own bedtime. "Hope springs again on the weekends," he notes, but Saturdays and Sundays are also packed with chores involving children and pets. Once, "finding ourselves unexpectedly without children or chores one afternoon," he recalls, "I raised the subject, and also an eyebrow. My wife looked at me as if I were speaking Urdu."[31]

Sean relates his complaints in a book entitled *The Bastard on the Couch: 27 Men Try Really Hard to Explain Their Feelings about Love, Loss, Fatherhood, and Freedom.* He acknowledges that "a modern marriage is held together by a thousand threads, of course. But if my wife doesn't depend on me for her financial solvency (and a good thing, too), she does depend on me for myriad other things—cooking and childcare, yes, but also for humor and companionship, for moral support and critical insight, for reality checks, and trivial information. Farther down the list, almost falling off the page, is sexual gratification."[32] Sean clearly believes his wife is taking him for granted.

THE INVISIBLE PARENT

Let me introduce you to two couples that have been married lots longer than Sean and his wife—thirty-eight years and fifty-eight years respectively. Happily for them, they do not share Sean's complaint. Despite their advanced ages they continue to enjoy passionate love lives with their spouses. Arguably, they are helped because the spouses share a religious faith, which provides them with a fifth "parent" who is all help and no hindrance. Christians, after all, do not call God their "father" for nothing.

Tony and June Giambalvo, married for thirty-eight years, have six children and seven grandchildren. They are both health professionals. He is an alcoholism and drug counselor as well as a dentist who works exclusively with HIV-positive patients. June is a school nurse. Their lives are pressured, and they have always fought a lot. But early on, Tony recalls, "We decided that no matter how angry we might get, no matter how much we might kick and scream, we'd never say to the other, 'I'm going to leave you.' Never put the marriage on the line."

"For me," Tony says, "I've realized how much more my marriage is when there's a spiritual aspect to it. I think spirituality is the key. I think God is present in our marriage in the sense that He's there in each other. He's present in the love and the kindness, the compassion and understanding.

"I think the most important sexual organ is the brain, and when things are right between me and June, and our spirituality is very strong, this affects us sexually. It's kind of like a love triangle with God and June and me. The closer I get to God, the closer June comes to me—like in an equilateral triangle, you know, the sides always stay equal—so if I get closer to God, June automatically gets closer to keep the three sides equal."[33]

Dona and Frank Irvin, an African American couple, are both in their seventies and have been married for fifty-eight years. Dona acknowledges that their marriage has required many compromises, and Frank adds, "Having been married so long, we've had to mesh someplace; and I think it's our differences that have brought us together."

Dona agrees: "There are problems and there are problems. We disagree on the minor things; but on the major things, like our belief in God or how we want our lives to go, we're in agreement. We've been through some situations that could either pull people apart or bring them together, like when our beautiful little son died in 1943, when he was just five years old.

"Part of the reason that Frank and I can still come together sexually is our spirituality, which has allowed us to become who we really are. We were inexperienced when we met, and we developed our sexuality together." Dona became an author at the age of sixty-five, celebrating a marriage that had retained its passion. She advised her readers: "If a 76-year-old man and a 78-year-old woman can do it, they can, too."[34]

On a recent Mother's Day, humorist Gene Weingarten paid tribute to his own wife and, by extension, all wives and mothers: "Thank you for being less competitive than we [husbands] are. This is a mature position, an essential position that must be assumed by one half of any two-person relationship that aspires to long-term success and happiness. We would have accepted this noble role ourselves, only then we would have lost.

"Thank you for believing, as we do, that love is forever—but not taking it for granted. This is an affectionate and respectful way of saying: Thank you for not inflating like a marshmallow in a microwave."[35]

⌗∞∞∞

STEPS IN THE RIGHT DIRECTION

Consider What It Means in Practice to Be Faithful

1. Fidelity is not just sexual. Do you celebrate and support your spouse's achievements, or are you competitive with your mate? Do you flirt

outside your marriage and consider it harmless? In social situations, are you quick to introduce your spouse and express your solidarity with him or her so people recognize you as a couple?

2. Are you "married" to your job or your interests? You may spend more waking hours at work than at home with your spouse. But your greatest satisfaction and accomplishment will come from your married life. If your career is your passion, then you are, in effect, a bigamist, and passion will drain from your marriage.

3. When you contemplate retirement, what first comes to mind? Playing more golf with friends, spending more time on gardening, traveling and your personal hobbies? Or do you look forward to having more time doing things together with your mate?

· 4 ·

Forbearance

Dealing with Differences

Anything worth doing is worth doing badly.

G. K. Chesterton

*C*hesterton, a brilliant but absent-minded Englishman, was famed for losing himself in the middle of London, whereupon he would phone his wife to ask her, "Where am I? And where am I going?" Many a couple will ask themselves the same questions during the course of a marriage. Having vowed to stay the course for better or worse, they can only pray for more of the former than the latter.

There are no trained professionals amid the ranks of husbands and wives. All spouses are lifelong amateurs, at the mercy of their own human nature and the whims of fate. Chesterton merely counseled humility amid uncertainty, because married life is preeminently something "worth doing."

Few challenges in life are greater than wedlock. Married life admits of no disguises, no dissembling, no pretense. Your spouse knows who and what you are and how you are likely to respond to the blessings, hardships, and tragedies ahead of both of you in your life together.

So it is wise—or at least practical—to expect that, however pure your mutual love, your marriage will not always be clear sailing in calm seas but will be tested by circumstances beyond your complete control. Even when you prevail, you will seldom emerge a total hero or heroine but only a battered survivor. Still, look at it this way: You are no longer left alone to be buffeted by life's disappointments. Now there are two of you to confront the same challenges and to celebrate your successes when they come.

49

MISERIES OF OUR OWN MAKING

"He who is not arguing is not married," St. Jerome observed. To which Ovid added: "Quarrels are the dowry which married folk bring to one another," leading Nietzsche to reflect that "if married couples did not live together, happy marriages would be more frequent."[1]

Judith Viorst tells the story of friends Sy and Hallie, married forty-five years, who survived his cancer only to encounter financial disaster just as they were preparing to retire. Sy says, "We've always been aware that, good as things can be, nothing's forever. We've seen many bubbles burst, and we know that when a bubble bursts, we need to get busy and blow another bubble." Wife Hallie clearly agrees. She keeps a Superman figurine on her nightstand on which she has pasted a photo of her husband's face.[2]

Couples *can* make life better for each other. Ever since we met, Becky has encouraged me to see to my health, to move ahead in my career, to choose friends and fights wisely, to spend and save sensibly, to expand my horizons without succumbing to ambition, to rest when I'm overextended, and to keep disappointment from turning into discouragement. When I was going through male menopause, she advised group counseling and, more recently, anger therapy. I grumbled, but took her up on it. Without her clear concern for me my life would have shriveled. Because of her it has expanded.

I can't pretend to have contributed as much to her. She is simply smarter and more sensible than I am. But I am her biggest supporter and promoter. We are both writers, but we do not compete. Indeed, we look forward to evenings when we read to each other what we have written that day. Nor do we shy from giving criticism and receiving corrections from each other.

When couples vow to wed "for better, for worse," they typically assume that the worse will come from outside the marriage—illness, debt, unemployment, problems with in-laws, and the like. But, too often, these are only precipitating factors that turn spouses against each other. The miseries of a couple's own making are those quarrels they have with each other when they could be joining together against life's inevitable adversities.

Couples fight for lesser reasons—often simply because they were individuals before they became a couple—and still are. Husbands and wives have habits and expectations that are legacies from childhood. Married life demands compromises, which can seem like threats to the husband's and wife's autonomy. Before we were even engaged I asked Becky what she might like as a modest Christmas gift. "Jewelry," she replied, adding after a moment's hesitation, "*Real* jewelry."

Translation: no cheap costume baubles. Her request was the initial revelation that my future wife was not a discount shopper, whereas I had been brought up to shop only for sales. Becky, I soon learned, is content to live simply, but she demands quality. I am, by nature, a cheapskate, happiest when prowling bargain basements and secondhand shops.

Instead of trying to change each other's predilections, we agreed from the outset to simply look at what we could afford together. It helped that Becky is a saver and an earner, while I had become inured during my first marriage to scraping along on the razor's edge of debt. I still postpone needed repairs and replacements, relying on her to tell me when we can't wait any longer for a new roof and furnace for the house or tires for the car. When she tells me, I comply.

WHY COUPLES FIGHT

Couples fight because they weren't born into the world as Siamese twins but as individuals, and marriage is a threat to autonomy. Before wedlock, we marrieds were used to having our way. Moreover, we were inclined to overlook our individual shortcomings, or at least forgive them. Marriage abruptly ends that self-deception forever. One cannot escape the X-ray vision of a spouse who sees all.

Still, married partners can afford to shed some autonomy while retaining their individuality. In point of fact, in the course of living together, husband and wife each change. It's called personal growth, and it can be accomplished without growing apart. Becky and I have each attempted and accomplished things in later life that we couldn't conceive of in our early years together. But a marriage becomes an endangered species when one spouse grows while the other stands still or slips backward. The trick is to encourage your partner to spread his or her wings without you fearing that he or she will desert the nest.

Love and hate are two sides of the same overwhelming emotion.

And so we fight. About money, sex, the relatives, the division of chores, the kids, and whether the painting over our couch should or shouldn't be two and a half inches lower. About when to eat and where to live, about what movie to see and whether to sleep with the window open or closed. We fight about you don't listen to me, and you don't treat me with respect, you're a slob, you forgot my birthday, you're too controlling. We fight because—despite the love that we had, and still have, for each other—there is so much to fight about.[3]

Instead of joining arms to fight their common enemy, couples can be inclined to opt for *civil* war, ready to burn Atlanta in their own bedroom.

Anger is a normal emotion. So throw things, kick things that don't break easily. But make certain that your emotion is on target, not on the unfortunate person who happens to be in the room when you're mad (and who just happens to be your soul mate). Even self-pity is okay on occasion, so long as you wallow deeply enough in it to want to get rid of it. But if you're hurting, don't deny your condition; that's deluding yourself and will only make it worse. Mourners used to signify their grief by wearing black arm bands. Don't wrap a black band around your spouse.

GET MAD

Anger is a positive attitude when it is properly directed. If you are angry, it's probably because something or someone hurt you—but not necessarily your spouse. Anger exists for a reason and deserves not only attention but also respect. The only permanently destructive anger is the kind we direct at ourselves; that is suicidal. It's pointless to berate yourself for failure; that only doubles the pain and will put a pall over your marriage.

We learn from our mistakes, but too often we get angry at ourselves because of an inflated notion of how wonderful we ought to be. No one really knows what it requires to be a perfect husband, or wife, or parent. We muddle through. When we hurt others by falling short of their reasonable expectations, we ask their forgiveness. That's only fair. But we must ask our own forgiveness as well, and give it to ourselves.

Understanding your anger will help you change the situation that hurts you. *Venting* anger is another thing. It seldom helps, especially when it is directed at the person you love, care for, and live with. When anger is used as a weapon of revenge, all it does is spread your pain to another person and mark you as "unreasonable" or worse.

Still, if your spouse is the cause of your distress, he or she has got to be told, and you must do the telling—calmly and courteously. Swallowing your anger changes nothing and will actually make you even more miserable than you are to live with already.

Thomas Jefferson said, "When angry, count ten before you speak; if very angry, a hundred." The rule is not to speak at all *while* you are angry. Aristotle was right: "Anyone can become angry, but to be angry with the right person, to the right degree, at the right time, for the right purpose, and in the right way—this is not easy." Anger should be your motive for making your situation permanently better for you and your spouse.

TIPS FOR EFFECTIVE ANGER IN MARRIAGE

Psychotherapist Harriet Lerner suggests these dos and don'ts for dealing with anger in a marriage:

1. *Speak up when an issue is important to you.* Trivial slights aren't worth confronting, but if you feel bitter, resentful, or miserable in a situation with your spouse, express yourself.
2. *Don't strike when the iron is hot.* If you start a fight when angry, someone is going to lose it, probably you, and possibly your spouse as well. Postpone the confrontation until you've cooled down and have identified a practical solution to the situation.
3. *Take time to think over the problem, then clarify your position.* Get to the real issue, decide what you want to accomplish, and determine whether the situation can be changed.
4. *Don't hit below the belt.* Don't demonize your spouse or the situation that caused your anger. You run the risk of winning a battle at the cost of losing the war and never attaining peace.
5. *Use the word "I," not "you."* Say how *you* feel rather than blaming your spouse. No one can dispute your feelings, but your husband or wife will reject being characterized as a villain.
6. *Don't make vague requests.* You can't expect your spouse to anticipate your needs. Tell your husband or wife specifically what it is that you want.
7. *Understand that your spouse is not exactly like you.* His or her values and sensitivities are probably different. Things that bother you may not faze the person to whom you are wed. But the spouse who loves you is likely to be accommodating if you will tell him or her specifically what it is that bothers you.
8. *Don't be self-righteous.* You are not trying to prove the rightness of your position and the wrongness of your mate's. Agree to disagree in principle. You just want a solution in practice.
9. *Acknowledge that each spouse is individually responsible for his and her own behavior.* Don't blame third parties for your unhappiness. Confront the person who is directly responsible.
10. *Don't tell your spouse what he or she thinks and feels or "should" think and feel.* The only feelings at issue are yours. You just want the situation to change.
11. *Don't pretend to speak through a third party.* If you're hurt, say so. Don't allege that your spouse is hurting someone other than you by his or her behavior.
12. *Don't expect changes from one hit-and-run confrontation.* Be patient with yourself and your spouse, who may test you to see whether you "really mean it." Be firm, but fair. Life is long—till death do you part.[4]

LAUGH

The best way to dissipate resentment is with laughter. Much of life is not nasty; it's just absurd.

Even when tragedies strike, humor may be the only way to overcome them. Humorist Eddie Izzard's family was very close. He was only eight when his mother died unexpectedly. Devastated by the loss, Izzard decided that he would devote his life to being funny. Today he ranks as one of the world's top comedians.

A disconcertingly accurate definition of marriage is that it is a situation comedy. If faith can heal, so can humor within the confines of lifelong wedlock. It's said that God laughs when humans make plans in order to insulate themselves from life's uncertainties.

We humans are distinguished from all other creatures by our ability and inclination to laugh. The Vulcan Mr. Spock on *Star Trek* was himself the object of amusement because he failed to recognize the humor inherent in the human condition. To him, much of human behavior was simply unreasonable. Indeed it is, and that's what's funny. Laughing at *themselves* is one of the healthiest habits a couple can acquire. By taking yourselves less seriously, the burden of being wonderful all the time will be lifted from your shoulders. Laughter actually releases chemicals that make us feel better. It also contributes to our health. A hundred laughs is equivalent to ten minutes of aerobic exercise.

Laughter will help a couple to live fully in the present moment rather than with regret for the past and anxiety about the future. Consider this age-old wisdom:

> Yesterday is history.
> Tomorrow is a mystery.
> Today is a gift.
> That's why it's called the present.

Forget your horoscope. There is no such thing as fate. Whatever cards you and your spouse hold, you can meld and play them together as partners. At most, only half of the quality of a person's life is dictated by the facts; the other half is determined by one's attitude toward the facts. With a positive, realistic approach you can often *change* the facts.

But first you must face them and see them for what they are. A stiff upper lip in the face of adversity is the way of retreat. Even anger and mourning are more realistic attitudes than denial. Laughter is even better.

FACING THE FACTS

Aside from Becky's and my life together, the marriage I know most about was my parents'.

My mother, who was born to two poor blind parents, never overcame her deprived childhood, but kept insisting that life was a cheat even when she was in comparatively comfortable circumstances.

My father had more to complain about, but seldom did. His education ended with grammar school, and he worked all his life for the same company in the same job, never receiving a promotion. Forcibly retired in declining health at age sixty-one, he spent his last dozen years, progressively paralyzed, in a nursing home. He often had black moods, but he met adversity positively. He was the kind of man who would stoop to pluck a wildflower from among weeds and wear it all day in his lapel.

Some misfortunes are predictable, and wishful thinking cannot deter them. But they can be dealt with positively. The first thing a newly married couple faces is a statistic: half of all marriages end in divorce.

But marriage is not the only risky business. In any given year one in every five new businesses fails, and one in twenty Americans loses his or her job. Four of every five women will be widowed in their lifetime. Everyone gets sick. We will all die.

Life is more than the sum of its tragedies. Especially when it is a life we share with someone who loves us, it is a perennial opportunity for growth and enjoyment. Each of us is more resilient than we think. Even after the worst accidents, when people have been injured and their homes destroyed, the survivors typically thank God "because it could have been worse." With a realistic attitude, you can make your life together better rather than worse. Disappointment needn't translate into discouragement. We just need to be reminded to make lemonade out of life's lemons.

Of course, to be palatable, lemonade needs to be sweetened, so couples will have to do something to sweeten whatever situation they find themselves in—to become proactive rather than defensive. When you're grieving, start thinking of what will make you feel better. Becky has the healthy habit of celebrating when confronted by disappointment. Above all, don't be deterred by rules you've imposed on yourself. Over a lifetime you've created your own character, so it's perfectly permissible to act *out*-of-character on occasion.

A close childhood friend of Becky's, now middle-aged, was served divorce papers by her minister husband on her birthday and set financially adrift, having never held a job. She pounded the pavements in New York, got employment, then temporarily lost her job when she was crippled for months by knee surgery. It's her habit at bedtime to write down all the good things that happened to her that day, then decide on the good things she will do for herself tomorrow. She counts her blessings, not her woes. Bad times are the very best times to be good to yourself. There are no medals for self-pity—only for courage. Becky's friend must count her blessings alone; you can count yours together.

GETTING AND STAYING TOGETHER

The prospects for remaining together for better or for worse are less likely if spouses consider each other to be merely the latest entries in their little black books of sexual partners. It used to be that only bachelors carried such pocket directories. Now many young women also keep score of how many sex partners they have gone through before settling into marriage.

When Jennifer Broussard was a student at the University of Pennsylvania, she used to keep track of the men in her life by name and date, then share her experiences with girlfriends, asking them, "What counts? What doesn't? I'm about to pass my benchmark. Is this guy worth it?"[5]

The "benchmark" of which Broussard speaks is a single girl's arbitrary determination of how many men she can safely have sex with before settling on Mr. Right as a husband.

Laura Sessions Stepp of the *Washington Post* notes that "these women analyze their numbers as if they were comparison shopping for the right size and color of shoes. They tell each other that sex is separate from love. And few adults tell them any different. Sex education teachers lecture on body parts and disease, and we know that parents would rather throw themselves in front of a truck than talk in depth about sex and romance."[6]

When student Kristen Thorne arrived at Georgetown University, two of her friends told her they each planned to have sex with no more than ten partners. If they did reach that number, they would target the next man for marriage. In fact, when number eleven did come along for both girls, he was not Mr. Right, so they both continued as searching singles.[7]

By contrast, Brown University student Veronica Searles worried that friends of hers who are still virgins "see themselves as odd, although they're not. They're almost ready to jump the gun because they're behind" their more sexually experienced classmates.

Broussard acknowledges that, over time, the quantity of girls' sex partners will matter less than their quality. When she informed her most recent boyfriend about her sexual record keeping, "he got all nervous and said, 'I know that you're free sexually and that's great, but . . .'

She defended herself, telling him, "I don't want to forget the names on my list, whether they're good or bad. I like to remember them, learn from them."[8]

But what is she learning? That sex can feel good even with a partner who is a poor marriage prospect? When single men and women shop in a super-market of easy sex, they are not assured of settling on the best prospect for a lifetime. Moreover, they will carry into any marriage the fantasy of choices they could have made among men other than their husband.

One-night stands and brief affairs fail to translate into the kind of com-mitment needed to sustain lifelong marriage with a single mate. Instead, they provide an easy excuse, once a marriage encounters difficulties, of concluding, "This is a mistake. I should have married Tom, Dick, or Harry instead."

SELF-ESTEEM AND MUTUAL ESTEEM IN MARRIAGE

Some years ago University of Texas psychologist William B. Swann Jr. noticed his young daughter sporting a T-shirt with the slogan "I'm lovable and capable" emblazoned on the front. When he asked where she got it, she replied that all her kindergarten classmates had one and wore them every Friday to school. In fact, the school counselor required the students to recite the mantra, "I'm lov-able and capable," before every class. Swann reports that during their conversa-tion "my daughter fell silent for a moment and then, with a quizzical expression, asked, 'Daddy, all the kids are wondering, what does "capable" mean?'"[9]

Aye, there's the rub! Most of us are caught up playing roles in life in which we are less than expert, and we can't escape many of them. I can't pretend that I was especially adept in all the jobs I've held to earn my living. If you are a spouse or parent, no one trained you to be expert in those roles, and effort alone doesn't guarantee success. As it turns out, confidence has a lot to do with courage, including the courage to come up short.

The value of self-esteem is that it keeps us rising to new challenges even when we're down. Thomas Hobbes, writing in 1658, affirmed that those "who estimate their own worth correctly . . . dare to try again," but warned that "those who estimate their worth too highly, or pretend to be what they are not, or who believe flatterers, become disheartened when dangers actually confront them." The philosopher's counsel stands up today and it applies to the "for bet-ter, for worse" vow couples make to each other in wedlock. Successful spouses pick themselves up, dust themselves off, and start all over again.

Being on good terms with yourself is essential, but it is equally true that few of us are truly satisfied with the reflections of ourselves that we see in the bathroom mirror and in plenty of human "mirrors" as well—our parents, children, employers, coworkers, and, above all, our mates. It is a cliché that low self-esteem can be traced to childhood and to demanding or indifferent parents and teachers. In youth and adulthood alike we are inclined to believe what others tell us about ourselves. Indeed, we tend to attract the kind of people who affirm our high or low opinion of ourselves. If we allow it, the self-confidence of husband and wife can be held hostage to the opinions of others, including their indifference to us. Don't allow it.

The self-affirmation movement assumes incorrectly that all people are consumed by a desire to think highly of themselves. Psychologists suggest the opposite: most of us are skeptical about ourselves, sensitive to our own faults. But we are nevertheless motivated to defend our self-image, because it can be frightening to change, even to a better opinion of ourselves from a poorer one.

As Dr. Swann notes, our sense of self "serves as the lens through which we observe reality, organizing our experiences and allowing us to predict and control important elements in our lives." They are survival mechanisms, *even when they are negative*. Life's losers take a certain perverse comfort in their self-pity. To start acting and thinking like a winner means giving up the stunted self you know for someone you don't yet know—a more capable self.

Another false assumption about easy self-esteem is that all persons believe themselves entitled to praise and feel good when they receive it. Studies reveal that people with low self-confidence initially welcome praise, but soon suspect that they have misled others and that the real truth about themselves will soon come out. Accordingly, they avoid opportunities for achievement and praise.

A final harrowing false assumption about the quest for higher self-esteem is that our spouses, friends, and coworkers will support our effort. That assumption flies in the face of the fact that others in our lives have a stake in our continuing to be the *same person we have always been*. Many a divorce can be traced to one partner "growing" while the other stays the same, and it is typically the steady spouse who feels betrayed by the change in the relationship. Newfound independence in one partner can threaten an intimate, interdependent relationship. For a marriage to satisfy and survive, husband and wife must believe that they are both winners.

THE SECRET OF THE SAINTS

Only a saint merits perfect self-esteem, yet saints are notoriously critical of themselves. They are effective nonetheless because they are confident. Their self-acceptance stems from their belief that their Creator loves them and requires that they share that love with others. Their self-confidence comes from working to justify that trust. Their humility is simply an acknowledgment of the truth about themselves.

Those of us who are not saints gain our confidence from small successes that encourage us to take further risks. It helps immeasurably, of course, to have a spouse who believes in us. Ironically, whereas children are constantly being evaluated by their parents, adults are often at a loss to know how well they are doing. That is why married couples need to summon the courage from time to time to ask each other, "How am I doing?" If you do, you will either be reassured, rechallenged, or made aware that your mate's expectations of you are unrealistic and need to be modified. Whatever your spouse's response, your confidence will not suffer because you will be exchanging illusion for reality.

Self-esteem is holistic. It encompasses our whole way of relating to the world—our strategies for establishing goals, our expectations, reactions to change, and how we deal with setbacks. People with low self-esteem tune out praise while amplifying anything derogatory said about them. They actually seek life partners who think poorly of them. Because of their low opinion of themselves, battered women tend to choose the kind of men who will mistreat them. They believe, perversely, that they deserve the abuse they get.

If they can afford the cost, people suffering from low self-esteem can consult expert counselors, who can guide them through lengthy therapy. A cheaper and faster alternative is to secure a prescription for antidepressants, which offer the illusion of a quick fix to personal confidence. It is true that Prozac and similar drugs can temporarily lift sufferers' moods, but pills do nothing to improve their faith in themselves. An honest, loving, plain-spoken spouse is better medicine.

So is a willingness to take reasonable risks. As a young girl growing up in the country, Becky was constantly warned by her parents to avoid the poison ivy that surrounded their home. Tired of being timid, and uncertain whether she was actually allergic to the leaves, she decided one day to roll in the stuff. Her experiment was successful. She proved to be immune to the poison—but only by taking a chance did she make that happy discovery. Suddenly, one facet of Becky's life became more predictable, and she became inclined to take more calculated risks.

In their quest for predictability, men and women with poor self-images take the opposite tack, embracing marriage partners who think poorly of them, while actually shunning those who think well of them. Lamentably, much of marital abuse is self-inflicted. Men and women with poor self-regard often choose confirming (but negative) marriage partners, feeling safer in abusive relationships.

Authentic fear can be useful, because it confronts real danger; but mere anxiety is useless, because it shrinks from the unknown and reduces us to inaction. One of the great blessings of marriage is the courage a husband and wife can give to each other to face the unknown together.

THE AUTHENTIC SELF

Anyone who aspires to be "all things to all men" is courting disillusion. But it is equally illusory to pretend *to yourself* to be someone other than who you are. Barbara Walters, who has made a career of interviewing famous people from all walks of life, acknowledges that actors and actresses have the poorest sense of themselves, possibly because their profession requires them to devote so much of their lives pretending to be someone else.

Nowhere is self-deception more dangerous than in loving relationships. Feminist Gloria Steinem reveals that she was so determined to get a particular man to fall in love with her that she assumed a false self—changing herself into the woman he wanted her to be. She was already well aware of the fearfulness of change: "Change, no matter how much for the better, still feels cold and lonely at first—as if we were out there on the edge of the universe with wind whistling past our ears—because it doesn't feel like home. Old patterns, no matter how negative and painful they may be, have an incredible magnetic power—because they do *feel* like home." Acknowledging change to be harrowing, Steinem nevertheless adopted a false identity to please her lover, in the process forfeiting her values and diminishing herself rather than lose a man she loved. Eventually she realized that "having got this man to fall in love with an unauthentic me, I had to keep on not being myself."[10]

To her credit, Steinem at length gave up the man, reaffirmed her true self, and found a mate who respects who she is.

FAITH TO FALTER AND SURVIVE

Confidence flows from faith in yourself and in each other. That faith begins with self-knowledge. Shakespeare's Hamlet remarks of the human animal:

> What a piece of work is man! how noble in reason! how infinite in faculty!
> in form and loving how express and admirable! in action how like an angel!
> in apprehension how like a god! the beauty of the world! the paragon of
> animals!

But in the next breath the prince's faith falters: "And yet, to me," he concludes, "what is this quintessence of dust?"[11]

Hamlet's faith in man lacks hope and love. You and your spouse deserve a fuller faith. Having linked yourself for better or worse with another fallible human being, you will need a faith that offers both of you a future, and engages your affections as well as your minds. For this you will need to believe in something beyond yourselves.

If you conceive of yourselves merely as accidental specks of life in a vast, impersonal universe, you are not likely to find a faith that holds out much hope. Believers and doubters are equally exposed to life's trials, but believers locate themselves in the universe and see the direction in which they are going.

If you or I attempted to live confidently on the basis of what we absolutely know for a fact, we could never get out of bed in the morning to face the uncertain dawn. People cannot help but live by faiths that fall short of certitude, but we can shed false faiths that are built on little more than habit, sentimentality, and wishful thinking. To be sure, even saints falter in action, but they maintain their faith despite their shortcomings. To be worthy of your belief, the faith that you profess in each other as husband and wife needs to be bigger and better than you both.

FALSE IDOLS

Have faith in yourselves as a couple, but beware of becoming the slaves of your beliefs. Much of the world's misery comes from people who devote themselves to causes "greater than themselves." Save the whales if you can, but save your marriage, your family, and your own lives first. Be suspicious of idols and ideologies. Unfortunately, many people find it easier to invest their faith in a crusade rather than in themselves. Devoting ourselves to causes can make us feel good about ourselves because they lift us above our petty personal concerns. But every crusade has its victims, destroyed by the assumed righteousness of its adherents. The allure of idolatry is as ancient as humankind. The Israelites found it easier to worship a golden calf than their invisible God. Idolatry prefers cheap substitutes over the real thing. To live confidently you must revere reality—and the most immediate real thing in your life is the person you married.

In the course of the last century more than 100 million men, women, and children died miserably and prematurely in time of war, the victims of faiths that turned their adherents into self-righteous killers. A true faith is not overbearing, but honest and humble, generous and true. It claims no victims.

Find a faith the two of you can share. Start by believing in yourselves, then keep faith with others. Better to reinvent your lives for better instead of settling for worse. Consider that the most celebrated couples of history and fiction seldom made marriages that survived. Recall Abelard and Heloise, Tristan and Isolde, Romeo and Juliet, Antony and Cleopatra. Real-life marriages are not played on the big screen of passion but on the small stage of domesticity. But good marriages enjoy this immense advantage: they play for extended runs.

STEPS IN THE RIGHT DIRECTION

Dealing with Differences

1. Become reconciled to your amateur status. Married life is not only an invitation to humility, but a humbling experience in itself. No spouse ever reaches professional status as a married partner. Situation comedies are funny precisely because they explore the plight of ordinary people like us, who are tested by situations that make them appear foolish. Be prepared to be wrong some of the time and to feel foolish when you are. Your spouse will still love you.
2. View your spouse as an ally, not an antagonist. Quiet, long-suffering spouses do not make a successful marriage. Most arguments in married life are no more than differences of opinion—not outright warfare—and admit solutions. An honest couple will often disagree but come to solutions without lingering hard feelings. When you "win" an argument with your spouse, your marriage loses.
3. Laugh. Life is full of absurdities, due to the fact that we try so hard to plan the future while taking ourselves too seriously. If you can each learn to laugh at life and at yourself, you will learn to laugh together. Then you will be a formidable couple.

· 5 ·

Finance

Budgeting for Bliss

Money talks.

Anonymous

$\mathscr{W}$hen money talks to an engaged or married couple, it typically tells them, "There isn't enough of me." In theory, two can live almost as cheaply as one, but marriage has a way of increasing a couple's expectations for the quality of their life together. Children, a home of their own, vacations, and entertaining all add to the cost of living happily ever after.

Unfortunately, whereas money talks, couples avoid talking about money. Their silence is a dreadful mistake, because conflict about money is the leading cause for divorce in America.[1] No, not sex, religion, in-laws, or disputes about child rearing. *Money* is the great divider in marriage.

There are obvious reasons. When a man and woman marry, they forfeit their previous autonomy. In earlier times, many women married seeking financial security. More often today both spouses worked prior to wedlock and were accustomed to supporting themselves financially. In many cases a newlywed wife these days earns more than her husband. Once married, it is rare for both spouses to be equally ambitious to get ahead in the workplace. Moreover, one may be a spender, the other a saver—a wicked combination for any couple hoping to live happily ever after.

Marriage is not just a merging of households but also of assets and ambitions. Even more daunting, it can also involve a merging of debts. Newlyweds often have outstanding college or car loans as well as leftover bills from their wedding and honeymoon. At the outset of wedlock it is not only an ideal but a practical measure to assume each other's debts as an investment in your life together, then pay them all off as a couple from your combined income.

Start by agreeing on what debts get paid first, then consolidate all of your outstanding debts at the lowest interest. Because credit card balances carry the highest burden of interest, that is where you will want to start. Your aim will be to pay off your credit card balance *in full* every month.

Whether or not you're aware of it, each of you has a credit history that is available to any inquiring merchant from whom you hope to buy on credit or any bank you approach for a loan. Newlyweds may opt to retain credit cards in their own names simply to keep their individual credit histories clean, but a joint credit card account (in both of your names) has the advantage of giving both of you a picture each month of what you are spending together and individually. That knowledge not only will help you manage your money together, but it will underscore your openness with each other.

THE CULTURE OF SPENDING

Barely fifteen minutes from my home is the one of the largest discount shopping malls in the United States. Potomac Mills is, in fact, the biggest tourist attraction in the entire state of Virginia. Every day its gargantuan parking lots are filled with thousands of automobiles. Tour buses roll in carrying shoppers from distant states for shopping sprees. Moreover, ranking with Capitol Hill and the White House, our nearby shopping mall has become a must-visit attraction for the millions of foreign visitors to our nation's capital every year.

Who can blame them? How can anyone pass up a chance to buy Limoges china or a Ralph Lauren suit at just half the retail price? The answer, of course, is anyone who doesn't really need them. Nothing is a bargain if you can't afford it, and even if you can, there are other options for spending your money. You can even save it now to spend later. But shop-until-you-drop has long since become America's favorite entertainment, with the result that we have been transformed from free citizens into a nation of debt-ridden consumers.

The fallout from this phenomenon has been dreadful. Every year one in seventy American families files for bankruptcy. These are not impoverished couples, but middle-class Americans spending way beyond their means. Stand in any store's checkout line and note how many people pay by check, using a credit card only for identification. Years ago I asked a clerk why anyone would use a credit card in such a strange way. Because they've passed their credit limit, I was told; the card is no longer good for anything except as an ID.

It was only after my remarriage at age forty-four that I permanently emerged from debt. Before then, I juggled bills against short-term loans, hoping each month that my paycheck would clear in time to cover the check to my landlord. But once I emerged from debt the full force of financial wisdom finally hit me: When you're in debt, others are profiting from your plight. Whereas when you have savings, *others pay you* for the use of your money. Your choice as a couple is to be financial winners or losers.

At the moment, the average American saves only one penny of every two dollars earned after paying essential living expenses. That is by far the lowest savings rate of any industrialized nation in the world. It accounts for our nation's anxiety about rescuing Social Security.

In addition to a monthly check from the government, our parents' generation could also count on retirement income from pensions from their employers. But pensions have long since been replaced by IRAs and 401(k) plans, which place the burden of saving on the employee rather than the employer.

Fewer than half of the nation's 77 million baby boomers have saved *anything* toward retirement. Many count on the equity in their homes to finance their later years. The problem is that a house is not a *liquid* asset. You can't sell it and still live in it. Moreover, the resale value of your home can plummet during a recession. I'm embarrassed to see men and women past retirement age toil in the heat and cold loading groceries into supermarket customers' station wagons. They're only working because they need the money.

THE ILLUSION OF AFFLUENCE

The appearance of affluence across America motivates us to spend, keeping up with our neighbors. But we actually have less to spend than we did a generation ago. Despite two incomes, the median American family has gained no ground in the past twenty years, and the earnings of the bottom fifth of wage earners have actually lost purchasing power. Meanwhile, despite the allure of "discount" shopping, real prices have risen. Because of the example of others, we have gone on a copycat spending spree. Rising expectations prompt Americans to spend more than ever at Christmas and for birthdays and anniversaries, not to mention Mother's Day and Father's Day. We purchase sneakers for our growing kids that cost more than our own dress shoes, and send our sons and daughters to colleges and universities we would never have considered for ourselves because we knew we couldn't *afford* them.

Here's the reality: Even if we could afford everything, we couldn't have everything. Where would we put all of it?

Lest you suspect that Americans are buying more but paying less, consider that the floor space of the average new home being built (and mortgaged!) today is more than double what it was in the 1970s. The average price of a new car increased by 75 percent in the last decade alone.

Not only are we spending more—we're demanding luxuries. Can you recall exactly when you started thinking that a cup of coffee was worth two or three dollars rather than twenty-five cents? The Starbucks empire was built on that sea change in values. Consider: sales of expensive wines have soared by 23 percent every year since 1980. Sales of wristwatches costing $2,000 or more rose 13 percent in a recent year alone. One of every eight new vehicles on the road is now a luxury automobile or SUV. A decade ago it was only one in fifteen. The worldwide financial crisis that began in 2008 left many couples with less to spend on luxuries and has even pinched budgets for necessities.

Oscar Wilde famously defined a cynic as one "who knows the price of everything and the value of nothing." His aphorism would have to be revised today, because none of us knows the price of anything until we check the sales ticket. But Wilde was wise about assessing *value*—not just the quality of the goods we buy and the pleasures we purchase, but the value they add to our lives. Once a couple agree on their values, they will know what measures to take regarding money.

CHOICES YOU CAN MAKE WHATEVER YOUR SITUATION

You Can Start Saving

Saving, like spending, is simply a habit. Breathing is a habit too; if we had to think before taking each breath, we'd have little attention left for anything else. A good habit is no harder to develop than a bad one. Saving and spending are not antagonistic. A couple is only saving now to spend later on something better.

You Can Reduce Expenses

But it's not easy. Cutting down is infinitely harder than cutting out. For example, let's say you spend $500 a month at the supermarket, mostly for food and household products. Reducing that expense will mean settling for cheaper products or depriving yourself of things you like. You will *feel* poor. You can't reduce your water bill, heating, or electric bill without discomfort either. So look to other parts of your budget to *eliminate* those expenses altogether.

The easiest expenses to jettison are those associated with your workday. Instead of eating lunch out and drinking those expensive cups of coffee on the run, pack your lunch and carry a thermos. Professional clothing is expensive and uncomfortable. Accessorize the suits and dresses you already have, saving instead for comfortable clothes you can wear at home and at leisure. Fire your cleaning lady and tidy up your house or apartment yourself. Who knows? You may just develop the habit of *keeping* it clean and enjoying the lack of clutter. Don't buy books or magazines you can get free from the library. Sell that extra car you seldom drive, along with anything you have but don't use. That's the idea: don't skimp—just eliminate.

You Must Live on a Budget

Budgeting simply means knowing where your money is going so you can be assured of having enough of it when you need it. The Internal Revenue Service requires you to file complicated returns each year to determine how much you owe your government. It's easier to construct a personal or household budget that shows you how much you owe *yourself.*

Just keep track of your joint and individual expenses, by category, for at least three months in a row, and don't forget to factor in those big annual and semiannual bills, like auto insurance, vacations, and Christmas gifts. You already have to balance your checkbook and pay bills every month, so keeping a budget will not be onerous. Once you determine, on average, how much you spend each month in each expense category, keep track in subsequent months to see whether you've gone over your limit.

Even celebrities live on budgets. When they entered their teens, Ashley and Mary-Kate Olsen were already worth millions, but each received just a seven-dollar allowance every week—a dollar a day for each day they completed their family chores. If they skipped a chore, like making their bed, they got a dollar deducted.

After more than twenty-five years of marriage, Becky and I still record every dollar we earn (by source) and spend (by category). In retirement, we can't expect our income to increase, so we have hunkered down to living on a budget that is 40 percent less than when we were working full-time. Decide at the outset which spouse will pay the bills and record expenditures. Then, preferably at the end of every month, sit down together briefly to review expenditures and agree on spending priorities.

Beware of Cash

It's practically impossible to keep to a budget when you spend cash. Of course, you could always save sales slips, but you won't. Instead, use checks and credit cards, which afford a handy record of what you are spending. Credit cards are best because they defer your payments. You can even get discounts or frequent-flyer miles by using your cards. Becky and I get a free trip to Europe every other year for using our joint card for every possible purchase and payment during the rest of the year.

Choose a card that has no annual fee, and pay off the balance in full every month. Couples should use one joint checking account and leave the desk-size checkbook at home where you both have access to it to note each other's entries and keep a running balance. Having separate checkbooks and individual credit card accounts are invitations to financial ignorance and marital disputes.

You Can Save Regularly

Make savings an integral category in your budget, preferably the same amount every month. It may be one of your smaller expense categories, but it should be at the very top of your budget worksheet. Savings are not what you owe others, but what you owe yourselves.

Set Aside Money for Predictable Expenses

You will need to replace your car or cars sometime, so prepare for it now. Otherwise, when the time comes and you're without wheels, you will feel tempted to buy a new model and pay for it on time with interest. By setting something aside now, a couple can build up a fund and pay cash for an almost-new car still under warranty that costs half the dealer's tariff.

Plan for Emergencies

In the space of a few months practically everything mechanical in Becky's and my household died and needed replacing: the computer, dishwasher, refrigerator, VCR, iron, vacuum cleaner, and two TVs. Moreover, the car needed expensive repairs, and the kitchen flooded and needed a new floor. Worst of all, the furnace failed in mid-winter and needed replacing. To boot, I needed expensive dental work.

Those were all emergencies, but predictable ones. We just didn't know they would all come at the same time. They did not bust our budget or depress our spirits, because we had set aside savings for the worst prospects. You can too. When I turned sixty-five, I took out an insurance policy to cover catastrophic illness for the rest of my life. It was a grim and costly addition to an already tight budget, but it relieved my mind and it ensures that Becky will not be left to fend for herself when she can no longer manage my care.

DEBT AND BORROWING

The instant you start saving, you will be able to invest. Instead of paying others, they will pay you for the use of your money. We'll consider some smart alternatives a few pages along. But if a couple is so deeply in debt now that savings are out of the question, you will first need to conduct a self-rescue mission.

Incidentally, if you assume that almost every couple owes money on their credit cards, you're mistaken. Forty-two percent of credit card holders pay off their balances in full every month. The cards are simply a convenience to them, as they should be—not a floating debt at high interest.

Everyone has to borrow money sometime (even millionaires have mortgages), but you don't have to go broke borrowing. When the U.S. Treasury is prepared to pay you less than 4 percent for the use of your money, why should you pay Visa or MasterCard 13 percent a year for the use of theirs? One of a couple's best moves is to join a credit union, probably the best available source of unsecured loans at low interest. Joining a credit union is wise in any case, because you can't borrow from it unless you also have a savings account there, so membership will support your saving habit. If there's no credit union at your workplace, find one through an organization you belong to. A credit union is like a volunteer fire department. Just as no one should expect to make a profit from putting out fires, no one needs to make a financial killing lending money to you.

Another source of cheap money is your life insurance policy. You can borrow on your insurance at low interest so long as you have a whole life (rather than simple term) policy. If you own your own home, you've already borrowed much of its value by taking out a mortgage. But with a home equity loan you can borrow against the portion of the house's value that is already yours. For example, if your home is worth $150,000, and your mortgage balance is $100,000, you have $50,000 worth of equity to secure a loan from a bank. Banks compete to lend you this money cheaply because they can't possibly lose (they'll take your home if you default).

A home equity loan couldn't be easier. You're given a line of credit indicating your borrowing limit, and a checkbook. You simply write checks, as needed, to yourself or your creditors and repay a modest portion of your balance each month. Best of all, the interest on these loans is *tax-deductible*. Becky and I used our home equity account to help pay for our daughters' college tuition. Now the account is still there ready to be reactivated should we suffer an emergency and don't want to touch retirement savings that are in investments earning much more.

CREDIT

If either you or your spouse has been refused credit you must discover why. Check your local Yellow Pages under "Credit Reporting Agencies" and write each of them requesting a copy of your report. In your request include your full name, Social Security number, current and former addresses, and the name of your spouse. Enclose a copy of the merchant's letter that denied you credit. By law, the agency must supply your report to you, explain your credit rating, and correct any errors contained in your record.

Becky and I request our report routinely every year even when we're not buying on credit, because every report has contained errors that needed correction. Although we are now more than thirty years into a second marriage, the agencies continued for years to recognize only my first spouse. Incidentally, you have the right to dispute your credit rating in person. You can also add information to your file that may help to explain any late payments or disputes with creditors.

If you ever get turned down for a mortgage or other loan, you have the right to know why. Write the lender within ten days. By law, lenders must explain their decisions, allowing you the opportunity to provide them with better information or to approach another lender with a stronger case. If any creditor refuses to file corrected information on you to the credit bureau, take that merchant to small claims court. For a small fee and no need for an attorney, you will get compliance. Creditors hate the prospect of going to court, so they'll likely comply immediately after your threat.

Financial advisers warn that you may be in financial trouble as a couple if your monthly debt payments exceed 20 percent of your take-home pay. Don't wait until credit is denied altogether to seek assistance. Fortunately, there is plenty of help to go around. Debt counseling service is a competitive field, and it's financed not by debtors but by creditors. That's right: the people to whom you owe money will pay anywhere from 6 percent to 12 percent to professional advisers to help you reorganize your finances and enable you to continue making payments you owe. Why are creditors so generous when the chips are down? Because the alternative is that you might choose bankruptcy, in which case they could collect nothing.

A counseling service will analyze your income and expenses, help you make payments, and tell you precisely how to stay out of debt in the future. If your finances are utterly out of control, your counselor will devise a formal debt-repayment plan, take a single payment from you, and distribute a portion of it to each of your creditors, whereupon they will instantly stop hounding you. In fact, some may offer to lower your monthly payment and interest rate, or waive late payment fees altogether until you've caught up.

However, you won't be able to run up any more charges on those accounts until that time. On average, it takes couples between four and six years to pay off their current debts through a counseling service. But you will still be able to put food on the table while you avoid bankruptcy and harassment.

BANKRUPTCY

You probably associate work houses with the novels of Charles Dickens. But as a child growing up in Depression-era Chicago, I remember my parents showing me a grim Cook County institution everyone called the "poor house." It was the twentieth century version of a debtors' prison.

Fortunately, at some point society decided that it was pointless to incarcerate people simply because they couldn't pay their bills (obviously they couldn't pay them any better from prison). Bankruptcy laws were passed because Congress acknowledged that it was better to give people a second chance to pay their way through life. If you are ever forced to file for bankruptcy you will need a lawyer (see the Yellow Pages for specialists, who will make sure they get paid). Once a judge discharges your debts, you will no longer be responsible for paying them. No creditor can even attempt to make you repay. You cannot be harassed—ever.

However, depending on the court's judgment, you may still be responsible for "nondischargeable debts," including alimony, student loans, and tax obligations. But your remaining assets will not be wiped out. Most states allow bankrupts to keep the equity in their home, their automobile, and their personal property.

Once the court relieves you of your debts, you will have only those assets and your job or jobs. Your wages will have to sustain you, because no bank will lend you money, and no merchant will extend credit to you. Should you change jobs, any prospective employer can request your credit report and learn of your situation. However, that's an unlikely prospect, so you and your spouse can keep looking for better-paying employment that improves your finances.

As soon as possible, you will want to restore your credit and get ahead of the game. First, correct everything in your credit reports that is false or misleading. Send corrections by certified mail, return receipt requested, so (if need be) you can later prove that the bureaus received your request. Unless corrected, bad credit information will remain in your file for seven years. By law, bankruptcy stays on your record for ten years.

If you have steady income and don't want to place yourself in the hands of a credit counselor, choosing Chapter 13 bankruptcy can restore your credit in just three years. Chapter 13 still requires you to pay your creditors what you owe them, but only over an extended period, during which time they cannot harass you. You will need a judge's approval to stretch out payments but won't need to pay a lawyer to make your case for you.

If you ever find yourself in this predicament and make this your choice, experts advise that you allocate no more than 25 percent of your combined income to debt repayment. You must list all debts with the court and show that you can pay them off in about three years. When your application is approved, you will make a single payment from each paycheck to the court itself, which will then disburse the money to your creditors. They cannot bother you or charge you additional interest for the extended repayment period.

TO REESTABLISH CREDIT

If you want to remove your bad credit ratings sooner than ten years, experts recommend that you write to each creditor and strike a bargain. For example, if you owed $1,000 to a furniture company, before having that debt discharged by the court, offer him $200 on the understanding (in writing) that the merchant will remove the bad-debt notice altogether from your report. That's not bribery, just a good bargain all around. The furniture store gets $200 (instead of nothing) and you get a second chance at a good credit rating.

If you have many creditors and little cash, that course may not be feasible. If that's the case, disregard your old bad credit report and start establishing a good new one. Here's how:

1. Establish a savings account in a bank or credit union and make small but regular contributions to it.
2. Later, go to a loan officer in the same institution and ask to borrow an amount equal to your savings on the understanding that your loan will be secured by your savings account. Make sure the loan is reported to the credit bureau.
3. Then take the borrowed money and open a savings account in another bank, making it collateral for another loan there. Now you have two savings accounts. Of course, you're paying interest on your two loans, but regular payment proves you're trustworthy. You're rebuilding credit.
4. Apply for a Visa or MasterCard using one of your savings accounts as collateral. Often a bank will offer you a credit line of 150 percent of your savings balance. With a $1,000 passbook savings account, you will have a credit card with a $1,500 spending limit. Warning: apply for these cards directly, not through a middleman who will charge you for the service.
5. Resume use of any accounts you did not include in your bankruptcy application—those that had a zero balance when you filed for protection. There is no reason these former creditors would know, or even think to ask, about your financial condition. As far as they're concerned, you've always been solvent.
6. Now, keep up with your payments. You'll soon be back on your feet.

COSIGNING

When I married for the first time, credit cards weren't plentiful. I had no debts, but no savings and no credit either. Still, I needed a car. Fortunately, I had a steady job, so I asked my father-in-law to cosign my auto loan. Clearly, he took a risk that I wouldn't keep up payments (in which case he'd be liable for the balance due), but he had already entrusted me with his daughter. And it didn't cost him anything. So he went along.

As you are aware, however, not just couples but whole families can break up over money matters, so it may be better to ask a friend rather than a relative to cosign with you on a loan. If you don't have a cosigner, you can still probably purchase a car on credit, but your required down payment will be larger. So, too, will be the interest on your loan.

How about housing while you're still under the cloud of bankruptcy? Assuming you can afford the payments, you can still rent a house or apartment if you explain your situation to the landlord *before* he sees your credit report. Then offer him a larger security deposit than he usually requires. That's free money to any landlord, and he can evict you before he is out of pocket on your monthly rent.

If you are in the market to buy a house or condo, start with the bank where you've established a savings account and taken out a loan. If the loan officer still rates you as too great a risk for a mortgage loan, try your credit union. Credit unions tend to be more liberal with auto loans and can be understanding about home loans as well. At worst, you'll be required to provide a larger down payment than usual and pay somewhat higher interest. But after a few payments your credit will be restored, and later you can refinance at a lower rate.

You can apply for a Federal Housing Authority (FHA) mortgage loan within just *one* year after your bankruptcy discharge and will need only a modest down payment and enjoy market interest rates. If one of you is a veteran, you can apply for a mortgage with no money down. Even if you're not a vet, you can still assume an *existing* Veterans Administration loan on the home you want.

INVESTING

Once you start saving, you are an investor—unless you're like Becky's late mother, who late in life kept gold Krugerrands under the bedroom floorboards. She worried that America was going the way of the Weimar Republic, when a loaf of bread cost a wheelbarrow full of deutsche marks. To be sure, her savings were safe, but they weren't earning anything.

Personal finance counselor Andrew Tobias provides a handy formula for making your savings multiply:

Make a budget, scrimp and save, quit smoking, fully fund your retirement plan and start early—*tomorrow*, if you possibly can—putting away $100 or $500 or $5,000 a month, whatever you can comfortably afford, in two places: short- and intermediate-term Treasury securities, for money you may need in a few years; and no-load, low-expense stock market "index funds," both U.S. and foreign, for everything else. According to Tobias, you will do better than 80 percent of your friends and neighbors.[2]

If you're under the age of fifty, many experts suggest that you put 80 percent of savings into stock funds, 20 percent in bonds. As you approach retirement, move more into bonds for stability. Remember: you are not saving for a rainy day. Rather, you are investing in sunlight for the rest of your life.

If you find investing tedious, you're like most people, including Becky and me. Happily, couples don't have to do the work. The nation's mutual fund companies will do it for you. Basically, they pool the savings of millions of Americans and invest for you, deducting only a small service fee you will never miss. You deal with the funds entirely over the phone (they don't put you on "hold"), by mail, or online. They regularly inform you how your money is doing, updating your account daily. If you're anxious, of course, you can check the newspaper every day. Mutual funds are for people who don't intend to speculate on the market, but merely ensure a solvent future. Incidentally, a couple's mutual fund savings aren't inaccessible. Just a phone call will return them to you for any reason whatsoever. However, if your savings are in *tax-deferred* funds, IRAs and 401(k)s, you will pay a penalty for early withdrawal.

A little consistent saving can make you a millionaire. Don't take my word for it. The magic is in compound interest. Say you're earning $35,000 and you put 4 percent of that in your employer's 401(k) retirement plan regularly. That's just $27 each week out of your paycheck (less if you figure the taxes that would be assessed if you pocketed that $27). What's $27? The price of a book you could borrow from the library instead of buying. Couples approaching retirement age are advised to invest less in stocks and more in bonds.

Assuming a 7 percent rate of return on your savings, you will have $590,134.11 in fifty years—or well over a million dollars if your employer matches your contributions. In fact, you'll probably have much more, because over the long haul stocks perform well over 7 percent.

To find mutual funds that appeal to you, consult the annual issues of *Money* and *Kiplinger's* magazines that list the performance of all funds. They're in your public library. You'll see how much the funds have returned over the past one, five and ten years. Despite some big winners, most funds don't perform as well as the market as a whole, so follow Andrew Tobias's advice and invest in "market index" funds that make investments that mimic the market.

SPENDING

Set priorities that satisfy your shared goals, not someone else's. Last year pet care was the third-largest expense in our family budget (after groceries and health expenses) because of our dog's and cats' serious health problems. We didn't mind. They're precious to us.

Sometimes cheaper products are best, because they are less complicated. Our new heating and air conditioning system is only the budget model, admittedly less efficient than top-of-the line units. But *Consumer Reports* warned that the more expensive systems need more servicing at extra cost. The more options you choose when you buy a car, the more things you have that can fail.

In my book *Spiritual Simplicity* I outlined easy strategies for saving time and money, and even a few ways of making extra money. I won't repeat them here except to warn that any sensible budget and savings plan will founder if a couple allows big expenses to overwhelm them. Divorce, catastrophic illness, college expenses, and major repair bills can rob you of the "happily ever after" years you're saving for.

Fortunately, you can purchase life, health, disability, and catastrophic illness insurance. You can even buy insurance that pays your mortgage if you lose your job. But some policies are rip-offs, and some are simply not worth the premiums. For example, purchase cheap term life insurance rather than whole-life policies. The money you save can be invested during your lifetime, and your survivors will still be protected by those savings in the event of your death.

College expenses rise faster than other prices. We knew we would have three daughters in college at the same time. To keep tuition and fees within reason, they attended community college, then transferred to state colleges. The exception was our middle daughter, who transferred to the private (and expensive) Corcoran School of Art across from the White House. When she ran out of money after her junior year, she dropped out to work for a year to save for senior-year expenses. Result: college degrees all around and no lingering debts for us or our daughters.

Many states offer savings plans that guarantee to cover tuition and fees for a four-year degree at a public college or university. Before you go into debt paying for prestigious college degrees for your children, be aware that employers seldom if ever ask where job applicants went to college, or even what their grades were, but only whether they graduated.

THE HIGH COST OF DIVORCE

This book is about lifelong marriage, but I'd be remiss if I neglected to acknowledge divorce. Divorce is not only an emotional disaster, but a financial one as well. Still, half of all marriages fail. The only divorce "insurance" is a prenuptial agreement, which is a cynical way to begin a supposedly lifelong, loving partnership. Fortunately, states now typically divide assets down the middle when couples break up. If you go into a marriage unsure of its longevity, a smart thing to do is to set aside some money for each of you should your marriage go belly-up.

In that event, hire a lawyer who specializes in divorce, especially if you have children. Be aware that the cost of a divorce in legal fees alone can be $20,000 to $50,000 per couple. A better course is to jointly hire a mediator trained in conflict resolution, who will charge $150 to $300 an hour but hammer out a fair agreement in fewer than 20 hours (rather than the typical 170 hours when both spouses retain lawyers). Some 85 percent of such mediated divorces cost less than $5,000 per couple. Find a mediator at *www.acrnet.org* and click on "Resources."

SPENDING ON OTHERS

There's a big difference between being money-wise and being cheap. The former is a virtue, the latter a vice. Generally, married couples are frugal with themselves, shopping for quality and discounts. But they can be cheap with other people, leaving a 10 percent tip for good service instead of 15 percent or 20 percent. It's not wise to save at the expense of other people.

One item in your budget should be devoted to saving the world, or at least a small part of it. It's up to you how you do it—through church or charities—but you must give something back as a sign of gratitude for what you have been given. It's not really expensive to be generous.

Ironically, the poorest one-fifth of Americans actually donate a larger percentage of their after-tax income to charity than Americans who earn $100,000 or more. Maybe that's because they understand from experience what "for richer, for poorer" is all about. Although wealthy people itemize their donations and get tax deductions, on average, they contribute less than 3 percent of their income to making the world a better place. Any couple investing in their own happiness needs to invest in others who have less to be happy about.

GET ADVICE

There's wisdom in the cliché that one must sometimes spend money to make money. That's not an invitation to take your chances at the gaming tables in Las Vegas or Atlantic City, but only a suggestion that you occasionally pay an expert for a little advice. If you are like most Americans, you already seek assistance with your income tax returns, but you may use a commercial tax preparer who learned the basics in a brief course and works only at filing time. Even Certified Public Accountants are too overworked at tax time to help you with your overall financial planning.

A warning: Don't ask anyone for advice who wants to sell you something. Some stockbrokers and insurance agents offer "free" financial planning that is biased. When my wife and I were approaching retirement, we went to a neighborhood CPA who had nothing to gain from her counseling but a seventy-five-dollar fee. For that, she told us everything we needed to do to protect our investments, reduce our taxes, and provide insurance against future disability. We've followed through on every one of her strategies to our mutual benefit.

A KIND WORD FOR POVERTY

When you take the marriage vow "for richer, for poorer," you are promising that you will hang together in hard times as well as comfortable ones. Just as everyone has a different notion of what it means to be rich, everyone has a different definition of what it means to be "poor." When housing was short during World War II, my parents, my blind grandfather, and I lived in a small abandoned storefront and bathed in a portable tin tub in the kitchen. We didn't consider ourselves deprived.

During Becky's childhood there were times when food was short and the house's only heat came from a single fireplace. She remembers being cold and hungry. To distract her and her siblings in winter, Becky's mother gathered snow, sweetened it, and called it "snow ice cream." The kids weren't fooled, but they humored their mother. Conditions eventually improved, but through it all, her parents' marriage stayed strong and the family prevailed.

In the course of any marriage a couple's mutual devotion will be tested by illness, accident, and financial strain, if not by true hardship. A healthy marriage is one that survives these tests by putting hope and trust ahead of anxiety. It's worth noting that Jesus of Nazareth actually praised poverty in his

Sermon on the Mount. His point was that it forces a person to focus on what really matters in life.

Tom Mullen, longtime dean of Earlham College, became a widower after forty-one years of marriage. As a Quaker minister he had counseled many couples over the years and has kind words for tight budgets: "Ask most long-married couples the Christmas they best remember, and their answers usually recall times when they were just getting started and could afford only modest gifts. Or they'll remember a time when one or the other was ill, and Thanksgiving, say, was spent in the hospital."[3] He recalls a woman who said of her late husband, "When we were down to our last dollar, we'd get fifty cents worth of gas and go buy one milk shake and two straws."[4]

What matters, Mullen suggests, is not how much money a couple has, but what money *means* to them and how it is *managed*. "In our heart of hearts," he believes, "we value a marriage that can be neither purchased nor starved to death. That's why Jesus born in a manger is our favorite Christmas story, more cherished than the one where royalty show up bearing gold, frankincense, and myrrh."[5]

You don't have to be religious to appreciate Jesus's counsel: "Don't worry about living—wondering what you are going to eat or drink, or what you are going to wear. Surely life is more important than food, and the body more important than the clothes you wear."[6]

Any loving couple will agree.

STEPS IN THE RIGHT DIRECTION

Invest Wisely in Your Life Together

1. Decide what it is you value. "Where your treasure is, your heart will be there also," Jesus noted. You don't have to be religious to agree with him. Decide as a couple what constitute the material *necessities* in your life together beyond food, clothing, and a roof over your heads. A car (or even two of them) may be necessities, but they don't have to be expensive or new. You may consider a college education to be requirement for your children, but an Ivy League campus is not a necessity. Write down your individual and joint priorities for spending.
2. Decide purchases you need now and those you can postpone. Before revolving credit became common, people put down small deposits on "lay-away" purchases, waiting until they had the rest of the cash to

claim the item. These days, it is acceptable to go into debt to purchase a necessity now, but irresponsible to commit yourselves to paying high interest in order to have something you want but can't yet afford.

3. Save. Even if a rainy day doesn't come into your lives, you will need to invest in yourselves and in your future on a regular basis. Marriage is more vulnerable to money worries than to anything else. If you have to reduce your standard of living to save, do it for love. If need be, you can live on love for long periods.

· 6 ·

Comfort and Care

Providing for Your Mutual Health and Well-Being

Sickness is the mother of modesty, putteth us in mind of our mortality . . . pulleth us by the ear, and maketh us know ourselves.

Robert Burton

*W*hen, as a single student in Paris in the 1960s, I contracted scarlet fever, I was confined to my tiny room and enjoyed the rare visitor, but no companion to care for me. I have never felt so lonely or helpless, before or since. One of the most reassuring blessings of marriage is that we gain someone to comfort us and care for us when we're ill.

When I first encountered Becky some twelve years later, I was living alone again in a spartan one-room apartment, cooking on weekends and eating leftovers the remainder of the week to save money. My daughters were living with their mother. It was another solitary time.

Although we hardly knew each other, Becky took an interest in my health, insisting that I take vitamins and eat wholesome food. I was touched. Even before she cared *for* me, Becky cared *about* me. For close to thirty years now we have nursed each other through illnesses and promoted our mutual good health.

But for many of those years I was a reluctant patient. It wasn't until the age of fifty that I awakened to my need to take Becky's caring advice if I expected to live long and well with her.

My wake-up call came as I stood on a subway platform during evening rush hour in Washington, D.C. At the time I suffered from chronic insomnia and was so sleep deprived that I ached from head to foot. It took immense effort to focus my attention on my stressful job and get from task to task and moment to moment.

In my family life I had become a short-tempered zombie, increasingly prone to infection. In the previous year I had suffered two bouts of pneumonia plus strep throat. Standing there in a tiny orgy of self-pity, I peered down at the subway rails and realized why some people would favor oblivion to the lives they are leading.

As I nursed that dismal thought, a young woman standing next to me on the crowded platform keeled over and fell onto the tracks below. Shocked from my reverie, I jumped down onto the roadbed and dragged the unconscious stranger from the rails. Other commuters reached down from the platform and pulled her limp body back before the next train arrived, lifting me to safety as well. Whatever prompted her fall, it was clearly not a suicide attempt, but a near-tragic fainting. All I could conclude was that, if an attractive professional woman still in her twenties could find herself in such danger, a fifty-year-old man had better start looking after his own life.

Becky insisted I get serious about my health. My employer referred me to his personal doctor, who tested me as never before in my life. Although I had suffered from allergies since childhood, I now learned that they were so severe that they were robbing me of my resistance to infection. Over time I was informed that I also suffered from hyperglycemia, an overactive liver, high blood pressure, an enlarged prostate, and glaucoma, not to mention sinusitis, arthritis, and fallen arches, and I had became prediabetic. A heart murmur had kept me from competitive sports in my teens. In advanced middle age, it became potentially life threatening.

HOW MUCH HEALTH CAN A COUPLE EXPECT?

Americans spend more per person on health care than the citizens of any other nation—more than $4,500 per year. But the evidence is that the investment has not ensured a higher quality of life. In Costa Rica, for example, the personal investment in health is less than $300 per year, and the country has only half as many doctors per capita as the United States. Yet life expectancy at birth is nearly identical there as here.

Although Medicare expenditures have doubled in the past decade, the Social Security Administration reveals that life expectancy among women at age sixty-five is shrinking. Meanwhile, men and women in their thirties are 130 percent more likely to be disabled than twenty years ago, primarily because of obesity. The age-adjusted death rate from diabetes increased by 39 percent over the same period, chronic lung disease by 49 percent, and kidney disease by 21 percent. Every year some 200,000 older Americans suffer fatal or life-threatening effects from improper drug use or interaction, and 90,000 patients in our nation's hospitals die from infections they contracted there.

To be sure, marriage is not the remedy for these dire prospects, but a couple that takes seriously their vow to care for each other in sickness and in health are bound to have less of the former and more of the latter.

The reason Americans don't live longer than Costa Ricans is because of bad health habits. We eat more, exercise less, spend more time in our cars, smoke more, and pursue more socially isolated lives. Phillip Longman, a senior fellow at the New America Foundation, acknowledges that "even at its best, modern medicine can do little to promote productive aging, because by the time most people come in contact with it their bodies are already compromised by stress, indulgent habits, environmental dangers, and injuries. Today, about 127 million adults in the United States are obese or overweight, 47 million still smoke, 14 million abuse alcohol, and 16 million use addictive drugs."[1]

One of the major missions in marriage is for husbands and wives to keep each other healthy. Tom Mullen, the Indiana Quaker minister, knew that his young bride had suffered from diabetes since childhood and was insulin dependent. From the outset their daily schedule required choosing food carefully and eating on a regular schedule. Still there were episodes when an insulin imbalance caused his wife to act as if she were inebriated—incoherent, with muscle spasms and slurred speech, and bizarre behavior.

"Over the years," he recalls, "I waited with her through many insulin reactions, sitting beside her pouring orange juice down her throat or putting honey in her mouth while she was semiconscious."[2] Ironically, in middle age, he became an insulin-dependent diabetic as well. He writes movingly about a time he and his wife were hospitalized in adjoining rooms, she to have a leg amputated, he to have his colon removed. "Loving your spouse doesn't cease when age brings wrinkles, you settle for a semicolon instead of a colon, and your wife loses a leg to disease," he reveals.[3]

During bouts of illness Mullen and his wife speculated about which of them would leave the other widowed. "She always said she wouldn't remarry herself, but she thought I should," he remembers. "Then she'd smile her glorious smile and add: 'Given the fact that you're a diabetic, have an ileostomy, and have Crohn's disease, you probably should limit your courtship to doctors, nurses, and pathologists.'"[4]

PICK YOURSELF UP, DUST YOURSELF OFF, START ALL OVER AGAIN

Today, in my seventies, thanks to Becky's urging, I am healthier than I was in my thirties, less prone even to common colds. None of my medical conditions has been *cured*, to be sure, but all are neutralized by dint of new habits, diet, and medication, and I feel better than I did when just half my present age. I credit Becky and my doctor, who both remind me that I am not just an intellect carried around inside a body, but a complete creature consisting of body, spirit, and emotions. We've learned that good health requires tending to all three.

Governor Adlai Stevenson was fond of quoting this conversation between an aunt and her favorite niece. *Aunt to niece:* "What do you want to be when you grow up?" *Niece:* "Alive."

Wouldn't we all? Dr. Walter M. Boritz II of Stanford University Medical School insists that the human animal is designed to last over a hundred years, but most of us manage to survive only a fraction of that span. Unfortunately, our Creator did not provide couples with 120-year factory warranties. The problem with prematurely deceased people, as with short-lived automobiles, is poor maintenance. By our habits we consign ourselves too soon to the human junkyard.

Few of us live long enough to die of old age. Our doctors are not to blame. Most of us die from self-administered abuse and indifference. One of the great advantages of marriage is that we gain a "better half" who has an investment in our caring better for ourselves and sharing a longer life with us.

Life expectancy has risen by more than 50 percent since 1920, and infant mortality has plummeted 2,000 percent since the turn of the century. Infectious diseases have been largely controlled by a combination of public sanitation, antibiotics, and inoculations. Heart surgery and organ transplants have literally given millions a new lease on life.

At the same time, every one of us is constitutionally weaker or stronger because of our genetic makeup. Becky's father favored a diet of chili dogs and candy bars, shunned exercise, and smoked until he was seventy. He survived a heart attack and gall bladder operation, and lived a long, robust life. By contrast, her mother took impeccable care of herself. A vegetarian, she was partial to organic foods, neither smoked nor drank, practiced yoga, kept slim, and exercised regularly. But she died of lymphatic cancer just six months after her husband.

Perhaps as important as a couple's health habits is their outlook. Becky's father was a born optimist and shared a spiritual kinship with Emerson and Thoreau. Her mother was a worrier and possessed no religious faith to make her feel at home with the universe.

TAKING CHARGE OF YOUR LIFE

Happy couples live longer. So do people with religious beliefs. Over 250 studies have demonstrated that, regardless of the type of belief, those who employ religious or spiritual practices in their lives will, on average, live longer, be ill less regularly, and be less prone to cancer than nonbelievers. Although there is anecdotal evidence that faith healing works, you won't want to rely on miracles to keep you and your spouse healthy. When you are ill you will need your doctor's counsel and care. But to *stay* well you must also be your physician's understudy, dispensing prescriptions that include sleep, diet, and exercise, along with positive thinking, steady breathing, proper posture, a calm mind, and frequent laughter. Contentment is good medicine. Joy is even better. Love is the very best prescription. Marriage can deliver all three. If as a couple you have your health you may not have *everything*, but you will have a foundation on which to build a satisfying life together.

There's more to health than popping pills. The two of you must take charge of your lives so you will have the prospect of golden years together. "Wellness" is not just the absence of illness, but the positive pursuit of contentment. A Gallup poll reveals that 85 percent of Americans acknowledge that their physical well-being depends on how well they take care of themselves. In a sense, medical science looks through the wrong end of the telescope, focusing on disease and dysfunction. By contrast, health maintenance concentrates on wellness of body, mind, and spirit. Because there are two of you, you have a partner to help you be well.

Author Greg Anderson was diagnosed in 1984 with metastatic cancer and was given thirty days to live. Instead, he rallied to his own aid and became cancer free, largely by altering his attitude and lifestyle. He became persuaded that life's joy, not its length, is the measure of wellness, and that couples are responsible for their own wellness, which includes health of mind and spirit. They must keep physically and mentally active, eat for nourishment and enjoyment rather than compensation, choose the least-invasive medical treatment when ill, be positive, control stress, respect themselves, and acknowledge that they already possess everything in their life to be happy—jettisoning regret for the past and worry for the future.

He urges couples to focus on life as a journey rather than a destination, and to act from vision and purpose, pursuing personal growth rather than the fountain of youth, gratefully appreciating their lives as both a gift and a responsibility.

PAIN, PAIN, GO AWAY

Biotechnologists predict that in the twenty-second century men and women will live indefinitely long lives, dying mainly from accidents, murder, or war, rather than from disease or old age. Humans will be like classic automobiles, kept going with spare parts and periodic overhauls. Regular injections of stem cells will revitalize human organs. However, there will still be pain.

Pain, of course, is not an illness but only a sign of something gone wrong. Unfortunately, pain *shouts* when a whisper would be a sufficient reminder to seek a remedy for the underlying malady. Most people can be reconciled to chronic conditions but few to the pain that accompanies them. So we need to neutralize the agony that goes with illness.

Fortunately, because pain is subjective, it can be managed through our reaction to it. Unfortunately, many doctors expect "good" patients not to complain of pain, but to grin and bear it. If that is your doctor's attitude, don't buy into it. Every couple is subject to illness from time to time, but no one need be victimized by pain. Fortunately, new drug-delivery systems allow pain-relieving remedies to be absorbed at consistent levels without side effects such as drowsiness and nausea. Transdermal patches, nasal sprays, and tiny electronic devices allow pain relievers to seep through the skin. Moreover, some new pills apply steady medication for twelve hours.

Don't hesitate to ask your doctor to prescribe something effective for your pain. Medical schools still provide scant training in pain management, and many physicians persist in dismissing chiropractors as quacks. Best-selling author Dr. Bernie Siegel alarmingly reveals that many doctors care inadequately for their *own* well-being, so you may have to prod them to pay full attention to yours. On average, physicians have more problems with drug and alcohol dependency than their patients, as well as a higher suicide rate. And they die sooner after the age of sixty-five than the rest of us.

Many doctors hesitate to prescribe narcotics even to terminally ill patients for fear it will lead to addiction, hasten death, or involve them in malpractice suits. Dr. B. Eliot Cole of the American Academy of Pain Management protests that "a patient who wants to commit suicide to get relief from pain is not receiving the kind of care he or she needs. That care is available—patients and their families need to demand it."[5]

Everyone's pain is personal. Anyone who says, "I feel your pain," is fooling you. Because suffering is subjective, spouses tend to be inarticulate in describing it to each other, let alone to their doctors. Experts in pain control suggest the first step in relieving pain is to *confront* it by describing it to ourselves. All pain is not alike. Once you meet your pain and define it, you can be on your way to mastering it with the support of your spouse.

The trick here is to separate oneself from the pain. Instead of complaining that "*I* hurt," just acknowledge, "The pain is *there*." Your spouse can help you follow these steps when you're hurting:

- Create a vivid image of your pain, objectifying it.
- Begin relaxing with slow, steady breathing.

- Detach your mind from the weight of your body.
- Concentrate on the image of your pain as something "out there."
- Imagine your pain draining away.

SLEEP

The three pillars of a couple's health management are sleep, exercise, and nutrition. By rights, sleep should be the easiest of the three to manage, because it literally involves doing *nothing*. But you both need enough sleep. If you are tired and inattentive during the day, you are probably not getting enough sleep. The best rest regimen is for both of you to maintain the same hours for retiring and waking every day of the week. "Catching up" by sleeping late on weekends or taking the occasional nap does not remedy sleep deprivation.

If you sleep well, be grateful. But if you are like Becky and me (and one-third of your fellow Americans), you have trouble sleeping well consistently. Being bedfellows is romantic only if you both sleep well. If poor rest is seriously interfering with your waking hours, sleep clinics can reveal the causes. Often the culprit is troubled breathing, or apnea. Snoring is not simply a trial for your bedmate but can be dangerous to your health.

Dr. James W. Pearce, director of the Sleep Disorders Center of the Pacific in Honolulu, admits that even he manages a truly refreshing night's rest only on vacation. His prescription: Don't oversleep because of the previous night's wakefulness. If you can't sleep, stop trying. Sleep can't be forced. Have a light snack before bedtime. Avoid drugs, including nicotine, alcohol, caffeine, and antihistamines before bedtime. Practice relaxation techniques and don't worry if you don't get eight hours. You may not need that much rest.

Dr. Pearce advises exercising earlier in the day, using the bedroom only for sleep and lovemaking, not eating, TV watching, reading, or working. If your sex life leaves you excited rather than relaxed, he counsels moving your love life to a different room and time of day. If either of you can't get to sleep until 3 A.M. but must wake at 7, go to bed at 3 A.M. After a week of sleeping well for just four hours a night, retire fifteen minutes earlier the next night and work your way incrementally to a full night's sleep.

In my own struggles with insomnia, I tried both over-the-counter and prescription nostrums for sleep. The former leave you feeling drugged next morning. The latter may induce amnesia, sleepwalking, and personality change, and can become habit forming. I was prescribed the drug Halcion when it was the state-of-the-art remedy. It turned me into a cantankerous Mr. Hyde before I fell asleep. When I awoke, my family told me what a monster I had been the night before, but I had no recollection of it. I felt innocent because I had total amnesia. Because of similar reports, Halcion was banned in Great Britain.

EXERCISE

Just because exercise is fashionable doesn't mean it is popular. Despite Nike's urging the population to "Just do it," only one-third of us do. Older couples are even less inclined to be active. Part of the appeal of exercise is that it enhances our feeling of well-being, but nowadays it is also used as part of a regimen to keep weight down and make men and women look and feel more attractive.

Its real importance is to keep a couple healthy. Ironically, as our lives becomes more stressful, we become more sedentary—a life-shortening combination. Darwin was right about the survival of the fittest. But don't expect your doctor to tell you how to exercise. Most physicians were never taught about exercise in medical school, and physical fitness is not mentioned in many of the leading medical textbooks even today.

The first time I ever heard the word exercise from my doctor was when I developed high blood pressure in middle age, then again when I tested as pre-diabetic. Still, it's never too late to start. The benefits of exercise for longevity are proven. The *Journal of the American Medical Association* reports that for every hour spent exercising, two to three hours of life are added to your lifespan. The benefits are most apparent after the age of seventy. Happily, the positive effect of exercise on a couple's *mental* health is almost immediate.

One purpose of exercise is cardiovascular conditioning. The heart, lungs, blood vessels, tendons, and bones are brought to their highest working efficiency. We make better use of oxygen, make the best use of food, and even eliminate body wastes more effectively. This requires endurance (or aerobic) exercise, not just touching our toes. Three sessions a week of sustained, moderately vigorous exercise for thirty minutes is adequate. You must loosen up beforehand by stretching so you won't strain muscles. In aerobic exercise you will break into a sweat.

Researchers suspect the three-times-a-week optimal exercise regimen has roots in our primitive makeup. Eskimos and other hunter-gatherer populations chase their prey three times a week, resting on alternate days.

Textbooks tell us that for optimum results we should exercise at 70 percent of our maximum. That requires couples to determine their individual pulse rates. For a sixty-year-old the 70 percent level should be something like 112 beats per minute. Couples at all ages can exercise together with little danger of overdoing it. Walking isn't boring when you have each other to talk to.

NUTRITION

The words nutrition and diet are often used interchangeably, but increasingly diet describes weight-loss regimens. Perhaps you need to lose weight to be healthy (obesity is increasingly killing people in their thirties!), but everyone at every age requires good nutrition.

As a child I observed meatless Fridays and occasional days of fast and abstinence with my parents. Jews have dietary restrictions, and Muslims prescribe fasts as well. The purpose of fasting is to make believers think of food (and life itself) as a gift, not a given. In our secular fast-food, snack-food, eat-on-the-run culture, too many couples not only don't think about their food but also don't *enjoy* it sufficiently.

Eating is a pleasure. Arguably, it is the most reliable and democratic pleasure, and the one most open to variety. Sex may be ecstatic, but food preparation can be an art and is a renewable feast. If you doubt me, check any large bookstore and count the titles devoted to food and drink. There are more cookbooks in print than books devoted to pleasing all our other senses combined.

Marriage means homemaking. The kitchen is arguably the most important room in a couple's house or apartment. At a couple's wedding reception, the newlyweds traditionally serve each other the first slices of their wedding cake. Eating at the same table has been a ritual from ancient times.

Eating sensibly does not deny anyone the pleasure of the palate. Although I was brought up with Popeye cartoons promoting the nutritional advantages of canned spinach, I loathed canned spinach. But as an adult I discovered fresh spinach—a revelation. Now, on the annual occasion when Becky and I treat ourselves to dinner at the Savoy Grill in London, I request creamed spinach even though it is not on the menu.

Food manufacturers increasingly cater to good nutrition with tasty low-salt, low-fat, low-cholesterol and sugar-free versions of their regular products. But they can't force us to eat them. If you do, you will live longer and protect yourself from disease. The late Dr. John Knowles, administrator of Massachusetts General Hospital and president of the Rockefeller Foundation, insisted that "over 99 percent of us are born healthy and are made sick as a result of personal misbehaviors and environmental conditions."[6] Since you are cooking and eating together as a couple, you are responsible for each other's nutrition.

Even competing diet gurus agree on nutritional guidelines endorsed by the National Academy of Sciences, which call for reducing your consumption of saturated and unsaturated fats, avoiding fried foods, and cutting back on butter, cream, and salad dressings, or switching to low-fat or no-fat versions.

Also, favor fresh fruit and vegetables and whole-grain cereals, avoid salt-cured and charcoal-broiled foods, and drink moderately.

Needless to say, it's easier to stick to the rules if your spouse joins and encourages you.

DEALING WITH DOCTORS

Becky and I share a physician who routinely runs late on his appointments. We've learned to tolerate his tardiness, because he spends as much time with each patient as that person needs, treating *people*, not ailments. Despite disincentives from the HMOs that insure his patients' health care (and provide him a living), he regularly refers them to specialists for additional tests, as needed, and encourages annual physicals, flu shots, exercise, and diet regimens. Our doctor is not getting rich, but his patients are staying healthy.

However, despite his insistence on patients taking charge of their own health management, his waiting room tends to be filled week after week with repeat offenders, who expect him to work miracles on bodies that have been abused through the years. An additional advantage for the couple that settles on the same primary physician is that each can bring the doctor up to date on the spouse's health.

Just because each of you is a patient doesn't mean that *patience* is the virtue you bring to the relationship with your doctor. Dr. Bernie Siegel, who assists men and women stricken with cancer, reckons that 60 to 70 percent of patients present themselves to their physicians like actors auditioning for a part. They perform the way they believe their doctor has scripted their role—passively taking their medicine, letting the physician do all the guessing, and only balking when the doctor urges them to make radical improvements in their lifestyles.

Dr. Siegel reveals that 10 to 15 percent of patients actually *welcome* serious illness as a diversion from their everyday problems. Emotionally attached to their maladies, they chronically fail to maintain their end of the doctor-patient relationship.

At the opposite extreme are 15 to 20 percent of patients who refuse to play the victim. They choose to take charge of their health rather than expect the doctor to *make* them well. They question every procedure, digging in their heels until they are satisfied that it makes sense. They read everything they can about their affliction so they can have intelligent conversations with their doctor. Hopefully, both you and your spouse are members of this demanding group.

Physicians have slowly come to acknowledge that the patients they consider feisty and uncooperative are the ones determined to get well, and who do actually improve. In a London sample, cancer patients with a "fighting spirit" enjoyed a ten-year survival rate of 75 percent, compared with only 22 percent for those who felt hopeless and helpless, passively accepting whatever the doctors did for them.

A century ago, America's founding psychologist, William James, wrote, "The greatest discovery of my generation is that human beings, by changing the inner attitudes of their minds, can change the outer aspects of their lives." You can too—all the better because you have each other.[7]

PRACTICAL PRACTICES

It is wise to write your doctor in advance of *every* visit, reminding him or her of the regimen you are on, the medications you are taking, and the progress you are making. That is the proactive way of presenting yourself and engaging a physician as your collaborator. Rest assured, your letter will be read, go into your permanent file, and be taken seriously.

If you're unhappy with your doctor, ask a nurse to refer you to the physicians she recommends in your area. Nurses are knowledgeable about what doctors can and cannot do, and how they deal with patients. Nurses are not bedazzled by medical alchemy. And they go to doctors too when they are ill.

Most important is that spouses become each other's advocates. That means not only nursing and supporting, but dealing forcibly with doctors and health care professionals. Parents do this automatically for their sick children. They must also stand up for each other when dealing with health professionals.

Unfortunately, the last thing a person in ill health is inclined to do is make demands on his or her doctor. As it is, physicians too often prescribe patience and a stiff upper lip as the best medicine, which is just another expression for "grin and bear it" and is unacceptable. When either of us is suffering from a serious condition, Becky and I visit our doctor *together* to vouch for the symptoms and to explain the effect of the illness on our lives together. It's difficult for a doctor to dismiss a patient's report when he or she must answer to a concerned spouse.

A word of caution: It is also important that the sick spouse be honest with husband, wife, and doctor about how badly he or she feels. Sadly, my own father was of the stiff-upper-lip school and didn't want to "bother" my mother, his doctor, or me when, in middle age, he became slow in speech and clumsy in gait. We just thought Dad was getting absentminded.

In fact, he was covering up the hardening of the arteries to his brain, which caused permanent damage and resulted in his forced retirement at the early age of sixty-one, followed by some twenty years of progressive physical and mental decline, more than half of them in a nursing home. Lesson: Complain when there's something to complain about and something can be done to remedy or alleviate the condition.

SEVEN COUPLES WHO CARE

In the popular novel and film *Love Story*, a young bride died prematurely. In real life most young newlyweds can't envision "in sickness and in health" ever applying to them. But as marriages mature, the need for husband and wife to care for each other becomes inevitable. When I reflect on this traditional marital vow, the picture that comes immediately to mind is Ronald Reagan being devotedly nursed by his wife Nancy. For years prior to his death the former president, suffering from advanced Alzheimer's disease, could no longer even recognize the spouse who cared for him.

It is reassuring to have the spouse who shared your life when you were both healthy care for you when you are needy. *George and Eva Low* are Chinese Americans married for more than sixty years, enduring financial hardship together for many of them. In advanced age Eva was diminished. "One day I feel pretty good, then another day I'm down," she said. "I had internal bleeding, then a heart attack and a stroke. I had to call 911 and go back to the hospital six times after that. George was so nervous."

"I'm lost without her," he admitted. "I depend on her so much." Eva's eyesight was failing, so George helped her with the cooking, getting her medicine, and helping her in the bath. They don't go out much. "I don't know how she's going to feel," George Low explains. "A lot of times she gets an attack anywhere." The Lows admit they pray a lot together.[8]

Gil and Becky Johnson have been married for over thirty years. Gil was born with only limited vision and over time became totally blind. Becky is legally blind, with no vision at all in one eye. "I'm definitely more of a risk-taker than she is," Gil admits. "Now, if Becky found herself in the middle of the street with cars coming, she'd either panic or run like hell. . . . But the truth is, if I were going to insist that we cross when I think it's safe, we probably wouldn't walk anywhere together."

The Johnsons learned to accommodate their disabilities. Relying on limited vision, Becky reads the mail, writes the checks, and does most of the cooking and cleaning. Gil does the couple's budgeting with a calculator or a Braille ledger. "Our marriage isn't spectacular," Gil says. "It's not razzle-dazzle. It's something that has evolved, grown, and matured. . . . It won't evaporate, that I'm sure of." Becky adds: "We've never faced any real tragedies. . . . We'll stay healthy, knock on wood, for a reasonable length of time."

"Maybe 90, 95 years, something like that," Gil says with a grin.[9]

Mildred and Alden Wagner have been married for close to seventy years. They have two children, four grandchildren, and three great-grandchildren. When she was eighty-five, she announced to her husband, "I can't breathe, I can't breathe." She was having a heart attack. X-rays showed four blockages in her heart. Alden recalls, "We'd always made our decisions together, and now I have to decide whether to let them do this or that to her."

"No heroics," Mildred insisted, and Alden wondered whether to put her through the pain and discomfort. But when the doctor said he didn't want to install a pacemaker, Alden told him, "Well, if it's going to help her, do it." Mildred is still around, and Alden exults: "Look at her, boy, we've got the flag back on top of the hill now, don't we?"[10]

Sue and Emil Siegel have been married nearly as long as the Wagners. In 1990 after a heart operation Sue lost most of her memory, so Emil has since tended to speak for them both. "Now she is essentially dependent on me," he admits. "I cook, dress her, and clean the house, and she's learned to live with it. Since Sue got sick, we don't fight anymore. I don't look at it for better or for worse; it comes naturally. When I was sick when we were young, she stayed with me. One of the secrets of long-term marriage is to do something to make the other person happy all the time." For every anniversary of their marriage he has given her roses "because I love her."[11]

David and Marnie Wood have been married for over forty years. They met as dancers with the Martha Graham dance company. In 1982 David was diagnosed with muscular dystrophy, and fourteen years later learned that he had Parkinson's disease. By 1994 he was confined to a wheelchair, but continued to be a choreographer for the Martha Graham Studio while Marnie ran the dance department at the University of California at Berkeley.

As her husband's caretaker, Marnie says, "We've always related to dancing, teaching, and parenting in terms of the total involvement of both of us. The same goes for his illness. I'm glad I'm here with him and that there are two of us to deal with it. We're two different sides of something that becomes a unit, and that's family."[12]

Frank and Margaret Cruz have been married for nearly half a century. Margaret, a community activist, became a lawyer at the age of sixty-two, determined to run for public office as a Hispanic American. When their only child was just two years old, Margaret contracted polio and spent a year bedridden, immobilized from the neck down. Then in 1994 she contracted cancer and had breast surgery. Since then Frank shops, cooks, cleans, and does the laundry. "I think that cemented our relationship," Frank says.

"My family really loved me through that cancer," admits feisty Margaret. "They took care of me, warts and all."[13]

Tandy Beal and Jonathan Scoville, both artists, met on a blind date when she was fourteen and he was nineteen. They were married after living together for twenty-seven years. Three weeks before the wedding she underwent a hysterectomy, and Jon's father lost his vision and began his final decline.

"Marriage has altered our relationship," Tandy admits with pride. "Since then there's been this magical pixie dust that's settled in around us. In your 20s you feel so thoroughly immortal, but when you take vows in your mid-40s, as we did, at a point when you realize that life is short, the mystery is richer and therefore the impact is greater."

"When the part about richer and poorer, sickness and health came up," Jon says, "I lost it because we'd lived through those things. When you marry at 20 you don't really know what those words are going to mean. But suddenly saying them and knowing what they have meant over the last 30 years, just really broke me up."

"One thing that I'm grateful for," Tandy says, "is that Jon and I both realize the fragility of our lives. . . . It's a deep river that connects us and inspires us to treat each other with respect." Her husband agrees: "I think it's a form of prayer."[14]

STEPS IN THE RIGHT DIRECTION

In Sickness and in Health

1. Playing doctor and nurse. No, it's not a sex game. These are the roles you need to assume in the course of any marriage. Physicians no longer make home visits, so you must play both doctor and nurse whenever your spouse is sick or disabled. That may mean taking time off from work for the duration and caring for your children while tending to your mate. These ordeals test whether you are mature or still *dependent* yourself. An even *bigger* challenge comes when both of you are ill at the same time. Be philosophical and loving: at least you're not suffering alone.

2. Caring for a sick child. Be prepared for a call from the school nurse telling you to come pick up your child, even when the tyke is suffering little more than the sniffles and when your place of business is far from home. Decide which of you will respond to these calls. Husbands and fathers are not automatically exempt.

3. Monitor each other's health. If your spouse is suffering, your marriage can suffer. But your spouse might not admit to his or her complaints. Be sensitive to changes in attitude and behavior. Depression can be no more than the "blues," but it can also be a chronic illness that requires treatment. Don't nag, but offer to accompany your spouse to a consultation and explain to the doctor any changes you've noticed in behavior or mood.

4. Be prepared. If either spouse becomes disabled, or when both become limited by reason of age, their vow to care for each other in sickness and in health becomes a daily responsibility. Some of the couples I've quoted are truly heroic as loving caretakers.

   Occasionally, however, caregiving can become a heavy burden and your home can seem like an infirmary. Don't let it happen.

   Marriage requires mutual assistance, but not martyrdom. If your spouse becomes housebound, don't become a hermit yourself. Hire someone to relieve you for an hour or two during the day. If you can afford it when you enter your retirement years, invest in a long-term care insurance policy that will pay for residential nursing home care or for nursing assistance in your home.

· 7 ·

Loving and Cherishing

There Are Many Parties to a Good Marriage

> For this is one of the miracles of love; it gives . . . a power of seeing through its own enchantments and yet not being disenchanted.
>
> C. S. Lewis

𝒢eorge Mason, author of the prototype for the Declaration of Independence, married his wife, Ann, when she was only sixteen. She gave birth to twelve children before dying at the age of thirty-nine. On Ann's death Mason composed this eulogy:

> In the beauty of her person and the sweetness of her disposition, she was equalled by few and excelled by none. . . . She was an easy and agreeable companion, a kind neighbor, a steadfast friend, a humane mistress, a prudent and tender mother, a faithful, affectionate, and most obliging wife . . . formed for domestic happiness, without one jarring atom in her frame.[1]

Nowadays we shy from expressing such expansive sentiments, fearing that we will sound maudlin and merely sentimental. With easy access to e-mail and cell phones, spouses have lost the habit of composing love letters, leaving them in danger of forgetting what it is that they no longer express to each other in words.

In his famed tribute to love, Saint Paul underscored that it is not merely a sentiment but a virtue that must be acted out:

> If I speak with the eloquence of men and of angels, but have no love, I become no more than blaring brass or crashing cymbal. . . . This love of which I speak is slow to lose patience—it looks for a way of being constructive. It

97

is not possessive: it is neither anxious to impress nor does it cherish inflated ideas of its own importance. . . . Love has good manners and does not pursue selfish advantage. It is not touchy. . . . Love knows no limit to its endurance, no end to its trust, no fading of its hope; it can outlast anything. Love never fails. . . . In this life we have three lasting qualities—faith, hope and love. But the greatest of them is love.[2]

The saint never married. But what he wrote about love for God, humankind, and all creation remains the perfect recipe for married love as well.

THE TRUTH ABOUT BEING SINGLE

Shane Wilson, who has been single most of her life, believes that, for all that has been written about the single life in the twenty-first century, the unmarried state is misrepresented. Forget "swinging singles," she says. "The first thing you should know is that being single makes you unbelievably selfish. . . . Singleness spoils you. . . . Someone annoys you, or life has tired you out—you just go home, lock the door and take the phone off the hook . . . you are answerable to nobody. This total lack of responsibility and please-yourself existence is addictive and, like all addictions, it simply isn't normal."[3]

Really *normal* people, in Wilson's estimation, are those who are married: "Normal people jostle along together and compromise and make do, and spend a significant amount of time considering the needs of their partner and their children."[4]

Wilson lives in England and has a special take on how a woman there eventually discovers the single life to be more restrictive than being wed:

Talk of gardening, you never have a garden if you're single, do you? You can't live in the country because you would get too lonely. . . . You can't dress unbelievably tartily if you're single (if there is a man in the background, it's sexy; if not, it's desperate). You can't get a dog, or everyone will think it's a baby. You can't go on romantic holidays. You can't have delicious food at home for no particular reason (nobody cooks for one). Plus, it is so expensive being on your own. There is nobody to share the mortgage with, or the car.

Her conclusion: "Help—better find someone quick."[5]

THE HEART IS A STUBBORN ORGAN

In his own words Tennessee Williams affirmed as much. Later, David Weinlick proved it when he abandoned bachelorhood for a life of loving and cherishing.

In 1998, the University of Minnesota graduate student posted a "bride wanted" notice on the Internet and received over 500 responses. After narrowing the field to twenty-eight potential mates, he invited them to the Mall of America in suburban Bloomington, where he interviewed them all, finally selecting Elizabeth Runze. David proposed to her on the spot, she accepted, and they were married in the mall just six hours later, their match approved by both sets of parents.

The Weinlicks are still married, living in a home of their own with a little dog, Thor. From the outset they agreed to have children. "We've been pleasantly surprised at how easy it's been," Elizabeth confided about their life together. "When people ask me how come our relationship's still working, I ask them: 'What about all the other couples who meet on blind dates and get married?' We're not so different."

The only apparent glitch was David's snoring, which occasionally drove his wife from the bedroom. Actually, husband and wife are compatible: both of them were twenty-eight-year-old students with similar values and goals when they met and wed. "It was an unusual way to get married," David acknowledges, "but we're very much in love." Elizabeth adds: "It's worked out far better than I ever dreamed. He is everything I prayed I'd have in a life partner."

Not many men or women anxious to shed the single life for marital happiness seek their mate at the local mall. But it's worth analyzing what David and Elizabeth did right that many others in intimate relationships do wrong. Both had long known what they expected from marriage and were willing to make a lifetime commitment to someone equally committed who shared the same standards.

According to statistical averages alone, the Weinlicks might have only a fifty-fifty chance of making their relationship a lifelong success, but they have already vastly improved their odds. Couples who live together before marriage have a higher rate of divorce than those who plunge in. Experts agree that couples who opt for trial runs of sexual compatibility remain tentative about commitment even after making their union legal.[6]

LOOKING FOR LOVE

All humans look for love. Unfortunately, many of us look in the wrong places because we know neither our options nor our minds. Sex can be purchased, but affection is priceless. Love is free, but it must be reciprocal, and it comes without a lifetime guarantee.

Nor is romance the only connection worth human quest. Men and women alike need friendship, respect, and affection to season and strengthen an exclusive and passionate relationship. All are ingredients of a marriage partnership that satisfies for a lifetime.

Many people require second chances at loving and cherishing because they got off on the wrong foot the first time around. Becky and I, together over thirty years, dearly wish we had met each other long before. Instead, each of us is the survivor of an ill-advised and painful first marriage. We represent each other's second chance at happiness. Accordingly, we have invested a lot in making us a success together. If you are in a similar situation, you can, with discretion and effort, be a success in a marriage the second time around.

Today half of American high school students have already engaged in sexual intercourse, and one in six teenage boys and girls has had four or more sexual partners. Sex is no longer the mystery it was when Becky and I were growing up. But, oddly, the casualness of passion among contemporary young people has made them wary of one another. *Washington Post* columnist Carolyn Hax, who regularly advises the "under-thirty crowd" about relationships, advises:

> These modern times are utterly devoid of dating rules and methods, courtesy of the free-love freaks of a certain generation that I won't name except to say that it rhymes with "maybe tumors." Now we're supposedly unfettered by stiff social rituals, and therefore free to mix and match with people based purely on character and chemistry. Thanks guys! Except you forgot those rituals helped people meet in the first place, which strikes me as a rather crucial step, and they came in very handy when it was time to send men home to their own beds.[7]

In 1997 Arthur Levine, president of Teacher's College at Columbia University, having surveyed 9,100 students, including focus groups on thirty campuses across the nation, discovered that they preferred casual sexual liaisons to emotional intimacy and commitment. "When students talked about relationships, the majority said they'd never seen a successful adult relationship in their lives," his study revealed. "They're scared of relationships, of deep involvement, and that doesn't happen. Sex does happen. One way you overcome the fear of a relationship is you get loaded first, and after getting loaded you go back to somebody's room and do it."[8]

CONNECTING

So here we are in the twenty-first century trying to grasp something that used to come naturally. From the *Washington Post* classifieds:

Women Seeking Men

40-year-old, pretty, vivacious, classy, fun DWPF, non-smoker, fit, loves hiking, biking, tennis, travel, Golden Retrievers, nights by the fire. ISO DWPM, N/S, college graduate, successful, sincere, warmhearted, 5'8" plus.

Men Seeking Women

Tall, handsome, complex, successful, 45-year-old SWM ISO intelligent, tall, attractive, fit, active, romantic 35-ish WPF. Ready to give and receive 100 percent commitment and full partnership with lifelong best friend.

Assuming he can fit golden retrievers into a "100 percent commitment" and will budge five years in his search for a younger woman—and assuming she can handle his "complexity"—one would hope these two might exchange letters and photos through their anonymous mail boxes at the newspaper, and meet face-to-face. Clearly they haven't run into each other by any of the traditional ways: at church, the office, in college or clubs, or being introduced by married friends. Those were the old options, and they worked. Sadly, they have long since been consigned to the dustbins of romantic history.

But wait: they *still* work. Even arranged marriages work. Indeed, such marriages function better than the typical romantic union, wherein passion is expected to precede and promote commitment. Around the world, most marriages are still arranged either by families or introductions by third parties. Those unions last because husband and wife enter the relationship with eyes wide open. Only later do their hearts open as well. So, if you are still single and searching for a marriage that will last, you might consider checking the Yellow Pages and calling a matchmaker. There's a "Hello, Dolly" out there to assist.

Men and women who publish personal ads are like fish swimming in the ocean. Unless you swim with your own school of fish, you will move alone through the waters and risk encountering a shark. Matchmakers realize that successful marriages rest more on commonalities than on hormones. In love, opposites often attract, but they don't remain attached unless they have a lot in common. In all likelihood, you may not even know what is uniquely attractive about yourself in the eyes of a potential mate. So you're likely to concentrate on advertising "evenings by the fire" and golden retrievers rather than your true character and ideals. If so, better to rely on matchmakers—not necessarily professionals, but friends who know you well (perhaps even better than yourself!) and have a circle of friends and acquaintances with interests in common. Most mature matches begin not with physical attraction, but with mutual interests and beliefs that lead to friendship and respect before love. Leave the passion for later; it will still be there waiting for you when you're ready for it.

HE LOVES, SHE LOVES

HUGS isn't exactly what it sounds like, but intimacy is its ultimate purpose. HUGS (Helping Undergraduates Socialize) was the brainchild of Brown

University student Rajib Chanda: a computerized dating service on that Ivy League campus. Fully one-third of the university's students—1,500 in all—subscribe to the service. They include athletes and artists, the geeks and the glamorous, fraternity brothers and rebels, heterosexuals and members of Brown's gay and lesbian alliance.

Chanda, a fraternity president, sensed that his fellow students yearned for old-fashioned courtship—an innocent way to sample intimacy without plunging into sex. "In a normal Brown relationship," he explains, "you meet, get drunk, hook up, and then either avoid eye contact the next day or find yourself in a relationship." That's neither love nor passion. HUGS offers the alternative of friendship between like-minded peers that may, or may not, blossom into something more.

Computerized dating services like HUGS offer better chances of success in romance than running personal ads in newspapers. With a personal ad you expose yourself to a world of potential predators at the same time you attempt to take cover behind come-hither copy that could describe countless other men and women looking for love.

A reputable dating service offers a better chance to express who you are, what motivates you, and what you seek in a partner. These services will match you only with prospects whose profiles complement yours, saving you from some dull (and perhaps a few scary) encounters. Some services offer the opportunity to present yourself on videotape and, in turn, to view the tapes of potential dates.

It's wise to narrow the field from the outset. African Americans, Latinos, and Jews who publish personal ads typically seek partners from the same group. So, obviously, do gays and lesbians. Unfortunately, too many seekers specify only height, age range, physical beauty, and nonsmoking as prerequisites. Needless to say, those qualifications hardly speak to friendship, let alone a future of loving and cherishing.

It's wise to acknowledge from the outset that Mr. or Ms. Right will probably also share your religious beliefs, your cultural interests, and your level of education and intelligence. Your prospective mate will also feel the same way as you do about wanting children and caring for aging parents. So, before advertising your yearning for golden retrievers and evenings in front of the fire, state clearly that you seek someone who will affirm who you are and what you stand for.

PREMARITAL AGREEMENTS

Some contemporary couples—more than 50,000 every year—won't enter a new marriage without a written contract. Premarital agreements are especially attractive to couples who have substantial income or assets and who consider themselves the victims of former failed marriages. By contrast, most first-timers at the altar consider a premarital contract to be an unromantic betrayal of trust. However, if a marriage is to have a chance, couples must agree from the outset on things that matter—on lifelong fidelity first of all, but also on children, work, home, recreation, money matters, and in-laws. Marriages have failed merely because couples couldn't agree on whether to vacation every year at the beach or in the mountains.

It isn't a bad idea to put your agreements in writing even without benefit of attorney. Look at it this way: agreeing in advance puts the health of the marriage ahead of each spouse's individual welfare. It means "we" are more important than "you" or "me" from now on.

Elizabeth Posner and Peter Shouten of Washington, D.C., had three failed marriages between them when they decided to try again with each other. Before they wed, Elizabeth insisted that they go out to dinner at least once a week. Now, if they disagree on trips, entertainment, or vacations, "the one who really wants to go will choose and pay for the entertainment," she says. "That way, neither of feels burdened financially, and it seems we enjoy each other's choices more."

The Shoutens are unusual in having agreed before wedlock that they would keep their finances separate. Joy and Rob Brillante of Bowie, Maryland, are more typical. They pool their income, and both agreed from the outset that Joy would handle the finances. "That was twenty-three years ago," Rob says, "and we have not had an argument about money since."

Rex and Teresa LeGalley of Albuquerque, New Mexico, had few assets when they wed in 1995, but they both bore scars from divorces, so they filed a sixteen-page prenuptial agreement with the county clerk. It spelled out virtually every aspect of their prospective married life, including shopping habits, which gasoline to buy, who does the laundry, and even how often the couple has sex. Details include: "Nothing will be left on the floor overnight, lights out at 11 P.M., and (staying) one car length away from other cars for every 10 m.p.h." The LeGalleys even agreed in writing that "Teresa will stay on birth control for two years after we are married and then will try to get pregnant."

Indeed she did, right on schedule, and their agreement allowed for two more children "after which we will both get sterilized." Teresa is proud that she and Rex haven't had a fight since they were married. "When you look at why people get divorced," Rex says, "the biggest reasons are money, sex, children, or some pet peeve the other one can't stand. This gives us a list we can live with."

The LeGalleys may be suspected of being control freaks in their marriage, but they agree on their mutual expectations, and they are still married.

MAKING MARRIAGE WORK

Strictly speaking, marriage is a contract, but few couples embrace wedlock as a purely business proposition. Unlike business negotiations, love rests on feelings. Moreover, lovers negotiate with one another as equals, friends, and supporters, not as adversaries. They trust one another, seeking mutual payoffs rather than deals that favor just husband or wife.

Whereas success in business consists in getting what you want, love is about getting what you *need*—even when the partners don't completely comprehend at the outset just what that is. Still, business negotiations have two advantages over lovers' quarrels: (1) They are guided by law, and (2) They often employ mediators. Whereas, when couples face conflict, they typically lack both guidelines and referees to guide them to agreement.

Success in marriage rests on respecting differences, accepting apologies, letting go of the past, treading softly on your partner's scars, and always leaving the door open after disputes. Wedlock can become a lockout when partners compete with each other, blame each other, and insist on being right. Outsiders recognize good marriages by what intimate couples do: spend time together, preferring each other's company, sharing their vulnerable feelings, their hopes, and their dreams. Solid spouses compliment each other. Finally, they touch each other often, and not just in the bedroom.

Psychologists concur that anger and anxiety are more intense passions than love and joy. Anger and anxiety destroy relationships. So do silence, indifference, and manipulation. Anyone entering a loving relationship who expects to change his or her beloved is doomed to disappointment. Psychologist Barbara De Angelis lays out rules for women seeking life partners. Most of them apply to men as well, and to couples already married. Here are a few:

1. Treat others the way you want them to treat you.
2. Remember that the opposite sex needs as much love and reassurance as you do.
3. Choose partners who play by the rules.
4. Don't play games.
5. Be yourself.
6. If you like someone, express your feelings.
7. Ask questions before you get too involved.
8. Don't become involved with partners who aren't completely available.
9. Look for a person with good character.
10. Pay attention to warning signs of possible problems.
11. Judge persons by the size of their hearts, not the size of their wallets.

12. Be fair: don't practice double standards.
13. Don't fall in love with a partner's potential.
14. Be honest about your feelings.
15. Show your most attractive feature—your mind.
16. Be emotionally generous, not emotionally stingy.
17. Wait until you are emotionally intimate before becoming sexually intimate.
18. Don't lower yourself to behaving like a sex object.
19. Love, honor, and respect—and expect the same in return.
20. Be monogamous, develop a partnership, and spend the rest of your life together.[9]

WHAT NOT TO EXPECT

When I was a college student in the 1950s I was engaged to a small-town girl, who wore my fraternity pin, knitted argyle socks for me, and ironed my shirts. Back then, many of my classmates married their college sweethearts as soon as they graduated, postponed sex until their wedding night, soon started a family, and are contented grandparents today.

Here is how a home economics textbook counseled girls to prepare for married life in that legendary time:

1. Have dinner ready. Plan ahead, even the night before to have a delicious meal—on time. This is a way of letting [your husband] know that you have been thinking of him and are concerned about his needs. Most men are hungry when they come home, and the prospects of a good meal are part of the warm welcome needed.
2. Prepare yourself. Take 15 minutes to rest so you will be refreshed when he arrives. Touch up your makeup, put a ribbon in your hair, and be fresh looking. He has just been with a lot of work weary people. Be a little gay and a little more interesting. His boring day may need a lift.
3. Clear the clutter. Make one last trip through the main part of the house just before your husband arrives, gathering up schoolbooks, toys, paper, etc. Then run a dust cloth over the tables. Your husband will feel he has reached a haven of rest and order, and it will give you a lift, too.
4. Prepare the children. Take a few minutes to wash the children's hands and faces if they are small, comb their hair and, if necessary, change their clothes. They are little treasures, and he would like to see them playing the part.
5. Minimize the noise. At the time of his arrival, eliminate all noise of washer, dryer, or vacuum. Try to encourage the children to be quiet.

Be happy to see him. Greet him with a warm smile and be glad to see him.

6. Some don'ts. Don't greet him with problems or complaints. Don't complain if he's late for dinner. Count this as minor compared with what he might have gone through that day.

7. Make him comfortable. Have him lean back in a comfortable chair or suggest that he lie down in the bedroom. Have a cool or warm drink ready for him. Arrange his pillow and offer to take off his shoes. Speak in a low, soft, soothing and pleasant voice. Allow him to relax and unwind.

8. Listen to him. You may have a dozen things to tell him but the moment of his arrival is not the time. Let him talk first.

9. Make the evening his. Never complain if he does not take you out to dinner or to other places of entertainment; instead try to understand his world of strain and pressure, his need to be home and relaxed.[10]

Times have clearly changed since then. Feminists would cringe at such counsel. Today one-third of all families are headed by a single parent, usually a mother who works outside the home. For her there is no spouse to come home to. Even women in intact marriages have only half as many hours to spend with their family as women did thirty years ago. Work for pay takes them away. Even if she stays home, nowadays marriages are more equal and most men find they can take off their own shoes when they cross the threshold. Nevertheless, care and consideration continue to be ingredients for marital contentment. The quaint courtesies of yesteryear no doubt were part of what made marriages endure, but they didn't necessarily make for good marriages.

CARING FOR AGING PARENTS

Most marriages involve more persons than just husband and wife. Children also need to be loved and cherished. Increasingly, couples must also make provisions for their aging parents. In recent memory, adult children expected to be on the receiving end of care from their parents. Today they are often responsible for their parents' care. The lengthening of life expectancy means that many couples whose own children have already left the nest must now turn to looking after as many as four elderly parents. For the middle-aged couple looking forward to the freedom of retirement this added burden is often financial as well as emotional. But here as elsewhere in life there are options to ease the burden.

When I reached the age of sixty-five I took out a long-term-care insurance policy on the chance that I might one day have to enter a nursing home. But nursing homes need not be alternatives of *first* resort. What a married couple wants to accomplish with an aging parent is to maintain a relationship of love and trust. Most aging parents are fiercely independent spirits who resist being dictated to, least of all by their children. As long as both parents are alive, they will prize their freedom together, but when one dies, children will want to step in, not necessarily with solutions but with suggestions.

If you are like most adult children, you haven't a clue about your parents' finances, but it is not intrusive to assure yourself that a surviving parent is protected in your deceased parent's will. The survivor may never have balanced the family checkbook, let alone paid a bill in fifty years of marriage, so offer to review his or her finances.

If your parent is clueless about paying bills, you do not have to take over that responsibility personally. For a small fee, the trust department of your parent's local bank will pay Mom's or Dad's bills, track investments, receive Social Security and pension benefits, secure savings, and arrange state and federal tax filings. Make a checklist of your parent's doctor, dentist, banker, lawyer, investment advisor, and trusted friends, as well as the location of safe-deposit boxes, insurance policies, credit cards, titles, personal valuables, and checking and savings accounts. Share that list with your parent's lawyer.

Make certain that your surviving parent has a will. You do not have to pry into its details, but reassure yourself that your parent's lawyer has an updated copy on file and that someone has power of attorney to make decisions on your parent's behalf should he or she become incompetent. If your parent is reticent to talk about failing health, consider speaking discreetly to his or her doctor to get a prognosis.

It is imperative that you and any siblings know how your parent wants to be medicated when close to death. When my mother lost consciousness toward the end of a fatal illness, she had left no living will to instruct her doctor about how much effort he should expend to prolong her hopeless condition. Fortunately, he trusted my word that Mom wanted to be allowed to die naturally, not hooked to machines.

Because you will always be your parent's child, it will be difficult for Mom and Dad to assume the role of a dependent, authorizing you to make decisions for them. So suggest a third party—someone you mutually trust. It could be a priest or minister, a social worker, nurse, lawyer, or doctor who can better sound out your parent on his or her wishes.

Older parents slip easily into denial, hoping for the best even as conditions get worse. Unless you live nearby, you will want to reassure yourself that your parent is covered in an emergency. Buy or rent a medical alert system that immediately contacts the local hospital should your parent fall or become ill. Leave a duplicate of your parent's house key with a trusted neighbor or friend, and keep your telephone answering machine on.

Make sure that your parent is taking advantages of property tax and other tax deductions offered by the county or community. Should your parent run out of financial resources, do not be ashamed to tap Medicaid to cover nursing home and medical bills. All Americans agree that we have a right to Social Security and Medicare benefits. Medicaid is no different. Once your parent's savings are gone, there is no need for you to deplete yours for his or her final years.

FRIENDSHIP

Aristotle counted friendship as a virtue and "one of the most indispensable requirements of life." Cicero went even further: "Without friendship," he said, "life is not worth living." Blood may be thicker than water, but friendship is not nearly as burdened by emotion and expectation as family life. Nevertheless, husband and wife must be bound by friendship. Romantic love is, of necessity, exclusive and possessive, whereas friendship is open and free. Marriage is bound by contract, while friendship is voluntary, beyond legal and formal control. But, happily, your spouse can also be your best friend.

Becky and I each have a close friend. She hasn't seen her friend in years, but they converse daily by e-mail or phone to share advice, complaints, and laughter. Although my own male friend lives nearer, we too seldom see each other, but still keep in constant touch. When I dedicated a recent book of mine to him, I borrowed these lines from Coleridge: "Friendship is a sheltering tree."

Some years ago my wife and I became Friends—the kind with a capital "F," better known as Quakers. The Religious Society of Friends, although founded by Christians, welcomes Jews, Buddhists, Muslims, and all others, persuaded that there is something of God in every human being. That is a sound basis for friendship. Friends don't just happen; they must be cultivated. The cultivation of friendship within a marriage demands effort.

Pets are friends of a different sort, but likewise require love and cherishing. During the course of our marriage, Becky and I have been blessed with the companionship of three dogs and six cats, plus the occasional injured bunny, bird, and squirrel. When we mourned the loss of our six-year-old tomcat, Fred, to an inoperable brain tumor, we still enjoyed the constant companionship of Fred's twin sister and a Scottish terrier. And Fred was succeeded by Rufus, a cream mackerel tabby, who is the happiest creature we have ever known.

Your life as a married couple can be enhanced by a creature with four paws or even wings. As a young girl, Becky cared for a pet lamb, and my mother's last years were brightened by her canary's song. Mom named the bird "Happy," for it made her so.

Loving and cherishing all these parties to your marriage can make you happy too.

STEPS IN THE RIGHT DIRECTION

Your Spouse Comes First

1. Make friends with your mate. Lots of people claim they have spent many years of their lives "finding themselves." Once married, you will no longer have that luxury. Your mate chose you as a partner in life not because you are a perpetual seeker, but because of who you are right now. You need to be self-assured in order to assure your spouse that he or she made the right choice. Get a grip. Make your mate your best friend as well as your lover.

2. Keep a rein on your in-laws. Men and women leave their families in order to marry. But parents can persist in believing of marriage that "We haven't lost a son; we've gained a daughter." Don't countenance that fiction. The truth of the matter is that each of you has gained two in-laws. Still, your first priority is your marriage. Decide together just how comfortable each of you is with parents and in-laws intruding on your lives.

3. If you want a friend, get a dog. That's what President Harry Truman advised about surviving political life in Washington. It applies to married couples as well. Before you decide to embark on the rigors of child rearing, it might be wise to test how responsive you are to the lesser demands of a furry, four-legged creature. You may find that your love grows as a couple when you have a pet on which to shower your affection.

· 8 ·

Children

Surviving the Blessings of Offspring

Children are what holds a marriage together.

August Strindberg

I found myself a parent for the first time at the age of thirty-three, having been wed for only nine months. Fast work, eh? Two years later, twin daughters arrived, so their mother and I were already outnumbered in the household just three years into the marriage. As an only child, I had no experience of sibling rivalry, but was soon to learn.

From the outset there were more serious problems. Even before the twins were conceived, my eldest daughter suffered convulsions, diagnosed as *grand mal* seizures, and became deaf for over a year. Even when her hearing returned, there was residual brain damage and she was left permanently learning disabled. When the twins were born more than two months premature, they were confined to hospital incubators for months. Both weighed less than five pounds, and the smaller of the two required surgery to remedy an intestinal obstruction.

Although they proved to be otherwise healthy, it soon became clear that the twins, too, were learning disabled, although not nearly to the extent suffered by their older sister. Becky, who brought to our marriage no children of her own from her previous marriage, knew what problems she was inheriting when she adopted them.

Raising any child is an ordeal. Raising three handicapped children and equipping them for responsible adult lives is an even greater challenge. Fortunately, all three (now in their late thirties) graduated from college and now lead independent, productive lives. But along the way they drifted back to their birth mother, who never remarried and who experienced a series of disabling illnesses, including cancer. Opting to be responsible for their birth mother, they became alienated from the two of us who actually raised them.

SO YOU WANT TO HAVE CHILDREN

The Swedish playwright August Strindberg argued that many marriages survive intact "because both partners have one interest in common, the thing for which nature has always intended marriage, namely children. . . . Long before a child arrives they discover that their bliss is not so heavenly after all, and their relationship becomes stale. Then a child is born. Everything is new again and now, for the first time, their relationship is beautiful, for the ugly egoism of the duet has vanished. . . . Children are what holds a marriage together."[1]

Judith Viorst disagrees with Strindberg, and she has a different take on how kids instantly affect a marriage: "No sleep. No sex. No privacy. No let's-catch-the-9:20-movie spontaneity. No leisurely Sunday mornings just hanging out. The arrival of our first baby can bring us a joy that's perhaps unattainable by any other means under the sun. But it's also an astounding assault on our marriage. Nothing we've read or heard or observed can prepare us."[2]

Many, if not most, couples believe that having children is both a sound emotional investment and a blessing on the marriage. But progeny are decidedly not good financial investments. Perhaps in an earlier era, when they could help with farm chores, children were a financial asset, but no more.

At the outset of the new millennium, the U.S. Department of Agriculture estimated that a couple with a combined income of just $60,000 should expect to spend $228,000 on each of their children by the time that child completes high school. Adding four years of college can easily increase their investment by upwards of $100,000 *more* per child, making each baby a projected expense of one-third of a million dollars.[3]

So the old song that claimed to find a million-dollar baby in the five-and-ten-cents store was correct. If, perchance, you expect the outlay to end when the kids leave home, reconsider. More than half of the nation's eighteen- to twenty-four-year-olds still live with Mom and Dad.[4]

In twenty-first-century America more than three in five households have no children at home. In one-fourth of those that do, Mom is the only parent around for the kids.

The percentage of parents who choose to stop with just one child has doubled in the last twenty years.[5] Claire North, of suburban Washington, D.C., acknowledges that she can stay at home because she and her husband limited their family to just their son, now four years old. "We have so much freedom that other parents don't have," she exults. "We go away overnight with or without him. We just go and (other parents) are envious of that. Also, I know I don't have to worry (about) money . . . whereas if I had a couple of kids by now, I'd be back to work, and I'd be crazed about it."[6]

BABIES AT ANY COST

Anyone unfamiliar with Americans might conclude from our 1.3 million abortions every year that we, as a people, hate babies. They would be wrong. Granted, some women (married or unwed) terminate pregnancies when they are inconvenient. But on the whole, married couples are only too happy to obey the Creator's command to "increase and multiply" at least once during their life together.

Americans love babies so much that an increasing number of couples are willing to pay upwards of $50,000 to special-order an infant that shares at least some of the buyer's genes. Of course, there is nothing new about sperm banks for the fertile woman who craves a baby without the burden of a husband. But today, courtesy of in vitro fertilization and surrogate mothers, anyone with a nest egg can purchase either sperm or egg and even pay another woman to bear one's child.

If *Consumer Reports* rated ways to have children, its editors would probably not consider surrogate parenting a "best buy," and would suggest adoption instead. Truth be told, there are plenty of foundlings condemned to be raised in orphanages or be bounced from one foster home to another for want of a couple who have enough love left over in their marriage to welcome a child who looks like neither of them.

In any case, whether or not your child is the spitting image of you and your spouse, at times it will have strange ways of showing love to you. President Harry Truman noted famously that if you want a friend in Washington, you should adopt a dog. Even the federal government has come around to Truman's wisdom, running full-page newspaper ads that shout: "For Mom and Dad: I Hate You." Here's the text:

> Scared of these three little words? Get used to it, because you've got a teenager. A teenager who's making friends, testing boundaries and trying pot and alcohol. You probably weren't going to win any popularity contests anyway, so be the parent and set some rules. Because dealing with an addicted child later is a whole lot scarier than hearing a few I-hate-you's now. To help them with their problem, first you have to get over yours.[7]

That's the message of the Office of National Drug Control Policy, cautioning parents that cute little babies grow up in ways you can't fully control.

LIKE OLIVE PLANTS AROUND THE TABLE

Poet and novelist Erica Jong is Jewish, so she is aware of Psalm 128 that depicts a married couple with children as a tiny peaceable kingdom. But when her own daughter published her first novel at the age of twenty, it turned out to be a thinly disguised account of life with her famous mother that suggested a different story than the psalm. "Mummy, I hope you don't mind," Molly announced, "but I've made you a total narcissist and a hopeless alcoholic in my novel."

The elder Jong acknowledged philosophically: "In her fledgling book my role is clear: I am the Mommy monster."

The daughter complained to the reading public that her mother was too often absent from the hearth when she was growing up, only to smother Molly with affection when she returned.

"It's true that I don't recognize myself in the character Molly calls 'my mother.' . . . But who am I to censor her? . . . I've been using my family as comic material for twenty-five years—how can I deny that right to my daughter?"

The elder Jong rebelled against her own mother many years earlier, yet admits that "I even listen to my mother now," even when she demands: "Tell (Molly) you're sorry you were such a dreadful mother. And apologize."

"Yeah, yeah, yeah" is Molly's response to her mother's contrition. "She looks at me with the sheer contempt that is grounded in excessive love," the penitent mother affirms, and concludes that "raising a daughter is definitely tougher than writing."[8]

NEEDED: MORE BABIES

Granting that children are expensive, demanding, unpredictable, and resistant to the commandment to "Honor thy father and thy mother," we need more, not fewer babies. The United Nations predicts that by 2010 most of the world's women will be having fewer than two children, and by mid-century the world's population will be shrinking for the first time since the Black Death in the fourteenth century.

At the moment, world fertility is just half what it was in the 1960s. The prevailing wisdom has been that, as nations develop their economies, women favor conventional families of two parents and two children, stabilizing the human race at 10–12 billion people compared to 6 billion today. But now it appears more likely that world populations will peak at just 8 billion, then decline in the second half of the century.

Joseph Chamie, who directs the UN's population division, reveals that fertility in over sixty nations is already below replacement levels, and that actual population decline has been postponed only because people are living longer. Religion, which traditionally encourages childbirth as God's blessing on a couple, is effectively being ignored in favor of routine contraception. Chamie points out that although Catholic Church opposition has long resisted state family planning, Brazilian women cut their nation's birth rate by half in just one generation. There are 40 million fewer Brazilians as a result! In Catholic Italy and Spain most women now choose to have just one child. Nor have the mullahs been able to prevent three-quarters of Iranian women from using contraceptives and cutting that nation's birth rate by two-thirds.

The notion that nations need to become prosperous before abandoning large families no longer holds. Most of the world's people now live in towns and cities where, unlike on farms, children are a financial burden rather than an asset.

With fewer births and longer life expectancy we now contemplate a world in which the old are the rule and the young will be the exception. Social Security in the United States is increasingly funded by the working young for the benefit of their seniors. The formula worked while young wage earners vastly outnumbered retired Americans. But fewer babies will result in deferred retirement as well as shrinking government benefits for their parents. Moreover, it is estimated that only 15 percent of aging Americans can expect financial and living assistance from their children.[9]

SO YOU WANT TO HAVE CHILDREN ANYWAY

Congratulations. You have embarked on an adventure like no other. Happy families may be all alike, but there are no parenting experts to offer foolproof advice on how to get that way. You will learn as you go and never be certain you have arrived. Family relations are like international relations, a mixture of diplomacy and firmness, peace and war.

Sandra Hardin Gookin, a mother and author of *Parenting for Dummies*, suggests, "Admit it, you're not in charge. Your children are. And both of you know it. Children draw you out and then pounce for the attack. They know when to cry. They know how to get you to say 'Yes.' They know when you're not looking. It's like playing a game of chess with someone with an IQ of 300."

She continues: "Welcome to *The Parenting Game*. The object here is not total victory, but a mutual solution that keeps everyone happy. You want to raise a child who turns into a well-adjusted adult, and you want to do it without being escorted away by men in white coats while wearing a jacket that has way-too-long sleeves."[10]

Not to put too fine a point on it, the initial step is to become pregnant. In an age in which contraceptives are reliable and widely accepted there need be no surprise pregnancies. Having a child is a mutual decision. If getting pregnant is the wife's decision alone, she runs the risk of her husband resenting fatherhood or not pulling his weight with the children.

Pregnancies can be hard or relatively easy; so can childbirth. Babies do not necessarily come easy and leave the mother feeling chipper. Kate Figes writes on parenting for London's *Times* and *Guardian* newspapers. Here's her cautionary tale:

> Thirty-six hours after I had delivered my first child by caesarian section after an arduous but failed attempt at a natural breech birth, a junior house doctor settled down for an intimate chat on the chair next to my bed.
>
> "And what are we going to do about contraception now?" he asked cheerfully, hugging his clipboard for moral support.
>
> I could barely move, still used a catheter, and everything hurt, even breathing. My breasts throbbed and my nipples stung. I was already hallucinating from sleep deprivation and I never wanted to go near a penis again. I wanted to tell him to piss off and leave me alone. Instead I stared incredulously at him and said politely, "I beg your pardon?"
>
> When it became clear that he was not going to leave until he had a satisfactory answer to write down next to my name, I mumbled condoms to get rid of him. I then watched him cross the ward to talk to a woman who winced with pain as she shuffled slowly around her bed to pick up her baby.
>
> "Piss off and leave me alone," she said when he asked her the same question. "If you think I'm ever going near a penis again you need your head examined."[11]

Figes faults pregnancy books for suggesting that parents' sex relations return to normalcy in six weeks. "Research shows that 30 to 60 percent of couples have 'resumed' sex within six weeks, but they've probably only done it once and it was more likely a bungled and unsatisfactory experience," she reveals. "Many couples do not resume sex for months after childbirth, and most couples find that frequency of sexual relations is severely reduced for years, if not permanently."[12] Don't conclude that couples must choose between children and a sex life. But it is true that young mothers and fathers must make time for intimacy. It's like learning to date each other all over again.

PERILS OF PARENTHOOD

G. K. Chesterton once reflected that the only tenet of the Christian faith that can be proved without the shadow of a doubt is Original Sin. The gentle Quaker philosopher Elton Trueblood went further, lamenting that all one need do to experience Original Sin is to become a parent. Both men traced the self-centeredness and perversity of human nature to infancy.[13]

By contrast, many parents of the baby boom generation raised their offspring as though they were born utterly innocent. Their bible of permissiveness was written by Dr. Benjamin Spock, who urged parents to indulge their babies, feed them on demand, and cuddle them when they awoke screaming during the night.

As the boomers themselves became parents, many of them had second thoughts about indulging their own youngsters, opting instead to equip them for the vagaries of the real world so they might grow into self-reliant adults. New York psychoanalyst Ruth Sharon applauds them.

> "The adult who was given 24-hour womb service when he was growing up, excessively pampered and indulged, will *not*, quite surprisingly, recall any of this fondly," she warns prospective parents. "Indeed, he will honestly recall his childhood as a miserable time and blame his parents for mistreating him, when in fact they did just the opposite. . . ."
>
> Having been shielded from frustration, challenges, and painful experiences in childhood, the adult lives not in the real world, but in a kind of cocoon. He is, in essence, an infant in an adult body. Not equipped to overcome problems, he grows up limited both in his personal relationships and in relating to his peers, still hoping that his needs will be anticipated and met. He says "I can't" with great frequency.[14]

Dr. Laura Schlessinger's book on child rearing is subtitled *Don't Have Them If You Won't Raise Them*. She argues that the responsibility of an effective parent is to tell a child "No" when appropriate. "'No,' out of the mouth of a reasonable, sensitive, involved loving parent, is a necessity in teaching children important lessons about life's limitations, the blessings inherent in self-control, the essence of values, and how to avoid danger," she says.[15]

Clinical psychologist Patricia Dalton warns indulgent parents that "there is an unspoken assumption that a child who feels good will never need to behave badly."[16] Dr. Schlessinger agrees: "Saying 'no' is not the antithesis of love. It is the very proof of the love that a parent has for a child. In setting limits on possessions, experiences, activities, behavior, and words, parents help their children become centered (as opposed to self-centered), secure, confident, and able to negotiate life in a healthy and productive way."[17]

"Jacqueline," one of Dr. Schlessinger's listeners, writes of her own experience growing up:

> The number one worst thing my parents (more so my mother) did that caused me difficulty was to never let me feel anything but happy. . . . Everything I did was perfect—I was never disciplined, never spanked, never told "no," never grounded, never made to do my homework. There were always excuses for me and blame was placed elsewhere. I lived with unrealistic expectations and perceptions of who I was. . . . I eventually became very angry . . . to the point of violence.[18]

PARTNERS IN PARENTING

The late Fred Rogers was fond of quoting the old Quaker saying that "Attitudes are caught, not taught."[19] Children are natural mimics. They will "catch" their parents' good example but resist the command, "Do as I say, not as I do." They will also pick up on your bad behavior, so parents must resist cursing, sarcasm, yelling, arguing, and lying.

Single parenthood can be heroic, but it is seldom chosen except by wealthy celebrities who can afford nurses and maids. I found my brief experience as a single parent to be exhausting, and I was constantly cutting corners with the kids.

It takes two parents to make a child and two parents to raise one. More often than not, family finances require both husband and wife to work outside the home. It is counterproductive to point a critical finger at the working mother, as if the only characteristic of mothering that is crucial is her constant presence.

Linda Mason, cited by *Working Mother* magazine as one of the "25 Most Influential Working Mothers in America," has three children and the benefit of an "equal partnership" marriage. Here's how it works:

- Wife and husband share the domestic responsibilities: both care for the children and household chores.
- Wife and husband also share household management responsibilities: being aware of what needs to be done at home, prioritizing tasks, and scheduling the tasks.
- Both parents share wage-earning responsibility; they may not have equal salaries, but they share the financial concern and planning.
- If one partner goes away for several days, the other partner can run the home successfully with no extended "to-do" lists or other direction and guidance.[20]

Sandra Hardin Gookin counsels prospective parents "how to be of one common mind without brain surgery," warning that "reality sets in when you actually have *your* child and nothing happens like you thought it would." She advises:

- *Don't argue about discipline*, especially in front of your kids. . . . They'll store this information away and eventually use it against you.
- *Respect each other's ideas.* Your child-raising ideas most likely will come from your background. . . . Don't always assume your way is the right way.
- *Talk out disagreements.* You need to be in agreement about household rules and how to handle it when those rules are broken.
- *Don't jump into an ongoing situation.* If you walk into a room where your partner is already handling a situation, try to keep quiet. . . . You probably don't know what's going on.
- *Don't gang up on your child.* If you both see something going on that shouldn't, let one parent deal with it. . . . If you see that your partner is having trouble, offer to step in and help.[21]

TANTRUMS

Just as missionaries sought to civilize savages, the parents' mission is to civilize their child. Truth be told, it is far easier to domesticate a dog or cat than one's own offspring. While parents of newborns are charmed to hear it speak its first words, very soon the words turn into screams and demands. A child's defiant behavior starts in about the fifteenth month, reaches a peak around twenty-two months, and slowly dissipates until the child's third birthday. The "Terrible Twos" are aptly named. They mark the child's Declaration of Independence.[22]

The best case against spanking a child is not that it is cruel and unusual punishment, but that, while it may temporarily end bad behavior, the youngster will soon forget why he was spanked. Marguerite Kelly, who writes the Family Almanac column for the *Washington Post*, suggests diverting the child's attention, isolating him, or giving him the silent treatment when he throws a tantrum.

Alternatively, bring him into the conversation: "Although a toddler can't follow half of [a parent's] running commentary, he loves to have adults talk with him as if they were talking with their friends." She also counsels being specific with a toddler: Tell him exactly when you're going to the store, not just "in a while."[23]

This may appear to be pandering, but it's really just paying attention. Although a child deserves respect as a person, it is a mistake to treat the child as an adult. A child knows better and expects the parents to make the rules and be consistent about them. Still, any child will test your resolve repeatedly.

Sandra Gookin counsels parents to build their expectations on a sense of humor. Instead of demanding of a child: "Just eat those peas!" you could say, "I bet you can't eat just twelve peas! No kid has ever eaten that many. You might set a record."

Instead of shouting "Didn't I tell you to make your bed?" you could say, "Let me time you to see how long it actually does take you to make your bed."

And, rather than growl, "You left your shoes out. Get them picked up now!" you could say, "Oh my gosh! Your shoes must have walked right out of the room. Why don't you help them back to the closet where they belong."[24]

GOOD HABITS, BAD BEHAVIOR

Becoming parents presents a strong incentive for a couple to scrutinize their own bad habits, because they are now permanent role models for the next generation. Indulging a child will not make him love his parents and is sure to make him an unhappy adult. Alternatively, if a child pitches in on household chores, he can earn some things he wants without demanding them of you gratis. A modest allowance allows a child to choose things for himself. It is neither a wage nor an entitlement but an incentive to be responsible for helping out. Work deserves a reward.

When you witness any child's bad behavior in public, you know that those habits were learned or are at least tolerated at home. Children who behave badly in restaurants clearly have bad table manners at home as well. If you expect your child to grow up to be kind and considerate of others, the habit must be formed at home.

Manners are civilized behavior, gracious and grateful. It is always a mistake to take others for granted, so it is important to set a good example, saying "please" and "thank you" to your kids and expecting the same consideration from them.

Becky and I were never so proud of our daughters as when they volunteered (without our prompting) to work summers as volunteers helping younger children with disabilities. They knew firsthand about handicaps and, instead of feeling sorry for themselves, made life better for other children facing lifelong obstacles.

There is a difference between punishment and discipline. They are both forms of teaching. "Discipline," Sandra Gookin writes, "is about setting ground rules and boundaries—and making your children live and follow those rules." Sounds easy enough. The only problem is that your kids, for their own reasons, aren't always going to want to follow those rules and boundaries. They'll always seem to have their own agenda, and it may not match yours.[25]

Tolerance ceases to be a virtue when it acquiesces to intolerable behavior. But parental nagging sounds to a child like a broken record and inspires resentment. A good tip for effective discipline is to put rules in writing. Sandra Gookin suggests that a child who persists in leaving the toilet seat up can be reminded with a note above the toilet that reads: "Please, close me when you're done with your duty! Thank you, (signed) Mr. Toilet."[26]

Our eldest daughter's disabilities included an impaired sense of her surroundings. As a consequence, her room was a complete mess, and she was frustrated because she couldn't find things. A wise counselor advised us to put labels on drawers, countertops, and in her closet, so she would be aware of where things belonged. Putting things in writing worked for her and us.

PUNISHMENT AS A LEARNING LESSON

Public authorities insist that ignorance of the law is no excuse from punishment. But around the house a child must be made aware of the rules—all the more reason for putting them in writing. A parent must make the punishment fit the crime. The most effective punishments are those that involve the loss of a privilege or that require the child to work to replace something he has broken. A child must be reminded why he is being punished.

Just because he annoys you is insufficient, especially if you are angry about something unconnected with your child.

Kids will make mistakes that are just that: errors, not indications of malevolence. The two most destructive things I did as a child were (1) accidentally wounding my father during rifle practice, and (2) backing the family car out of the garage with the driver's door open, bending it badly. My parents were spankers, but on those two serious occasions they didn't punish me, because I was instantly and honestly contrite. Goofing up is not the same thing as being bad.

Repeat offenses after punishment could mean the child is not getting enough attention, is bored, or resents the parent being involved with a sibling. The answer is to give him something to do, preferably something that gets him involved with you. Wise parents don't set punishments when they're angry. They give their child the chance to fix the mistake, then they forgive and forget, reassuring the child of their love. Parents of children who are at the crawling stage know that they must fix locks on cabinets the child can reach. It's a matter of childproofing the home and removing the sources of temptation.

WHEN DISCIPLINE FALLS SHORT

Unfortunately, some children respond poorly to both discipline and punishment. I met some of these barely controllable children when our eldest daughter spent some years in a private school for the learning disabled. Stanley Greenspan, former director of the National Institute of Mental Health's Clinical Infant Development Program, estimates that upwards of one in four children suffer from one or more neurological and behavioral ailments. These include distractibility, impulsiveness, depression, and bipolar disorder, as well as autistic-type behaviors, which can make a child detached, antisocial, and explosive.

Jeanne and Chuck Harple's nine-year-old son Austin is just such a child. Although he takes the mood stabilizers Depakote and Trileptal, as well as Ritalin to help focus his attention, he has been sent home countless times since kindergarten for violent behavior toward his fellow students and his teachers. He curses his parents and tells them to shut up, and tells his sister "I'm gonna *kill* you." He manipulates his parents and brags, with a smile, "I *love* negotiating. I *always* get my way."

Washington Post staff writer Peter Perl notes,

> Psychiatrists and behavior therapists who have worked with Austin have told the Harples they believe his cursing and verbal threats come from a lack of impulse control arising from a complex combination of problems: They include an underlying neurological disorder that disrupts his sensory abilities; attention deficit hyperactivity (ADHD); obsessive-compulsive disorder (OCD), which creates constantly recurring anxieties; and oppositional defiant disorder (ODD), which makes him inflexible and explosive.[27]

The Harples also have two daughters to care for. For a time the pressure of raising Austin put such a strain on their marriage that they separated, but they got back together after counseling. Austin's teachers tell them they hope he will eventually earn the equivalent of a high school diploma, but his mother is adamant: "He will *absolutely* go to college. Absolutely. It is *not* an option." Still, she worries that her son's behavior will keep him from really growing up, marrying, getting a job, and raising his own family. Otherwise, she says, "Austin will probably be living with us forever."[28]

SUFFER THE LITTLE CHILDREN

Jesus of Nazareth said, "Suffer the little children to come to me." But an increasing number of Americans complain that they suffer too much from *other* people's children, as well as from the public expectation that they be perfect parents of their own offspring.

Professor Susan Douglas of the University of Michigan has one child and complains,

> I'm completely exhausted, and unlike Sarah Jessica Parker, I did not weigh less after my child was born, so I was wearing my husband's sweat pants, which were the only thing that fit. And I had some spit-up-splotched sweater and hair that hadn't seen a comb in a couple of days, and a screaming infant in the checkout cart. Then I look over and there are these racks of magazines screaming on the cover that motherhood was sexy . . . and a perfect, doting husband. And they would tell you all the perfect things they were doing with their kids, like somersaults in the park.[29]

Fifteen years later, Douglas produced a book, *The Mommy Myth: The Idealization of Motherhood and How It Has Undermined Women*. She complains that "'having it all' has morphed into 'having to do it all' and it's about time women stood up and made the choice to say no."[30]

No wonder the baby boom that followed World War II is being replaced by a babyless boom, with couples deciding to altogether forgo the joys of hearing the patter of little feet. They call themselves "child free," not childless, and they put the accent on the word "free." Social commentator Peter York believes we may be witnessing a real schism in society. "There are many who, in a previous era, would have had children but now put them off until their 40s, or do not have them," he notes.

"It's a group that is growing ever more rich and selfish and will increasingly object to public policies that they believe discriminate against them," he predicts.[31]

Elinor Burkett is fanning the flames of a new civil war between parents and couples without children. Her book, *The Baby Boon: How Family-Friendly America Cheats the Childless*, argues that "employees with children get thousands of dollars a year in benefits—extra insurance and unpaid leave, scholarship aid and tax credits—denied to nonparents.

"Those who remain childless save untold sums for our employers, yet these sums are not repaid in other benefits, such as extra holiday time or greater pension contributions." She is especially galled by the flextime given by employers to employees with children but denied to the childless. Moreover, maternity and paternity leave sanctioned by government discriminate against the childless, she argues.[32]

Childless couples with a grudge have turned to the Internet (see www.childfree.net) to battle the "breeders" and hallow the child-free life. And they are organizing. Groups such as No Rugrats!, Zero Population Growth, and No Kidding provide support for those who claim discrimination and demand equal treatment from business and government. One clear inequity: childless employees with adult dependents such as a sick parent are overlooked by employers' subsidized health plans.

Great Britain's childless warriors possess a livelier sense of humor than their American counterparts. Their manifesto concludes: "Comfy child-free couples of the world, unite! You have nothing to lose but your bank holidays (and perhaps care in old age)."

Don't count on it. Remember that the cost of raising a child to the age of eighteen is $228,000 for a couple with a combined income of $60,000, and only 15 percent of aging parents can expect to be looked after by their adult children.

THE CASE FOR PARENTHOOD

As an incentive to obey his command to "increase and multiply," the Creator attached the most exquisite physical pleasure to the act of procreation. Of course, humankind has long since contrived to separate the pleasure from the actual creation of offspring.

Moreover, the mere perpetuation of species is no grand affair. There are insects that are born, reach maturity, breed, reproduce, and die in the course of a single day.

For most species the act of procreation is instinctive and mindless, not a matter of conscious choice. Humans are the notable exceptions. We choose to participate in the act of creation, fully aware that we cannot insist that our offspring love us. The only legitimate motive for choosing to have children is *our* love for *them*.

cᗒᗕᗒ

STEPS IN THE RIGHT DIRECTION

Children Can Complement a Marriage; They Can't Replace It

1. Choose parenthood for more than sentimental reasons. If children were born as teenagers, there would be a drastic reduction in the

birthrate. Yet all babies grow up, and their independence takes the form of parental rebellion. Moreover, siblings will compete with each other and for your affection. Be certain your marriage is already strong before you take on this new responsibility that will sorely test your life as a couple.

2. Don't steal from yourselves to enrich your children's lives. You give your children life, love, values, and attention. But they are also financial and personal burdens on their parents. Don't sacrifice your own quality of life as a couple to assure them more comfortable lives than you enjoy. The best thing you can give your children is the example of a loving marriage.

3. Don't expect your children to be wonderful—or grateful. Parents want to be proud of their children, but it is a mistake to expect more of them than you do of yourselves. Be prepared to love a child of yours who is average or even troubled or handicapped. Remember, you didn't create them; they are God's creatures. Alternatively, if they are accomplished, they are not *your* accomplishment, but their Creator's. You are first of all husband and wife, and only secondarily parents. Don't live through your kids. You have lives of your own. Keep living through each other.

· 9 ·

Intimacy

Being One Flesh and One Spirit

How am I blest in thus discovering thee!
To enter in these bonds, is to be free;
Then, where my hand is set, my seal shall be.
Full nakedness! All joys are due to thee

John Donne

$\mathcal{A}$s he approached death, England's poet laureate John Betjeman was asked whether he had any regrets. "Yes," he replied, "that I didn't have more sex."[1] There is no record of his wife's reaction to Sir John's confession.

Granted, there have been some successful marriages in which sex played little or no part. George Bernard Shaw and Jacques Maritain and their wives come to mind. "But the sexual rapport is a sensitive barometer of a relationship as a whole."[2]

Sex, of course, is easily abused, both in and out of marriage—as a threat, a trap, or a weapon. G. K. Chesterton cautioned that "the moment sex ceases to be a servant it becomes a tyrant. There is something dangerous and disproportionate in its place in human nature . . . and it does really need a special purification and dedication."[3]

Although sex sells fiction, surprisingly few novels depict happy sexual relationships between husbands and wives, preferring physical passion to be expressed in seduction and adultery. Most novels featuring husbands and wives are about unhappy marriages. Just as pornographers are wary of depicting tenderness and romance, novelists prefer conflict to comfort, and shy from all but rough-and-tumble couplings.

It may simply be that we are embarrassed by the intimacy of others who are joined not only in body but also in soul. We can feel left out, even when loving spouses are only holding hands in public. Sex within marriage, like the bond itself, is exclusive, and at its best is a source of mutual pleasure, comfort, affirmation, and joy. But it is also intimate and private. Men and women who freely discus details of their sex lives before wedlock suddenly become guarded once they are wed.

No one these days marries just for the sex. Cohabitation provides sex free of commitment, so marriage is expected to deliver much more than easy access to a warm body. By the same token, sex within marriage is never just about sex but about an entire ongoing relationship. It sends messages about how well the entire relationship is working.

That married couples swiftly dispense with *Kama Sutra*–style acrobatics only means that sex within wedlock is *meant* to be routine. Routine means familiar, reassuring, safe, and comfortable. Less inventive and short on fireworks, perhaps, but more loving. Judith Viorst quotes married friends who say of their spouses, "We know what turns the other on, and we can each say what we want during sex."[4]

Strictly speaking, once married, couples no longer "have sex." They have each other. They are saying, without words: "I don't just want 'it'; I want you."

WITH MY BODY I THEE WORSHIP

Of course, routine can degenerate into dreary domesticity. At the conclusion of Tolstoy's *War and Peace*, Natasha and Pierre have substituted predictability for passion. They are just another aging couple, examples of the novelist's contention that happy families are all alike.

In semiretirement Becky and I relish the freedom for lovemaking whenever we want. Today, rather than being the victims of sudden and frequent passion or stolen moments when children are out of the house, we often make dates with each other, sometimes days ahead of time. The satisfaction we find in each other has deepened. We have become leisurely about enjoying each other. We take our time. No "fast food" sex for us.

Julia Bourland, former sex columnist for the *San Francisco Chronicle*, is young and much newer to marriage than we. She advises young couples that, contrary to the premise of *Sex and the City*, sex within marriage is not confining but liberating. But lovemaking is no substitute for commitment through thick and thin. Sex cannot get a couple through the hard times; it only distracts them from problems they must solve together. At worst, sex may only be a stalling tactic, delaying the inevitable disagreements that could lead to divorce if not confronted head-on during the course of a marriage.

From interviews with newlyweds, Bourland reveals that women experience a surge in sexuality that they attribute to the commitment of love and monogamy they have made. She argues that lovemaking is an expression of one's spirituality. Many women told her that "making the 'till death do we part' vow to their lover and future father of their children gave their sex life more reverence and meaning."[5] For young marrieds who felt guilt about indulging in sex before marriage, "the freedom from guilt could be the rebel yell that awakens your sensuality."[6]

Marriage makes a man and woman feel grown up. That's a heady experience. Without the pressure to perform, a couple can be tender with each other. They are no longer the victims of their hormones.

In athletics, practice makes perfect. Marriage affords the practice time, free of inhibitions, to attune yourself to someone who desires to make love to you exclusively for a lifetime. In marriage, a man and a woman see each other literally with their pants down, which is an invitations to drop their pretenses and inhibitions as well. Spouses can't fool each other for long. They are constant witnesses to each other's imperfections, affirming that love is more important than perfection. In marriage, humility and humor are the best medicines.

"Contrary to Hollywood myth," Bourland argues, "married sex is the most satisfying [a couple] can get. It's familiar, it's emotional, it has experience, it has depth and a sense of humor, it's safe, and it has many faces: It's trampy when it wants to be, serene when desired, and, at a minimum, a good stress reliever when your mind is wrangling with your most recent credit card statement."[7]

IS THIS ALL THERE IS?

There is no such thing as bad sex within marriage. There is better sex, or not enough sex, or rough sex, or unwanted sex, but (short of rape) the act itself delivers pleasure. Rest assured, the joy of sex is no keener for celebrities than for the rest of us. But, while routine is good, complacency isn't. That's when sex becomes the equivalent of fast food. Spouses need to pay attention and savor their love while accepting that each repetition will not be the equivalent of the Big Bang.

Dr. Michael McGuire of UCLA Medical School calculates that if a couple enjoy sexual intercourse twice a week between the ages of eighteen and seventy-two, they will have achieved ecstasy for a total of only nine hours and twenty minutes. No wonder our overwhelming national addiction is to eating, not to making love.[8]

When man and woman become husband and wife, they are still lovers, but that is no longer the exclusive role they play. After I finish writing today I will shop, clean the bathrooms, and vacuum and mop the floors. Not very sexy, eh? These days, the only occasions when I put on a business suit are when I give a lecture or record my TV show. My tux has been in mothballs for years. Becky and I seldom dress up anymore, but we "date" more often than ever. Now it's vacations together, celebrating holidays, lunches out, dinners at home, dancing in the kitchen, and reading aloud before the fire.

In short, although we are determined to continue being attractive to each other, we no longer see ourselves as sex kitten and tomcat. We are not just lovers; we are cooks, cleaners, shoppers, caregivers, gardeners, and pet parents, not to mention writers. Playing all those roles, plus living in close proximity 24/7, doesn't exactly fuel a couple's libido.

Familiarity can be hard on passion, which feeds on mystery, anticipation, and surprise, all of which must be renewed in the marriage. Stress stems from a hundred other aspects of everyday married living. Ironically, although sex is an effective prescription to deal with stress, everyday preoccupations dampen desire. Do not fret: your sizzle is still there, but it may require a vacation from everyday cares to heat up.

It is the conceit of every new generation to believe it has invented sex. Adult children are repelled by the very notion that their elders still enjoy sexual relations. In fact, sex has been here from the beginning of time and accounts for the fact that the world is still populated. There is nothing whatsoever novel about it. We are all the products of sex.

Because the culture is saturated with sensuality, even newlyweds are tempted to believe that other couples are indulging and enjoying it more often than they are. From her interviews, Julia Bourland learned that even in the first year of marriage, many couples are content to make love just once a week. What is problematic is the discrepancy in libidos: one spouse wants it more—and more often—than the other. That complaint is aggravated once there are growing children, demanding careers, and ailing parents to burden the marriage.

KEEPING LOVE ALIVE

Marriage does not mark the end of dating. Just as your times together had to be planned before you wed, lovemaking needs to be scheduled once you're wed. Sex on a regular basis must become a mutual priority, and time must be set aside for it. The old excuse of "Sorry, dear, but I have a headache" was never very convincing, but in fact sheer physical and mental exhaustion is a fact within contemporary wedded life.

The solution is to confront the causes of exhaustion. That means good diet, sufficient exercise, less partying, and more sleep. Making it a habit to go to bed together earlier ensures both sufficient rest and time to make love if the couple wishes. Sex can actually be more spontaneous when a couple schedules time for each other.

However, even for men and women who long wondered whether they would ever find a mate, marriage can make them complacent and less demanding of their need to keep themselves attractive to each other. Sex will not stay spontaneous unless husband and wife alternate in taking the initiative. That means being both seductive and vulnerable. Rather than rejecting outright your spouse's advances when you are utterly not in the mood, it's permissible to bargain: "Okay, but only if you're willing to do most of the work."

Unless your idea of a vacation together is to climb Pike's Peak, holidays are the best thing to rekindle a couple's love life. You have to get away from every routine and pressure in order to relax and simply enjoy yourselves. On vacation couples temporarily "vacate" their obsession with career and routine in order to recommit themselves to pleasing each other.

Some vacation destinations are sure-fire invitations to romance. Long before I met Becky I had been an impoverished graduate student in Paris, lonely and nearly immune to the city's charm. After our children left the nest, we dipped into our savings to spend a winter week in a tiny Left Bank hotel near the Sorbonne. All my earlier disenchantment with the City of Light dissipated in Becky's company. Today, when fortune frowns, we repeat Rick's line to Elsa in *Casablanca*, reminding each other: "We'll always have Paris!"

Vacations anywhere, preferably without the children, are renewable honeymoons. Erica Jong, tantalized by the notion that a couple can make sex "tantric"—melting into each other body and soul—acknowledges that a couple may have to settle for less when in-laws call, the dog throws up, and your child is high on drugs. "You want to be tantric lovers transported to nirvana," she concludes, "but for that you'll have to go on vacation to Uttar Pradesh and meditate on the Taj Mahal."[9]

Still, even when married sex falls short of nirvana, familiarity need not breed contempt. She continues:

> Good sex is what satisfies a couple's exquisitely specific physical, spiritual, and emotional needs—and if both partners like it more tender than lustful, more playful than earnest, more kinky than straight, more cool than hot, or even more "wham bam thank you ma'am" than slow and sweet, then that is exactly what good sex is for that couple.[10]

INFIDELITY

Most couples commit to restricting their sex lives to their life partner. Surveys of marital infidelity are notoriously suspect in any case, because spouses are reluctant to admit to cheating on each other. Still, it's worth noting that nearly half of all husbands and as many as 40 percent of wives admit to having been unfaithful at least once during their marriages.[11]

Spouses stray for more reasons than sexual adventure. Some feel they are taken for granted and want to feel desirable and cherished again. Sometimes straying is a kind of revenge on one's spouse. Or it can be a battle against aging, or just a way to rekindle excitement. Therapists warn that the urge to wander can come at any time in a marriage. The vaunted "seven-year itch" is a fiction.[12]

When "open marriage" became fashionable during the 1960s and 1970s, hip couples believed they could maintain their marriages so long as both spouses were honest about having sex with others. I spent most of the years during my first marriage on college campuses, where spouse swapping was considered a fail-safe way of having one's sexual cake and eating it too. The swapping was typically instigated by male professors, titillated by their young female students and bored with their wives. Even when couples survived their quest for "openness," the quality of the marriages suffered. Most, alas, ended in divorce.

It's not uncommon for a straying spouse to insist to a close friend that his or her extramarital affair actually *preserved* the marriage. But all bets are off if the affair becomes known to the innocent party. If one strays and is found out, the other now feels free to stray as well, and the marriage is compromised. Even when, over time, a couple comes to terms with adultery, it is most often for the sake of the children or financial security. Even when adultery is kept under wraps, it is at the price of a life of lying and sneaking around. When a spouse confesses to cheating, it often stems from the burden of feeling guilty, but justified as well. Then the confession becomes a weapon that tells the spouse, "I went elsewhere because *you* failed me." Psychoanalyst Henry Dicks believes infidelity is sometimes "a last desperate attempt to get blood out of a stone."[13] Failing that, the adulterer often concludes that he has already paid for his sins.

What is permanently lost in a marriage, even with the revelation of a one-night stand, is "a deep knowledge of the other and a profound trust that what one knows is reliable," says Annette Lawson.[14] Faithfulness is not just sexual exclusivity, but mutual trust. "The opposite of monogamy," says Adam Phillips, "is not just promiscuity, but the absence or the impossibility of relationship itself."[15]

TWO BODIES, ONE SPIRIT

In Dante's *Hell*, the lovers Francesca and Paolo are condemned to spend eternity locked naked in each other's embrace. That is more sex than any couple seeks, and a dramatic reminder that marriage is not about lust, but about love. Wedlock is an exclusive sexual relationship, to be sure, but a spiritual one as well. No one marries just for the sex.

A lasting marriage is one of shared values. Opposites attract to some extent, but only if the spouses' lives are enhanced by absorbing the new values a husband and wife bring to their life together. Newlyweds ultimately reconcile themselves to their spouse's behavioral shortcomings, but not to their flawed values. Over time, a couple can alter the script of their relationship, but they can't change each other's character. Nor can they learn to respect a spouse whose values are callous, devious, and self-centered. The seven deadly sins are no friendlier to wedlock than to God.

Even before our marriage, Becky and I decided on a church together. It was not the one I was raised in, and she was brought up in no religious denomination whatsoever. But she had studied religion in college with some brilliant teachers, and we shared beliefs. Becky was about to take on the responsibility for my three little daughters and agreed that it was important that the girls be given the benefit of being grounded in faith, whether or not they reconsidered their beliefs later. As a couple, we wholeheartedly embraced our compromise.

Which was a blessing. A Creighton University study reveals that interdenominational marriages are 47 percent more vulnerable to breakup than when husband and wife worship together.[16] That's on top of the nation's overall divorce rate, and it doesn't even address the vulnerabilities of interfaith marriages or those in which one spouse is unbelieving or nonobservant.

I grew up with the mantra: "The family that prays together stays together." It's a cliché, of course, but the definition of a cliché is something trite but true. Today Becky and I worship as Quakers—a faith founded on silence, simplicity, generosity, inclusiveness, truth telling, and peace seeking. It's something we can wholeheartedly share. But we note each Sunday that, although most members of our modest congregation are married, more often than not only one spouse shows up. We never meet the other. We see only half of a couple.

THE HAPPY MARRIAGE

In the 1990s psychologist Judith Wallerstein recruited fifty couples who professed to enjoy happy marriages, in an attempt to discover the secrets of their success. The recruits were middle-class couples of all ages, married anywhere from ten to forty years, and included second marriages with children. What Wallerstein found strikingly similar in the couples' definition of marital happiness was their respect for and friendship with their spouses. Despite disagreements, they revered their spouse and embraced shared values. They were all adamant that their marriages would last.[17]

One long-married wife, when asked what makes for a happy marriage, told the researcher, "A bad memory." Which is another way of saying, forget trivial disappointments and conflicts in wedlock and cultivate a sense of humor. For every couple studied, happiness in marriage meant feeling respected and cherished, liking as well as loving their mate, and the joy they experienced in each other's company.

Even more telling was that every happy couple volunteered that their marriage was the most important commitment and achievement in their lives. They valued their spouse's integrity, not only loving but also admiring his or her honesty, compassion, generosity, decency, loyalty to the family, and fairness.

While confessing to serious differences, including conflict, anger, and the rare infidelity, all agreed that, over time, the satisfactions of marriage overwhelmingly outweighed the frustrations. Every spouse considered his or her partner to be "special" as an individual and himself or herself to be "fortunate," rather than entitled, to be wed to that person.

"Everything we have we did together" was the claim of happy husbands and wives alike. "Neither the legal nor the religious ceremony makes the marriage," the psychologist concluded. "*People* do, throughout their lives."[18]

On the basis of her studies, Wallerstein identified nine building blocks of a happy marriage:

- Detaching from previous commitments
- Expanding the sense of self to include spouse and children
- Managing inevitable stresses
- Making the relationship safe for expressing differences
- Creating an imaginative and pleasurable sex life
- Sharing laughter
- Being playful
- Providing encouragement
- Relishing memories of life together.[19]

THE GRAND PERHAPS

If a prospective couple's own parents neglected to leave them with the legacy of religious faith, newlyweds may be unaware that there is something missing in their marriage. More likely, the spouses may possess intuitive values that they are unable to articulate, because their good inclinations are grounded in mere sentiment rather than reason and revelation.

"My mind is my own church," Thomas Paine declared. But his intellect did not make him a spiritual man, only a cantankerous one.[20] Ralph Waldo Emerson preached, "It is by yourself without ambassador that God speaks out to you. . . . It is God in you that responds to God without."[21] In Emerson's time that was possibly a healthy sentiment, because he was preaching against narrow Puritanism. But today couples are not so grounded in traditional faith, so those who are sincere can find themselves lifelong "seekers," looking endlessly for a spirituality like wanderers in the desert.

The crunch comes typically with the appearance of children. Few couples can demand good behavior from their children with the explanation "Because *we* say so." Couples who lack a common religious faith soon realize that they cannot pretend to play the part of God in the family, making the rules. As a consequence, many couples will join a church or faith for the sake of their children, knowing the kids need more assurance and grounding than just the parents' approval.

Of course, good behavior can be separated from religious belief, but it takes extraordinary good will and a great deal of effort to love and serve one's fellow man if life is essentially aimless and there is no future to it. More often than not, secularism is not outgoing and humanistic, but selfish and self-centered. The aged playwright John Mortimer says he has made peace with his own atheism, because his parents were both unbelievers yet extraordinarily fair-handed and nurturing without reference to God or the hope of eternal life. But Mortimer is a rare exception.

Many couples shun religious faith on the basis that only a good God is worthy of the name, while the world is full of evil. So, if God exists, they conclude, he must be responsible for the world's pain and heartbreak. In fact, our experience reveals that most of the evil in life is of our own making. People neglect and abuse themselves and one another. The only way a good God could ensure that people act decently toward one another would be to strap us all in straightjackets.

"Is it easy to love God?" C. S. Lewis asked rhetorically, replying, "Yes, for those who do it."[22] But Mortimer is content with a life in which God remains "The Grand Perhaps." In a conversation shortly before his death, the novelist Graham Greene affirmed both his own faith and Mortimer's agnosticism by quoting from Robert Browning's poem:

> All we have gained then by our unbelief
> Is a life of doubt diversified by faith,
> For one of faith diversified by doubt:
> We called the chess-board white,—we call it black.[23]

In a happy marriage it is important that husband and wife agree on the color of life's chessboard.

THE MYTH OF COMPATIBILITY

Even compatible couples divorce. "There's no such thing as a compatible couple," says Diane Sollee, director of the Coalition for Marriage, Family and Couples Education. "There's no such thing as Mr. or Mrs. Right. Every couple has at least ten irreconcilable differences. Look, you're going to disagree. That's normal and expected, and will continue throughout marriage. What's important is that couples learn to manage their disagreements."[24]

But it helps immeasurably to identify what a couple is likely to disagree about. Which explains the growing popularity of premarital coaching. Traditionally, marriage counseling has been reserved for saving ailing marriages from divorce. Now the emphasis is on a kind of preventive medicine: ensuring the health of the marriage before it even happens.

It is a national priority. In 2004 the White House asked Congress for $1.5 billion to promote "healthy marriages" by means of premarital counseling. Acknowledging that family breakup breeds poverty and crime, an increasing number of states are promoting marriage education in an attempt to reduce the divorce rate. In 1998, Florida began requiring all high school seniors to take a marriage and relationship skills course before graduation.[25]

People in love shy from discussing their differences, in the hope that love will conquer all or that they can change their mate's ways once they are married. Premarital counseling requires that they confront their habits and values before taking the plunge. An inventory for both men and women contemplating marriage, called FOCCUS (Facilitating Open Couple Communications, Understanding and Study) is popular with both secular and faith-based marriage mentors. It was created by a nun in the mid-1980s and consists of 189 statements, with which each prospective spouse must agree, disagree, or acknowledge uncertainty.

Statement 53, for example, reads: "I am uncomfortable with the amount my future spouse drinks." Statement 90: "We agree on the religion in which we will raise our children." Statement 130: "I am concerned that a past sexual experience could affect our marital relationship in a negative way."[26]

MARRIAGE DOCTORS

Mike and Harriet McManus of Potomac, Maryland, are volunteer marriage counselors. Married for over forty years, they still bicker, occasionally in the presence of the couples they advise. Together they have assisted forty-seven engaged couples, nine of whom decided that what they learned about themselves over the course of five three-hour sessions revealed that they were not meant for each other.

The McManuses are founders of a nonprofit organization called Marriage Savers. Together they have crossed the country to train other couples to be mentors. Their own Fourth Presbyterian Church of Bethesda requires that any couple that wants to be married in the church must first complete the inventory and be mentored. From 1992 to 2000, 247 couples completed the program, with only seven of the subsequent marriages ending in divorce.

The results of the inventory are typically revealing. "Some of these thoughts have not been expressed," Harriet explains. "They're in love, but in the throes of love, when feelings are running very high, we tend to think that our partner always agrees with us and understands our every need. You don't understand anybody until you ask them what they think or feel or believe."[27]

Two emeritus professors at the University of Washington believe they can predict with near 100 percent accuracy whether a marriage will succeed based not on an inventory but on the manner in which they fight with their mates. In 1994 John Murray and John Gottman recruited 700 newlywed couples and videotaped their quarrels, scoring each partner's words and gestures.

For example, the spouse who rolls his or her eyes during a spat loses four points, but one who smiles through the fight gains three points. Getting defensive costs two points; injecting a note of humor gains four points. For the marriage to succeed there must be five positive points for every negative one. The professors have tracked the 700 couples every two years and find their predictions are uncannily accurate.[28] The scoring scheme can be learned in thirty minutes.

A COURAGEOUS COUPLE

Nigerian-born Joshua Obalua was twenty-seven when he was mentored by the McManuses along with his fiancée, twenty-six-year-old Kemi Adebiyi. Both are American citizens but were intent on returning to Africa for their wedding so their families could share in their happiness. As an engineering student at Syracuse University, Joshua composed a wish list to present to God describing the woman he wanted as his mate for life. On six sheets of paper he scrawled the 250 qualities he sought in a wife.

She would be a serious Christian like himself, a better manager of money than he was, even-tempered (to balance his occasional irascibility), and, if possible, a fellow Nigerian. He even specified her shoe size, "size seven, plus or minus point five."

He was introduced to Kemi by his own father. Born in America, she had studied economics at the University of Maryland and worked as an auditor for the federal government. So, he reasoned, she must be responsible with money. Remarkably, her shoe size was 7½.

After graduating from college, Joshua settled in New Jersey and drove every weekend to see Kemi in Maryland. Tiring of the travel, he moved to Maryland in 2001 to live near her, but neither considered living together during their courtship, considering cohabitation to be improper. A year later at a family gathering Joshua proposed marriage.

Kemi said yes, "but I didn't want to get married right then. I think his family had this idea that we were going to get married that year. But I was, like, I still have so many things that I want to do. You know, finish school. We couldn't really afford to get married then. He couldn't afford an engagement ring, so he gave me a promise ring, which I never wore. I hated it." Instead, Kemi held out for the real thing.

The couple found the McManuses through the Fox News website and asked to be mentored. Although it was not required, they both agreed to be chaste before the wedding, defined as no sexual fondling or intercourse. Kemi said she didn't want sex to become a crutch in the marriage, to be used as their way of making up after disagreements.

By the second session with the McManuses, the couple already confronted a conflict. Kemi was working ten- to twelve-hour days. Joshua thought she should have a choice of not working, but he wasn't earning enough to support them both, let alone a child. The McManuses made observations and tried to be nonjudgmental, but they were concerned that Kemi might not want children at all. Nonsense, she said, but she would expect Joshua to assume equal responsibility for child rearing.

The McManuses asked the couple to create a budget. It was clearly extravagant for young marrieds with modest earnings, calling for daily lunches in restaurants and $250 a month for Kemi's wardrobe. They compromised. Another conflict: Joshua is untidy. "But my bathroom is always clean," he insisted, as Kemi shook her head no. They would solve the problem by setting aside a bedroom in their home for his office. He could be messy there but nowhere else.

One evening with the McManuses is devoted to a ten-step strategy for dealing with conflicts, notably balancing a couple's careers with children. Together the engaged couple defined the problem, acknowledged solutions that soon failed, then came up with better answers.

Finally, the McManuses asked the couple to write love letters to each other. Joshua's was extravagant, calling Kemi a gift from God: "Of all angels in heaven you were meant for me. Today and tomorrow, I will always love you. For you are my angel, my baby girl, my Kemi." Kemi's protestations of love were more earthbound: "I want to marry you because you're a very good person. . . . I love you and wish you the best always."

Kemi and Joshua were wed in Lagos, Nigeria, two days after Christmas in 2002.[29]

"FULL NAKEDNESS! ALL JOYS ARE DUE TO THEE"

I prefaced this chapter with a portion of a love poem by John Donne (1572–1631). It was addressed to sixteen-year-old Ann More, who adored him and whom he married secretly in 1601 without her father's permission. It was a rash decision that prompted Ann's father to send the poor poet to prison for a time and lose all prospects for social advancement.

However, the couple's love, both physical and spiritual, never faltered. She died in 1617, delivering their twelfth child. Two years earlier Donne had taken holy orders. He never remarried but became the most renowned preacher and religious poet of his time, installed in 1621 as dean of London's St. Paul's Cathedral.

In Paradise the first man and woman were unaware of their nakedness. They felt shame only after they had something to hide.

The Donnes' marriage demonstrates that in wedlock there needs to be no conflict between the sacred and the profane, no barrier separating sex and spirit. The marriage bond, far from constraining the couple, made them free.

In the same spirit Donne could write to his wife:

> Come live with me and be my love,
> And we will some new pleasures prove,
> Of golden sands and crystal brooks,
> With silken lines and silver hooks.

And to his God:

> Yet dearly I love You, and would be loved fain . . .
> Take me to You, imprison me, for I,
> Except you enthrall me, never shall be free,
> Nor ever chaste, except You ravish me.[30]

Before the Fall, the first man and first woman walked together with their Creator in contentment and love. Any modern couple that shares the same generous values can recreate Paradise in their marriage.

STEPS IN THE RIGHT DIRECTION

Pursue Intimacy as Marriage's Gift

1. Worship each other on level ground, not on a pedestal. Don't be afraid of losing your individuality within marriage, but don't be afraid of being equal either. It's often noted that the longer a couple is married, the more the spouses look alike. That's because husband and wife are now halves of a new creature: *us*. They complement each other. Sex poses as intimacy, but as passion subsides, you will have to build true intimacy on friendship, shared memories, respect, and admiration. These, like your marriage, can last a lifetime.

2. Accept your vulnerability as a gift. Spouses who insist on winning every argument will never enjoy intimacy. Nor will those who cover up their errors and misjudgments. Marriage is a level playing field with no room to hide. It thrives on vulnerability, laughter, and trust in each other.

3. Build on your common values. That means cultivating similar interests and activities. Talk to each other—not just gossip or family business. Read to each other. Listen to music together. Worship together, or at least value and revere the same things. Cultivate your sense of wonder, and share it. Learn together.

• 10 •

Divorce

Surviving Separation, Finding Love Again

Marriage is like an endless visit in your worst clothes.

J. B. Priestley
(who was married three times)

$\mathcal{E}$arly in the last century, alarmed at the soaring divorce rate, G. K. Chesterton warned university students that B.A. would soon stand for "Bachelor Again," and M.A. for "Married Again."[1] The faithful, uxorious Chesterton lamented that "the modern man wants to eat his wedding cake and have it, too."[2]

T. S. Eliot was even harsher on divorce, calling it the death of the spirit—worse, he said, than extremes of physical pain.[3] Tolstoy famously remarked that all happy families are like one another, whereas each unhappy family is unhappy in its own way. So, too, are the parties to any divorce.[4]

With the advent of no-fault divorces, couples are now inclined to blame "irreconcilable differences" for marital failure, without identifying those differences. The even higher failure rate of second and subsequent marriages suggests that unhappy couples expend little effort in scrutinizing what went wrong the first time around.

"No-fault" is clearly a euphemism when applied to the breaking of the marriage bond. No couple parts without acknowledging or assigning blame. The fault and the pain of marital failure are personal, and the breakup is usually unexpected and often unwanted by one of the spouses. As much as sophisticated people would prefer to part amicably, there is no such thing as a civilized divorce.

Divorce is sometimes effectively accomplished by simple abandonment. My first wife had been previously married to an American in Paris who simply

141

announced to her one evening that he was going out for a pack of cigarettes. He never returned, and she never saw him again.

THE HIGH COST OF STRAYING

Fidelity, even more than love, is the glue that binds married couples. Today, in half of our states, adultery is no longer a crime, and in the others it is seldom, if ever, prosecuted. Nevertheless, sexual straying from marriage remains a very stupid, if not criminal, activity.

The average adulterous husband can invest almost $26,000 conducting an extramarital affair. After his wife finds him out, he can count on another $5,000 in legal bills, plus a deposit of $1,800 on a place to live after she ejects him from their home, then takes half their property.[5]

Adultery is a terrible investment. Consider: only 5 percent of men or women who leave their marriages for someone else actually end up marrying that person.[6]

The presumption that it is the husband who is more susceptible to the seven-year itch is no longer true. Grant Thornton Forensic and Investigative Services asked fifty divorce lawyers to name the most common causes of the cases they had represented in a recent year. Those who cited extramarital affairs reported that in 45 percent of the cases it was the *wives* who cheated. Predictably, a spouse's extramarital affair is the most common reason (30 percent) for starting divorce proceedings, followed by couples "gradually growing apart over time" (26 percent), and strains caused by family life (11 percent). Emotional and physical abuse is cited in just 10 percent of breakups.[7]

Lawyers specializing in divorce acknowledge that it is seldom decorous and often accompanied by acrimony and deceit. In most cases one spouse—in 90 percent of cases the man—attempts to conceal financial assets from the other, either by shifting accounts to other banks or passing assets to his new companion.[8]

Increasingly aware of such dire statistics, philandering spouses tend to avoid exposure as long as possible. They are aided by the Internet, which not only helps to introduce prospective mates but also assists strays. Doug Mitchell (an alias) started an extramarital affair after five years of marriage and two children. He sought advice on how to successfully live a double life.

"Therapy didn't work," he said. "Since my wife and I share the same friends, I couldn't turn to any of them for advice. I turned to the Internet and didn't find any answers, so I started a website and asked for answers." His site soon became a business, and Philanderers International quickly gained 2,000 active members. By 2003 it was receiving 80,000 inquiries every day. Visitors can meet other cheaters on the site, learn how to keep their identity secret for brief liaisons, and avoid tipping their hand to their spouse while they are wandering. Half of the subscribers to the service are women.[9]

THE DECLINE OF PASSION

In modern times, marriage typically begins with romance and passion. To survive long it must add love, companionship, shared interests, mutual help, patience, and fortitude.

Some scientists theorize that nature decrees that every marriage be a divorce waiting to happen. Robert Winston, a professor of fertility studies, explains that "love is, literally, a drug, and a highly addictive one at that. And like all addictions there is a law of diminishing returns. The positive effects wear off after a certain period of time." He believes humans are programmed to lose interest in every sexual partner.[10]

Helen Fisher, an evolutionary psychologist, agrees, comparing humans to foxes, which are serially monogamous, pairing up for just one breeding season and staying together only long enough to help raise their young together before splitting. Culling statistics from sixty countries, she discovered that divorce rates peak around four years into marriage—about the time necessary to raise a single child through infancy.[11]

John Carey, who chaired the committee that chose the best fiction of the year for Britain's 2003 Man Booker award, read 117 new novels. Afterward, he noted that "the commonest single topic . . . is marriage break-up—at least half of them deal with it," even those authors who managed to contrive happy endings.[12]

Are people programmed like foxes to couple with mates, then leave them? Michigan State University psychologist Richard E. Lucas is one who doubts it. He and a team of researchers followed couples from courtship through the early years of marriage, asking them along the way to rate how happy they were on a scale from zero to 10. Most scored between 5.5 to 8 throughout the period. Those who actually married scored higher.

During courtship and their falling in love, the couples' bliss peaked and got yet another boost during the first year of wedlock. After two years of marriage their happiness predictably moderated but it still remained higher than people who never married.[13]

Linda Waite, a University of Chicago sociologist, reveals that married people enjoy better physical and emotional health, live longer, and lead more satisfying sex lives. She cautions that couples who divorce to end an unsatisfying relationship may not end up happier. Indeed, she reports, they do not turn out to be happier than unhappily married people who stay together.[14]

LAMENTATIONS OF THE FATHERS

When people pity single parents, they typically have in mind a divorced mother of small children, all of whom were abandoned by a wayward husband and father. But what is increasingly clear is that wives are nearly as inclined as husbands to seek sex outside the marriage and to file for divorce. On the whole, mothers are still awarded custody of small children, not because the father is considered an unfit parent, but because he is likelier to earn more to support his broken family.

I know whereof I speak, having fought successfully for custody of my three little daughters long before they had reached adolescence. Today, there are many more divorced fathers raising children on their own, as well as "househusbands" who care for children while their wives work.

The typical deadbeat dad was never married to his children's mother in the first place, so there never was a divorce. He is a renegade from parental responsibility, not from marriage. By contrast, divorced dads deprived of the company of their children do not feel freedom, but loneliness and misery.

A survey by Datamonitor, "Trends in Women's Lives," reveals that many divorced thirty-something British women are reveling in self-esteem, as well as "mass affluence," much of it awarded by the divorce courts.[15] By contrast, divorce can be devastating to husbands and fathers. A divorced Englishman's chances of dying are 40 percent higher during the six months following the breakup. He is three times as likely to die of cirrhosis of the liver than when he was married. His life expectancy shrinks by six years. Before jumping to the conclusion that he deserves what he gets because the divorce was his doing, consider that it is women over 70 percent of the time who are initiating the divorce.[16]

Vanessa Lloyd Pratt, a divorce lawyer for twenty-six years, reflects that "women are often used to coping on their own. . . . It's not until another five years have passed that maybe they'll find they are lonely. Men, though, hate divorce instantly, they are as miserable as sin."[17]

Charlie Lewis, professor of family development and psychology at England's Lancaster University, notes that men typically underestimate the trauma of separation: "They feel very isolated and rejected by the very people they expect to rally round and help them."[18]

The irony, adds attorney Pratt, is that what divorced men seek to recapture after marital breakup is the very thing that attracted them to marriage in the first instance. The "main reason men cope so badly after divorce," she says, is because "they still want someone to look after them."[19]

Rock entrepreneur Bob Geldof nearly went bankrupt in his attempt to have more than infrequent access to his children after his wife, Paula Yates, left him for another man. He won custody of his three daughters only after his ex-wife died of a drug overdose. Geldof writes:

> I am only too aware of the pain that women suffer in divorce, but it is equally true that it is as nothing compared with the financial and emotional loss suffered by men. She may lose her man, he loses the lot:
>
> If he is the offending party, people believe that it's right that he should leave the house and kids and pay for them. He even half-thinks this in his guilt. But rarely does he think: I've got a new woman, I'm happier, so I'll just take the kids and go off to this new life. Indeed, society would view it askance if he took the kids. Why? We don't if she does precisely the same. Why?[20]

CHEERLEADERS AND SKEPTICS

Despite the dismal prospects for couples breaking up, there are those who actually favor divorce. Ellen Fein and Sherrie Schneider's rule number forty in their *Rules for Marriage* states: "Realize that your marriage is over if he cheats even once." They go on to advise, "We are not telling you that you must divorce your husband for one sexual infidelity. We are just saying that even if you decide to stay married to him, your marriage is really over. Even if he never cheats again, how will you know? How can you trust him?"[21]

In addition to infidelity they also cite alcoholism, drug abuse, compulsive gambling, rage, and physical violence as justifications for filing for divorce. Recall that these are the women whose other rules include: Be supportive. Let him win. Do things you don't want to do. And don't expect a lot of sympathy from your husband.

They are even skeptical of marriage counseling as a remedy: "Even if your husband is all for it, we are not convinced that marriage counseling is the answer. Sometimes it can add fuel to the fire. We've spoken to women who have attended marriage counseling with their husbands and tell us that all they did for the full hour was talk about what the other was doing wrong."[22]

When author Judith Viorst was more than forty years into marriage she acknowledged that it's not always a bed of roses. But speaking for many women of her acquaintance, she argues, "Bad as our marriage is, or so we tell ourselves, divorce is even worse."[23] Her friend Lola, whose husband of thirty-five years has been unfaithful for half that time, admits she has "very often thought of divorce. But what stops me is that, when I look around, I don't see my divorced friends being very happy."[24]

Viorst ponders, "Should we divorce if, although we married for better or for worse, the worse turned out to be worse than we ever expected?[25] She cautions: "The risk, of course is that, walking away, we take our unhappy self with us, that significantly unsatisfied self that imagines the grass is greener everywhere else."[26]

Ruth Caplin, a Maryland therapist, reports that "if one member of a couple very much wants to save the marriage, the chance of its survival increases enormously. One dedicated mate can change the climate."[27]

Most marriages that end do so between the second and fifth year, with the greatest likelihood of breakup coming during the third year.[28]

DOES RELIGIOUS FAITH DETER DIVORCE?

Although Jesus proscribed divorce except for adultery,[29] most Christian denominations today acquiesce in accommodating the subsequent marriages of divorced persons.

By contrast, the Catholic Church does not permit divorce, and will not recognize civil remarriage. However, it permits the physical separation of the couple. Moreover, it is willing to scrutinize whether the original marriage contract was invalid due to some impediment, typically because one or both of the spouses withheld full consent to the marriage vows. In such cases a church tribunal can declare that the marriage never existed, and the parties are free to remarry.[30]

Despite all churches' distaste for divorce, there are now parts of the Bible Belt where the divorce rate is even higher than in the nation at large.[31] This goes to show that Christians don't always act in accordance with what they believe.

The psychologist Ruth Caplin acknowledges that a strong religious orientation can enable an embattled spouse "to try again without losing self-respect."[32] But even the great Christian apologist C. S. Lewis acknowledged that some spouses are utterly wrong and bad for each other and find themselves "chained together mercilessly . . . two mutual tormentors, each raw all over with the poison of hate-in-love, each ravenous to receive and implacably refusing to give, jealous, suspicious, resentful, struggling for the upper hand, determined to be free and to allow no freedom, living on 'scenes.'"[33]

It is precisely the kind of mutually destructive marriage that Edward Albee portrayed in *Who's Afraid of Virginia Woolf.*

But few couples seeking divorce are at each other's throats. After twenty-two years of practice, Indianapolis marriage counselor Susan Cahn has concluded that "70 percent of couples who divorced didn't need to divorce, that they could have made it," if instead of leaving the marriage, "they'd understood that conflict is normal, that conflict is growth trying to happen."[34]

In Christian weddings, following the couple's vows, the minister or priest proclaims on behalf of the community: "What God has joined together, let no one put asunder." It is a caution aimed not just at interlopers who might tamper with the marriage, but at the couple themselves, who are responsible for maintaining a relationship that God has blessed and entered.

Couples experiencing difficulties with their marriage are less likely to consider divorce if they believe that God is the author of marriage and that it has been the divine plan that "they are no longer two, but one flesh."[35] As Jesus noted, the permission given by Moses to divorce was a concession "to their hardness of hearts."[36]

St. Paul, who never married, nevertheless made the greatest claims for the married state:

> The husband must give his wife the same sort of love that Christ gave to the Church, when he sacrificed himself for her. . . . So men ought to give their wives the love they naturally have for their own bodies. The love a man gives his wife is the extending of his love for himself to enfold her. . . . For this cause shall a man leave his father and mother, and shall cleave to his wife; and the twain shall become one flesh. The marriage relationship is a great mystery.[37]

MAKING SEPARATIONS WORK

No one has a notion how many unhappy couples decide against divorce for the sake of their children, or postpone their separation until the children are grown and leave home. But anecdotal evidence suggests that children are more of a glue in unhappy marriages than they are a cause for marital breakup.

"Birdnesting" is a compromise many unhappy couples embrace that respects the fact that the marriage is in disrepair without denying the children the care of two parents. Journalist Sarah Baxter describes it as "flitting in and out of the marital home while the children stay put."[38] It is an arrangement that recognizes a greater role of fathers in child rearing and the increase in joint custody judgments by divorce courts.

When Mari Frank broke up with her husband in the late 1980s, she had two toddlers to protect. She rented an apartment on her own, while her husband went to live in his girlfriend's beach house. The children remained in the family home, and the parents took turns caring for them there. The arrangement lasted only two years, but today Frank is a divorce lawyer who helps other unhappy couples with children to come up with birdnesting agreements.[39]

The agreements specify how the couple will behave with each other in the children's presence, which parent will be home when, whether they are both responsible for keeping the house clean and doing the laundry, and how dates and new partners can be accommodated. Rabbi Peter Netter and his wife divorced when their youngest child was seven and their oldest was twelve. He moved into the family home every other week, while the children's mother lived in his apartment.[40]

A strong financial incentive for birdnesting is that many couples with small children have negative equity in their homes and do not want to sell them at a loss when they separate.

Family lawyer Lowell Sucherman warns that children can take advantage of these agreements to pit their parents against each other. The kids can be tempted to think the house now belongs to them, and the arrangement perpetuates the children's belief that their parents will get back together eventually.[41]

Nevertheless, New Mexico judge Ann Kass believes that birdnesting can level the playing field in contested divorces before they become final. "When a divorce suit is first started," she says, "parents often jockey for position. They believe that whichever one can get to stay in the house and have primary custody of the children will have a stronger claim at the end." The judge wants parents to "walk a mile in somebody's else's shoes" so they better understand what the children are going through and will develop sensible custody-sharing arrangements.[42]

Divorcemagazine.com polled over 2,000 respondents in 2003 and discovered that more than 30 percent of divorced parents said they would consider giving birdnesting a try. Divorce lawyers caution that amicable custody-sharing arrangements typically falter when one or both parents finds a new long-term lover or mate. The parent's concern for the children remains strong, but the new lover or spouse is often unwilling to accept a role that is both more demanding and inferior to that of stepparent.[43]

GETTING BACK TOGETHER AGAIN

Leslie and Mort Gerson were husband and wife for thirteen years, starting with their June 1958 wedding. They separated in 1970, reconciled the next year, moved back together for six years while their divorce became final, then remarried. They are now both well into their sixties and have three children.

"I was fun-loving," Leslie says of her younger self.

> Trouble was, I didn't have a clue as to what raising children was about, and so much happened during our first year together: we got married, I got pregnant, Mort passed the bar, and our son David came along. That's when things really started changing—reality set in. . . .
>
> I think our marriage problems started that first year, but I kept rationalizing it as the years went on, even after our second son, Robert, was born, saying, "This is what marriage is like. Daddy goes off to work and mommy stays home with the kids."

"It all came to a head after our daughter Joanne was born," Mort explains, "when the two boys were seven and ten. Leslie would call me at my office, complaining and asking me to come home."

"That was right before our breakup," Leslie recalls. "During the first ten years of the marriage I had tried to be vocal about what was going on with me, but I was still extremely frustrated and resentful. I remember wanting to go to a marriage counselor, but Mort would say, 'You're the one who's unhappy, you go, I'm not having a problem.' That created a lot of distance for us."

After thirteen years of marriage Leslie moved out with Joanne, while David and Robert remained with their father. "I was so confused. I didn't want to be married to him, but I didn't want him out of my life."[44]

They both started dating others. Both were miserable.

A year and a half into the separation Leslie moved back in the house. Nevertheless, they allowed the divorce to become final after another six months. It was their way of not taking each other for granted. "That first year back together was tough," Mort recalls. "And later on, it was rough having two teenagers in addition to dealing with the process we were going through. . . . Life is not for amateurs."[45]

"People still want to believe that something magic happens when you marry and that everything will be wonderful," Leslie admits. "That was me thirty-eight years ago. Now I realize that successful relationships are very hard-working, on-going struggles, where people learn to compromise and give and take and give and take. We both realize that marriage is not fifty-fifty, it's seventy-five–seventy-five."[46]

If Tolstoy was right about families, the Gersons were unhappy each in their own way when divorced, but now share the kind of happiness other couples enjoy who stay together.

CONFESSIONS OF A DIVORCE LAWYER

The English octogenarian Sir John Mortimer is the son of a divorce lawyer and, before he turned to writing plays and novels, was a barrister himself. His first cases were in dreary probate court, but he soon walked in his father's professional shoes. "Divorce was sexier, more dramatic, and supplied our daily bread," he says, "so that in my childhood I was housed, fed, watered, clothed, and educated almost entirely on the proceeds of adultery, cruelty, and wilful neglect to provide reasonable maintenance."

He notes that ending a marriage today can be as simple as "filling out a form, dividing up the property, and saying, 'Cheerio!'" But when he began practice after World War II anyone who wanted to divorce "had to prove something extremely serious like cruelty or adultery."

One of Mortimer's earliest clients was a man so determined to divorce his wife that he attempted to persuade someone to commit adultery with her. Unsuccessful as a recruiter, he was reduced to disguising himself in a false beard, mustache, and dark glasses, "and creeping into his own bungalow in full view of the neighbors, pretending to be his own co-respondent." Mortimer adds:

> The plot was discovered and the unfortunate husband was sent to prison for "perverting the course of justice." I thought this was extremely hard. If you can't sleep with your own wife wearing a false beard, what can you do? His case showed, however, in an extreme form, and unbridgeable gap between the law, justice, morality, and even common sense.

When Mortimer starting pleading divorce cases, an English husband could still get damages from his wife's lover. "This," he recalls, "entailed an argument in court about her value in hard cash." He explains:

> In these unseemly proceedings, a husband had to argue that his wife was a fabulous cook, mother, and lover, and therefore worth a great deal. The ungallant lover, however, swore she was a cold fish in bed and never did the washing-up. There was no such thing as a divorce by consent; in fact consent was called "connivance" and was a bar to freedom from an unhappy marriage.[47]

SO WHY NOT DIVORCE?

Some marriages that survive beyond the first few years fail in midlife, Judith Viorst notes, because of a sense that time is running out. "Why not end a marriage—now that the children are almost all grown—which lacks shared interests, passion, excitement, pleasure? Why not try for a marriage with more emotional gratification?"[48]

Instead, she suggests renegotiating the terms of the marriage, quoting psychoanalyst Roger Gould about the transformations that are possible:

> The old conspiracies are abandoned. In their place is a relationship based on emphatic acceptance of our authentic partner, who is not a myth, not a god, not a mother, not a father, not a protector, not a censor. Instead there is just another human with a full range of passions, rational ability, strengths, and weaknesses, trying to figure out how to conduct a meaningful life with real friendship and companionship. From this new dynamic, many different forms of marriage may follow: two very separate lives, in which husband and wife come together only periodically, as their rhythm of relating dictates; total sharing of one's life in work and leisure; or variations between these two extremes. In any case it is a relationship of equals, without rank, position, or self-abrogation.[49]

Viorst believes that divorce is a loss like the death of a spouse, and is often mourned in closely parallel ways. But, she adds, "there are some important distinctions. Divorce evokes more anger than death, and it is, of course, considerably more optional. But the sorrow and pining and yearning can be as intense. The denial and despair can be as intense. The guilt and self-reproach can be as intense. And the feeling of abandonment can be even more intense—'He didn't *have* to leave me; he *chose* to leave me.'"[50]

Divorce confronts a marriage's midlife crisis by walking away from it. But to do so, you lose a mate and must still live with yourself.

MAKING A NEW COVENANT

We're all fortunate that the advent of no-fault auto insurance didn't encourage the average American driver to play bumper cars on the nation's highways. But no-fault *divorce* has arguably encouraged the destruction of marriages. Legislators in Louisiana believe it is too easy nowadays to get married and too simple to get divorced. They argue that a fender-bender can be fixed on an automobile, but the children of divorce are likelier to experience permanent damage. Every year about 1 million American children are added to the rolls of broken homes.

Lamenting that "till death do us part" is only a tattered remnant of romantic fiction in a nation in which half of all marriages fail, Louisiana's legislature decided a few years ago to encourage lifelong bonds. Its device is an optional contract called "covenant marriage," which is harder to enter and exit than ordinary no-fault wedlock. No couple can enter or leave covenant marriage without professional counseling, and divorce is permitted only for abandonment, adultery, physical or sexual abuse, long separation, or the sentencing of a spouse to hard labor or death.[51]

Some Louisiana clergy today will officiate only at covenant marriages. Moreover, many couples in the state, already happily married, have decided that, as a sign of their mutual commitment, they would also embrace the stringent covenant bond.

From the outset, naysayers lined up to attack the innovation as idealistic. Geraldine Levy, who cares for battered women at the New Orleans YWCA, said the law overlooks the psychological damage one spouse can inflict on the other, yet fails to qualify as grounds for divorce in a covenant marriage. John Shalett of Family Service of Greater New Orleans argued that starry-eyed young couples truly believe their love will endure, but are unprepared for reality to set in after the honeymoon ends. Other critics predicted that some prospective spouses would insist on covenant marriage as a kind of emotional blackmail.

Wedlock, to be sure, is not for the fainthearted. Covenant marriage addresses the likelihood that "no-fault" in marital failure is only a handy fiction. In real life there is always one spouse who is aggrieved, and one who precipitated the breakup, even when both contributed to it. I have yet to meet a divorced couple each of whom freely, wholeheartedly, and unilaterally desired to end the marriage. Bad marriages are caused not by the fading of romantic idealism but by unreasonable expectations and bad behavior. In two-thirds of American divorces, children are the permanent victims.

LIFE AFTER MARRIAGE

A. Alvarez compared divorce to suicide, with one significant difference: "Although both are devastatingly public admissions of failure, divorce, unlike suicide, has to be lived through."[52] If marriage is about companionship, divorce is about solitude.

But George Bernard Shaw, while lamenting divorce, looked upon it as a kind of insurance policy: "I take it as a fact there is no marriage, however judiciously and carefully it may be arranged, whatever may be the good faith of the parties to it, which is not an experiment. . . . Divorce, in fact, is not the destruction of marriage, but the first condition of its maintenance."[53]

But Goethe, who knew something about diabolical temptations, insisted that marriage must be indissoluble, arguing that "it brings so much happiness that individual instances of unhappiness do not come into account."[54] He advised feuding spouses to "let the moment pass, and you will count yourself happy that what has so long stood firm still stands." He added: "The human condition is compounded of so much joy and so much sorrow that it is impossible to reckon how much a husband owes a wife or a wife a husband. It is an infinite debt; it can be paid only in eternity."[55]

⸎

STEPS IN THE RIGHT DIRECTION

Pick Yourself Up, Brush Yourself Off . . .

1. Don't separate just because you're both tired of each other. Ask yourself why your spouse is tired of *you*. The two of you may just be in separate ruts, having developed annoying habits and routines over the years, no longer sharing your interests and enthusiasms with each other. Talk with each other. You are not enemies; you used to be friends. It's unlikely you will be happier alone or with someone new who simply puts up with you.

2. Don't play the victim. You may *be* the principal victim in separation or divorce, but it will do you no good to play the part as a long-running tragedy. Divorce proceedings attempt to sugarcoat the causes for marital breakup by citing vague "irreconcilable differences," but only you know what those differences were. There is seldom a clear villain and an obvious victim. Marriages are not made in heaven. Some are mistaken matches from the get-go.

3. Don't rush back into marriage. Not until you have reached some clarity about what contributed to the breakup. Second marriages fare even worse than first ones, often because the new spouses consider that they were the utterly innocent parties their first time around and are defensive, insisting that "no one will take advantage of me again." The world does not demand that you be married, nor value you as an individual just because you're wed. Get to know yourself better, and you will be better for a new someone.

Permanence

Maintaining Marriage in Changing Times

> No man or woman really knows what perfect love is until they have been married a quarter of a century.
>
> Mark Twain

$\mathscr{D}$espite the inclination of the rich and famous to hedge their marital bets by means of prenuptial agreements, ordinary Americans continue to enter wedlock assuming their particular lock is unbreakable.

But we have become increasingly tolerant of the infidelities of others. Nelson Rockefeller's divorce denied him his party's nomination for the presidency in the 1960s. But Bill Clinton, a serial philanderer, remained popular and survived impeachment in the 1990s.

Even the president's chief persecutor, Congressman Henry Hyde of Illinois, acknowledged that "infidelity is a private act," and Clinton's only public crime was to have sworn on the Bible to tell the whole truth.

Harvard University historian Nancy F. Cott believes the president survived his marital infidelities "because the majority generously (or cynically) tolerated a wide range of behavior in couples, seeing husbands and wives as accountable principally to each other for their marital performance. The debacle of the impeachment forced explicit public cognizance of marital conduct as private and of marital infidelity as too common a failing to prompt civic excommunication."[1]

Cott traces the devaluation of marriage to "a generation's seismic shift in marriage practices."[2] Beginning in the 1960s sexual nonconformity became youth's political statement and was soon assimilated by their elders. With the rise of feminism, women began to assume the sexual initiative, and sanctions against premarital, extramarital, and interracial relations lost their force.

The traditional link between sex and marriage was weakened by the mass marketing of the birth control pill, starting in the 1960s, effectively separating sex from pregnancy. The new freedoms demanded by heterosexuals also made it possible for gays and lesbians to reveal and indulge their own inclinations. Love and lust became the coinage of personal fulfillment, and an entire generation came to accept the mantra, "If it feels good, do it."

The sexual revolution was not confined to the United States but spread across the industrialized world. Between 1965 and 1980 the rates of marriages and births declined sharply, while divorces and out-of-wedlock births soared. The French demographer Louis Roussel dubbed this cultural transformation the "banalization" of previously condemned behavior.[3] Relationships once considered sacred and lasting were cheapened, and the notion of respectability in sexual relations lost its moral force.

EFFECTS OF THE SEXUAL REVOLUTION

The fallout was phenomenal. From 1960 to 1998 unmarried households multiplied tenfold—more than five times as fast as U.S. households overall. By century's end the National Opinion Research Center at the University of Chicago acknowledged that cohabitation had become the norm for American men and women, not only prior to marriage but after divorce. Nearly two-thirds of men and women born between 1963 and 1974 first cohabited without benefit of marriage.

Wedlock is no longer the predictable institution it once was. At the outset of the new millennium fully one-fourth of all American households consisted of men and women living alone. With the decline in marriage, the birth rate had already dropped from more than 3.5 children per woman in 1960 to just 2 in the mid-1990s. Households without children (62 percent) became the norm, while unmarried mothers now account for one-third of all births. At the millennium three-fourths of American women were in the labor force, including more than 60 percent of married mothers of children under the age of six.[4]

With the number of working women nearly equal to that of men, legal constraints on wives in the business world were weakened. Although the 1964 Civil Rights Act made gender a forbidden basis for discrimination in the workplace, feminists failed to persuade legislators to add an equal rights amendment to the Constitution. Nevertheless, "due process of law" and "equal protection of the laws" persuaded most judges to protect women in the workplace.

Divorce became easier in the mid-1960s with the virtual abandonment of the adversary principle. California adopted "no-fault" divorce in 1969, and by

1985 every state agreed that any incompatible couple could end their marriage without blaming either spouse. No-fault divorce converted marital breakup into a victimless crime—except for the couple's children.

Traditionally, a husband or wife petitioning for divorce was required to demonstrate that the other spouse was guilty of adultery or desertion. With no-fault divorce, the states stepped back altogether from passing judgment and allowed the partners themselves to define their own marital expectations.

The Supreme Court in 1979 made the awarding of alimony gender neutral, and the division of property between divorcing spouses became more equitable—the assumption being that the material assets of either partner belonged to them both when their marriage ended. A homemaker could even be compensated for her unpaid work. So could a husband whose wife earned more than he did during the marriage. As for supporting the children of divorce, by 1988 welfare reforms made *both* fathers and mothers responsible.[5]

PREMARITAL CONTRACTS

With the sharp increase in unmarried cohabitation, the states began to consider the legal obligations of the couple when their informal arrangements failed. In 1976 in California the actor Lee Marvin was sued for "palimony" by an actress with whom he had lived for seven years. The courts refused to consider the arrangement to be a common-law marriage, treating it instead like an agreement between business partners. When Marvin appealed a $104,000 award to the woman, it was overturned, but the right of cohabiting partners to sue was upheld.

Feminists urged that women contemplating marriage protect themselves by prenuptial contracts, not only specifying the division of property should the marriage end in divorce, but also the couple's shared obligations within the marriage—including budgeting, housework, childcare, and even frequency of intercourse. The courts tended to honor these premarital contracts as well as new agreements drawn up by already married couples.

But there were limits. A husband could not be required to abide by a no-sex contract with his wife or allowed to escape his obligation to support her financially. When in 1993 a wife claimed compensation for caring for her sick husband at home rather than placing him in a nursing home (which had been her preference), a California appeals court refused to uphold what it called "sickbed bargaining," reasserting instead the traditional notion that caring for a spouse is part of the "marital duty of support."[6] So the traditional vows of "in sickness and in health," and "for better, for worse" still retain some force in law.

Even before the U.S. Supreme Court in 1973 decriminalized abortion, the widespread use of contraception had been justified on the basis of a couple's right to privacy. But privacy was not physical protection. If the state could not enter the American bedroom, husbands were theoretically free to rape their wives with impunity. In practice, however, since 1970 police have claimed and exercised the right to enter the home to counter domestic violence. But it was not until 1984 that a New York appellate court agreed that husbands could be prosecuted for marital rape. Other states swiftly concurred.[7]

The upshot was that "the law of marriage no longer gave bodily possession of the wife to her husband," establishing instead "a new norm of the wife's self-possession, with the potential to reframe the roles of both marriage partners."[8] It can be argued "that by the 1980s the states and the nation had let go their grip on the institution of marriage along with their previous understanding of it."[9]

LOSING A GRIP ON MARRIAGE

An unintended consequence of this step back by public authority was the revival of polygamy among fundamentalist Mormons in Utah and Arizona despite official disapproval by the Church of Jesus Christ of Latter-Day Saints.[10] Today the courts are much less interested in Americans' living arrangements than they are in ensuring the *financial* responsibility of partners (married and unmarried) for each other and for their children.

Predictably, the retreat of the courts prompted a reactionary movement, especially among fundamentalist Christians who demanded the restoration of "family values." The religious right succeeded in blocking ratification of the Equal Rights Amendment while pressuring the states to establish limits to abortion on demand. Nevertheless, despite some misgivings, most Americans had no desire to return to the old patriarchal model of marriage.[11]

That model had already been rendered obsolete by the prevalence of two-earner couples. Americans are now, by and large, tolerant of others' heterosexual living arrangements, with the notable exception of adultery. At the millennium four out of five adult Americans pronounced adultery to be, without exception, wrong.[12]

Although antigay attitudes have declined and same-sex partners' rights have increased, there remains a widespread reluctance to award the term *marriage* even to lifelong same-sex partnerships. Eight of ten Americans affirm "old-fashioned values about family and marriage."[13]

Until fairly recently civil authorities were reluctant to extend marriage (by that name) to same-sex relationships. However, some churches bless faithful gay couples with wedding-like ceremonies, arguing that wedlock is contracted by mutual consent of the partners, not by political authority.

In a 1998 ruling in Alaska, a superior court proclaimed the right to choose one's life partner to be "fundamental." Judge Peter Michalski wrote: "The relevant question is not whether same-sex marriage is so rooted in our traditions that it is a fundamental right, but whether the freedom to choose one's own life partner is so rooted in our traditions."[14] He believed this freedom to be so rooted.

Rejecting his judgment, thirty-five states passed laws forbidding same-sex marriages, wherever contracted, and Congress in 1996 passed a Defense of Marriage Act that reserved the words "marriage" and "spouse" to only one man and one woman. Before voting, some supporters predicted that same-sex marriage "would start the descent down a slippery slope to licensing polygamy, incest, even marriage to animals."[15] The bill passed the House by 342 to 67 and the Senate by 85 to 14.

CRACKS IN THE CONSTITUTION

Nevertheless, Vermont, while reserving "marriage" to one man and one woman, made provision for a "civil union" of same-sex couples that awarded the same rights and protections as wedlock.[16] Massachusetts went further, as its courts required the state legislature to abide by the state constitution and extend equal rights to gay couples, joining the Netherlands, Belgium, and three Canadian provinces. In the summer of 2003 the U.S. Supreme Court had struck down all remaining antisodomy laws on the grounds of the constitutional right to sexual privacy, opening the way to legitimizing same-sex unions.

By early 2004 San Francisco and other municipalities were extending marriage rights to gay couples. It was a classic use of civil disobedience, not unlike that which won civil rights for African Americans in the 1960s. The 2000 census for the first time had reported 549,000 same-sex couples. There were undoubtedly many more who were reluctant to reveal their arrangements to the government.

With cohabitation and divorce so common, and strains on traditional marriage only increasing, politicians profess to want to make heterosexual wedlock more attractive. Yet public policy runs counter to political rhetoric. As two-earner couples became the norm and wives' take-home pay approached that of their husbands, marriage became a disadvantage when it came to paying taxes. Many working couples discovered they were victims of a "marriage penalty," paying more for filing jointly as spouses than they would as unmarried singles.

African American couples were even harder hit by the "marriage penalty" than whites, because a higher proportion of black husbands and wives are near-equal earners. Some affluent couples actually divorce on December 31 and remarry the next day just to qualify for single-earner status for tax purposes.[17] Older couples, either divorced or widowed, have also found it more advantageous to cohabit rather than marry and lose both partners' Social Security benefits. Along with reducing taxes, the younger George Bush successfully persuaded Congress to begin to eliminate the marriage penalty.

Constructive critics of same-sex marriage argue that it "does not simply extend an old institution to a new group of people, but changes the definition of marriage, reducing it primarily to an affectionate sexual relationship accompanied by a declaration of commitment."[18] From ancient times legal marriage was conceived as an institution assisting society in achieving not only sexual activity, mutual help, and affection, but also procreation and parental care and accountability. Critics hesitate to award the term "marriage"—and its rights—to relationships that possess neither the possibility of procreation nor the responsibility of child rearing. Nevertheless, whether it is graced with the nomenclature of marriage, committed same-sex couples will likely, over time, achieve the rights of wedded couples.

Jonathan Rauch, a conservative journalist, argues that marriage will impose a social discipline on same-sex couples. "The gay rights era will be over and the gay responsibility era will begin," he predicts. Concerning marriage, he argues, "no other institution has the power to turn narcissism into partnership, lust into devotion, strangers into kin."[19]

MARRIAGE, AND OTHER ARRANGEMENTS

Rauch worries that the real threat to marriage comes from casual cohabitation, warning that we are approaching the day when marriage—straight or gay—will be "merely an item on a mix-and-match menu of lifestyle options, a truffle in the candy box."[20]

Marriage as an institution is on the wane in any case, with only 2.3 million weddings a year, the fewest ever relative to the nation's adult population. Nearly half of Americans are still unmarried by the time they are thirty, and nearly 12 percent of women and 16 percent of men are still unmarried when they enter their forties.[21]

Two respected social scientists argue that, rather than expand the status and privileges of marriage to same-sex couples and, inevitably, to others committed to caring relationships, "society should find alternative ways of meeting the needs not only of same-sex couples but also interdependent friends, and dependent but unmarried kin."[22]

Marriage is, after all, only one of many mutually advantageous personal relationships. We all know of young children who have been raised by a single parent, a grandparent, or other relative, not to mention stepparents and foster parents. Adult siblings live together in mutually dependent relationships. So do friends. Because I am more than a decade older than Becky (and women have a longer life expectancy than men), she is already contemplating life when I am no longer among the living. The all-female household depicted in the long-running TV series *The Golden Girls*, spanned two generations and four women.

Without putting too fine a point on it, all these caring, protracted relationships are forms of "marriage," obviously absent sex, romance, and procreation, but including mutual affection and financial and emotional responsibility. Browning and Marquardt argue that "tax benefits, legal adoption, welfare transfers, and more refined and accessible legal contracts should all be used to meet these needs" of Americans living together and caring for one another.[23]

⸎

If public policy still fails to effectively encourage men and women to marry, love continues to be exalted in twenty-first-century America, romance reigns, and wedlock still appeals to those who seek lifelong intimacy and fulfillment. No one has contrived a more appealing alternative.

Far from stifling individuality, marriage still holds out the promise of mutual caring in place of isolation. More than ever, marriage can be conceived as both security and freedom. In the future, many Americans may postpone marriage indefinitely or shy forever from the risk of its failure. But for courageous couples, wedlock will be a safe harbor in a tempestuous and unpredictable world, offering an intimacy that exists nowhere else, and the promise of living happily ever after.

That is my hope for you.

⸎

STEPS IN THE RIGHT DIRECTION

Give Your Marriage a Lifetime Warranty

1. Remember that your marriage requires regular servicing. Just as your car can't be expected to keep running without periodic service and

checkups, your marriage needs regular attention. Deferred maintenance of your home will require expensive repairs or renovation.
Marriage is a living thing. With inattention it can decay or die. Birthdays, anniversaries, vacations, and other holidays are occasions for a
couple to consider their blessings. But they are infrequent. Schedule
celebrations of your life together, and surprise each other often with
gifts of gratitude.

2. Consider how fortunate you are and show it. You have someone who
   loves you exclusively despite being aware of all your shortcomings.
   Don't take that love for granted. Return it a hundredfold.
3. Savor growing older together. Your marriage is a lifetime investment
   in each other that, with attention, will continue to pay dividends to
   the end of your days. Don't be afraid to plan ahead, knowing that you
   have a permanent partner in life.

· 12 ·

Compatibility: Will Our Marriage Last?

A Self-Test for Couples

mar-riage \'mar-ij\ n. The institution whereby men and women are joined in a special kind of social and legal dependence for the purpose of founding and maintaining a family. An intimate or close union.

Webster's Seventh New Collegiate Dictionary

"*M*arriage, as my ferocious mother-in-law always used to say, gazing balefully about her, is not a love affair," recalls the English pundit Minette Marrin. "I always used to find that rather discouraging, especially when I was first married to her son." She continues:

> However, I do know what she meant. Marriage isn't only a love affair, though ideally it begins with one. Marriage is, most importantly, a social contract, the most important social contract there is in civil society. . . .
> I often wonder now, looking back, what my mother-in-law would have said if I had asked her what marriage is, as opposed to what it's not. . . . What strikes me now is that people still don't really talk about it. They talk ceaselessly about relationships and fulfillment and parents, but they don't actually say much about the wider demands and necessary conventions of marriage or of partnership.[1]

Marriage is not an equal-opportunity relationship, nor can anyone embrace it as a fifty-fifty proposition. More often than not, wedlock requires a lopsided investment by one of the spouses that never ends.

In any case, no marriage comes with a lifetime guarantee of satisfaction or your money back. Whereas insurance companies make a comfortable living by predicting when you and I are likely to die, they do not offer marriage

163

insurance policies, because so many marriages fail, most of them within the first five years. It's revealing that extramarital affairs typically begin within the very first two years of wedlock.

Still, at the outset, nearly all couples confidently embrace marriage, persuading themselves that they will beat the odds. One thing is certain: a marriage seldom fails because of forces *beyond* the couple's control. If both spouses contribute the proper ingredients to their life together, in sufficient measure, they can weather the inevitable challenges, repair the hurts, and strengthen their marriage to last a lifetime.

Tolstoy observed that, while happy families are all alike, unhappy families are unhappy each in their own way. That suggests that there is a recipe for successful lifelong marriage, which each couple can adjust to suit their situation.

Whether you are contemplating wedlock or already married, it's important to determine whether your expectations of married life are reasonable and likely to be met. Answer each of these questions *separately* before comparing your answers with your spouse or intended. Don't agonize over your answers. *Spend no more than three seconds on each question or five minutes overall.*

AGREE / DISAGREE

1. I believe our marriage was made in heaven.
2. Opposites attract, so our differences will actually strengthen our marriage.
3. We have different religious faiths but don't argue about them, so they don't matter.
4. Keeping embarrassing secrets from my partner isn't the same as lying and can't hurt us.
5. I trust my spouse will never be attracted to another man or woman.
6. As long as we each hold up our end of the marriage, we won't have to do more.
7. Because my partner belongs to me forever, I will never be jealous.
8. As long as the sex is good, other problems will pale.
9. True love means never having to say I'm sorry.
10. There are possessions I will bring to the marriage that are mine and not for sharing.
11. I won't mind if we each flirt with others in public as long as we trust each other.
12. My partner will never withhold information from me.
13. If my partner wants time to pursue his or her own interests, it robs us of time together.

14. No matter how long we're married we'll always be youthful.
15. We will sacrifice our individual interests for common interests.
16. When some of my partner's habits annoy me, he or she will change them out of love for me.
17. Money will not be a problem for us if we each handle our own personal finances.
18. We can discard old family traditions and start anew.
19. When we have an argument, we will call a truce and solve the problem in bed.
20. We agree completely on how many children we want, when to have them, and on sharing parental responsibilities equally.
21. Whoever has the bigger paycheck will enjoy no greater say about how we spend our income.
22. We can share equally the task of paying bills and keeping track of our expenses.
23. Since we love each other, we no longer need to say "please" and "thank you."
24. I needn't bother consulting my partner before agreeing to a business, social, or family commitment that affects us both.
25. We won't let our parents put pressure on us to be with them during holidays.
26. I expect my spouse to know instinctively what will make me happy.
27. Romance will last and marriage will fulfill all of my needs.
28. We agree completely on contraception, abortion, and frequency of lovemaking.
29. It's only necessary that one of us be a good listener.
30. I can't imagine any kind of behavior that would be grounds for ending our marriage.
31. As long as we have a steady income, I won't worry about our credit card balances.
32. Even when I am behaving badly or in a foul mood, I expect my partner to love me for myself.
33. Living on a budget robs marriage of romance.
34. If we both have jobs, we can afford to eat out rather than prepare meals at home.
35. It's essential that each of us drive a new car.
36. If sex ever gets boring, I might consider swapping with another attractive married couple.
37. Although I feel superior (or inferior) to my partner in important ways, I won't let on.

38. I resent my partner's friends when they enjoy time with him or her, leaving me out.
39. All of my partner's successes are due to my support.
40. I resent my in-laws' advice as interference in our lives.
41. It doesn't matter if one of us isn't clean, tidy, and organized so long as the other one is.
42. We share the same tastes in everything.
43. If it were possible, we would spend every moment of our time together.
44. My spouse must love me totally or not. Nothing I can do will affect the way he or she feels about me.
45. I can change my partner's habits by pointing out his or her flaws and inadequacies.
46. For better or worse, I compare my marriage to that of my parents.
47. My happiness depends on how my partner treats me.
48. I can't be happy if my partner is sad.
49. I can forgive abusive behavior from my partner, because he or she doesn't really mean it.
50. I will lie to protect my partner's feelings.
51. If I have an emotional or medical problem, I will resist going to a professional for help.
52. I know exactly what makes my partner "tick."
53. When my partner gets angry, I remain calm, proving me to be superior.
54. It doesn't matter if we have different attitudes toward celebrating holidays.
55. Even if our vacation destination is my idea, my partner will agree to it.
56. Around the house, there are some things that are "man's work," some that are "woman's work."
57. It's better to discuss any domestic problems with someone of my own sex rather than with my partner.
58. I expect to name our first child for my mother or father.
59. I enjoy time to myself, but when my partner is around, I expect him or her to want to be with me.
60. If my partner will only work harder at our marriage, I will be a happy person.
61. As we age, I expect us to grow together, not in different directions.
62. If I am ever unfaithful in the marriage, it will be my partner's fault.
63. I sometimes berate my partner for being clumsy, but expect him or her to maintain a sense of humor.

64. My partner has no right to be critical on occasions when I have too much to drink in public.
65. I reserve the right to veto any contribution my partner wants to make to a charity or loan to a friend or relative.
66. When I get angry at my partner I feel justified. That's just being honest about my feelings.
67. I don't need to resolve problems, but just end arguments by having my partner admit he or she was wrong and apologize to me.
68. I would never consider calling the police if my partner was physically abusive to me.
69. When I am ill, I will expect my partner to stay home to care for me.
70. Once we have children, we will do everything as a family and seldom go out as a couple.
71. If my partner is unhappy with his or her job, I will tell him or her to stick with it to ensure our income.
72. If a better job for my partner requires our moving to a new place, I will feel put upon.
73. If I am offered a better job elsewhere or one that involves longer working hours, I will expect my partner to support my decision.
74. As I age, I can't be bothered about continuing to be attractive and maintaining a good appearance.
75. A prenuptial agreement will help our marriage by making it more difficult for my partner to consider a divorce.
76. If I confess embarrassing secrets from my past, my partner will think less of me.
77. Marriage won't change my relationships with family and friends.
78. Once married, I can still maintain friendships with former romantic partners.
79. So long as *I* feel good, the marriage is good.
80. By being vigilant, I can perpetuate the marriage.
81. Small irritations have no place in a loving marriage.
82. I have everything to gain from marriage and nothing to lose.
83. Once we are married, love will conquer all.
84. I will judge our marriage's health by my partner's generosity and attention to me.
85. I can continue to enjoy the freedoms of single life after marriage.
86. I know better than my partner what he or she needs or wants.
87. Other couples have bad marriages because they don't love each other enough.
88. As long as I'm sincere in expressing my needs, and honest in making demands, the marriage will last.

89. Married life is serious, so I don't need a sense of humor about our life together.

90. I can always rely on food, alcohol, or a pill to put me in a better mood.

91. My partner is content with going to bed and rising at the same time I do.

92. Whatever he or she is doing, my partner won't mind being interrupted when I have something to say or ask.

93. I resent my mother-in-law's influence over my partner.

94. If I occasionally fall short of expectations in my marriage, it can be blamed on what I suffered as a child.

95. If I were to die, I would not expect my partner to want to remarry.

96. I expect my wedding day to be the peak experience of our lives.

97. I don't have to be absolutely right to justify refusing to admit I was wrong.

98. I expect my partner to be grateful and forgiving, because everything *I* do is for him or her.

99. I act the way I do because God made me this way.

100. We will live happily ever after because I believe it.

Finally, a brief essay question:

101. I married (or want to be married) because:

Before you share your answers with your spouse or partner, take a second look at your answers. You will probably acknowledge at the outset that some of these expectations are outlandish and deserve a firm "disagree."

But in fact, *all of them deserve to be rejected*, either as naive, self-serving, presumptuous, incomplete, or impractical. That's not to say that couples contemplating marriage while harboring some these expectations are courting certain marital failure. But each one of these expectations announces, in effect: I want to have my cake and eat it too, enjoy the comfort of relying on another person while remaining independent, and be loved and respected without reciprocating—an impossibility.

The most unrealistic expectation of all is that a successful marriage merely requires spouses to meet each other "halfway," dividing responsibilities equally at every turn. The reality is that marriage is, at times, a sixty-forty or seventy-thirty responsibility, and occasionally it's entirely on the shoulders of one partner.

To embrace a life together for better, for worse; for richer, for poorer; in sickness and in health envisions occasions when one spouse carries major burdens for the other. Becky and I have friends whose spouses became totally dependent on them when struck by Alzheimer's. The burden of love fell 100 percent on the healthy spouse. Yet these marriages lasted until death did them part.

Now, as a couple, compare your answers, including the reasons you gave for being attracted to marriage in the first instance. Use this exercise as an opportunity to define what each of you is prepared to *invest* in your life together, as opposed to what you expect to *gain* from marriage. Join your clear heads to your warm hearts.

How Long Has This Been Going On?

A Short History of Marriage

The Lord God said, "It is not good for the man to be alone.
I will make a helper suitable for him."

Genesis 2:18

*P*rostitution may qualify as the world's oldest profession, but marriage is humankind's oldest institution. Although both involve sex, the resemblance ends there. Prostitution is a brief, commercial transaction that requires neither affection, exclusivity, nor mutual responsibility.

By contrast, marriage is entered as a lifelong contract to share much more than bed and bodies. It is about sharing lives. Moreover, it is creative, ensuring the continuation of the human race. At its very best, marriage affords a man and woman the opportunity to create not only offspring but an entirely unique creature called "us."

I challenge anyone to enter a room full of strangers and discern who is married to whom. Spouses surely leave marks on each other, but they are seldom visible to outsiders. Over the years as I have addressed large groups, I have become wary of presuming that a man and woman who are sitting together are man and wife. Before speaking engagements I tend to work the room, introducing myself, but I no longer ask, "Is this your wife?" or "Is this your husband?" Indeed, I've made so many misidentifications that I now wait for couples to introduce themselves as spouses.

A related mystery, of course, is what attracts couples to each other. In the past, professional matchmakers identified something in eligible men and women that warranted introducing them to each other. In recent memory, when hosts entertained friends at dinner parties, they made certain that any single woman who was invited was matched with a bachelor. Romantic sparks

171

rarely flew, but it was a courteous gesture and an unpressured way to meet compatible people.

Alas, in our own frenetic century dinner parties have been consigned largely to history. In a more innocent time couples actually met in church, whereas now they are more likely to bump into each other in bars. Today in America men and women in search of a mate are typically reduced to advertising for them online. That venue requires the candidates to serve as their own matchmakers, selecting the right words to indicate the sort of person they are seeking, while describing themselves in the most tantalizing terms. It is a hazardous exercise, relying on the sincerity and truthfulness of strangers.

The very first couple required none of this effort. In Genesis, the Creator, having made man, determined that it was not good for him to be alone. By fashioning a mate for him, God became the first matchmaker. Since they were expressly made for each other, Adam and Eve had no options. Nor did they marry with benefit of clergy. God himself was their witness. It was an earthly match made in heaven.

Ever since, just as no one has contrived an alternative to the family, no one has devised a practical alternative to marriage. Both are the cornerstones of civilized life. But the *lock* in wedlock, once impregnable, is now easily broken, and we are all poorer for the fact.

MARRIAGE IN THE ANCIENT WORLD

It is commonly assumed that romantic love as the basis for marriage is a recent phenomenon, and that marriage prior to modern times was contracted for economic or political reasons. Admittedly, there are still many cultures in the contemporary world in which marriages are arranged by others, but even in such cases the spouses must consent, and couples tend to grow in mutual respect and affection, if not passion and romance.

The accepted view of the wife in the ancient world was that she was her husband's dependent and chattel, useful for producing and caring for his legal offspring, and serving as his cook and housekeeper. This is not an informed view, however, because we utterly lack the wives' point of view. Ancient literature was written almost exclusively by men. The macho image of marriage in the ancient world persists because men seldom recorded the love they bore for their wives, and women left scant records of their marital devotion. We can only guess how they viewed their lives together.

The practice of polygamy in biblical times perpetuates the perception that wives in simpler societies were merely a man's unsentimental property, useful for chores, childbearing, and sexual satisfaction. But here again we may misjudge. Polygamy ensured that nearly all women in primitive times need not face life alone. "Today," Marilyn Yalom notes, "men look for wives who can provide not only sex, love, children, and housekeeping services, but also wages and participation in community life. The requirements for today's wife give added meaning to the biblical proverb "Whosoever findeth a good wife findeth a good thing."[1]

Even in biblical times a wife was not expected to be a pushover. The Talmud calls her a "helpmeet," acting as a moral check on her husband: "When he is good, she supports him: when he is bad, she rises up against him."[2] The notion of marriage as perpetual wedlock is found in Jewish marriage contracts dating from eight centuries before Christ. Before witnesses, the groom pronounced, "She is my wife and I am her husband from this day forth and forever."[3] Although husbands could initiate divorce, separation required witnesses. But wives retained some leverage. A childless widow, for example, could demand that her late husband's brother marry her.[4]

BIBLICAL MARRIAGES

The overriding concern in biblical marriage was to produce children, but wives were prized for other reasons. Sarah, wife of the patriarch Abraham, passed herself off as her husband's sister so Abraham might curry the favor of a pharaoh and a king. Her sacrifice to her husband's ambition involved sleeping with foreign monarchs. Having passed childbearing age without conceiving, Sarah encouraged her husband to take as his second wife an Egyptian slave girl, who bore him Ishmael. But in old age she miraculously conceived Isaac. Upon her death, "Abraham came to mourn Sarah and to keen for her."[5] It could not have been less than a love match.

The marriage of Isaac with Rebekah was contracted even before the couple met, yet the bride's consent was not presumed: "'Let us call the young woman and ask her for her answer.' And they called Rebekah and said to her, 'Will you go with this man?' And she said, 'I will.'"[6]

"And Isaac brought her into the tent of Sarah his mother and took Rebekah as wife. And he loved her, and Isaac was consoled after his mother's death."[7]

If further evidence is required that biblical marriages were love matches, we have the story of Isaac and Rebekah's son Jacob, who worked for his uncle Laban seven long years to earn the right to marry Rachel, only to be given the girl's elder sister Leah instead. Altogether Jacob toiled twenty years in servitude to Laban before finally winning his chosen bride. How often could love survive such a lengthy courtship in our own times?

Proverbs pays tribute to marriage by exalting the good wife:

Who can find a virtuous woman? for her price is far above rubies.
The heart of her husband doth safely trust in her. . . .
She will do him good and not evil all the days of her life.
She seeketh wool, and flax, and worketh willingly with her hands.
She is like the merchants' ships; she bringeth her food from afar.
She riseth also while it is yet night, and giveth meat to her household, and a portion
   to her maidens. . . .
She stretcheth out her hand to the poor. . . .
Her children arise up, and call her blessed; her husband also, and he praiseth her.[8]

CHRISTIAN MARRIAGE

Although the New Testament lacks the Hebrew Bible's emphasis on couples and childbearing, Matthew's and Luke's accounts begin with a devoted couple, Mary and Joseph. However, the evangelists are clear that, while Jesus had a human mother, God was his father.

Jesus himself embraced a mission that precluded marriage and parenting. Moreover, many of his close followers were married men whom he persuaded to take leave of their families for extended periods to preach the gospel and heal the sick. Whereas Jews were inclined to believe that life ended in death, Christian revelation looked beyond earthly life to eternity, where Jesus remarked of the redeemed: "When they rise from the dead, they neither marry nor are given in marriage, but are as the angels."[9] Far from denigrating marriage, Jesus was merely stating the obvious—that immortality has no need of conception and birth.

But Christianity could not be more respectful of love, which it esteems as the highest virtue. And Jesus proclaimed the permanence of wedlock: "What God hath joined together, let not man put asunder."[10] And: "Whoever shall put away his wife . . . and shall marry another, committeth adultery."[11]

In Judaism men and women felt compelled to marry, because wedlock was the only sanctioned way Jews could fulfill God's command to "increase and multiply." Uncertain about eternity, they focused on earthly life. Whereas for Christianity, God's kingdom embraced not only this world but the next, so the quest was not for worldly prosperity but for immortality.

Inevitably, marriage, while prized and blessed by Christians, was appreciated not as a necessity but as an option. Taking Jesus and Paul as models, early Christians became inclined to regard celibacy as superior to the married state. As Paul argued, "The unmarried man cares for the Lord's business; his aim is to please the Lord. But the married man cares for worldly things; his aim is to please his wife; and he has a divided mind. . . . The married woman cares for worldly things; her aim is to please her husband."[12]

Later, Augustine argued that married couples should engage in sex *only* for procreation. Until the Reformation the tradition of a celibate Christian clergy was adopted principally to prevent church property from being passed on by priests to natural heirs, but it also reflected a suspicion within Catholicism that sex and spirituality were somehow antagonistic.

Still, Jesus himself had hallowed marriage with his first miracle, and Paul himself can be quoted in praise of marriage: "The husband must give the wife what is due to her, and the wife equally must give the husband his due. . . . Do not deny yourselves to one another."[13] Paul compared the love of married couples to the love of God for his church, and marriage was counted among the seven sacraments through which God graces human life.

GREEK AND ROMAN PRACTICE

Ancient Greece and Rome maintained the tradition that a bride was to be given by her father to her husband, along with a dowry. Even today it is traditional in church weddings for fathers to "give away" their daughters and, until very recently, (as a kind of dowry) the bride's parents were expected to assume the expenses of the wedding. Today in America, however, couples marry later than ever in our nation's history and, since both spouses typically have been employed for some years, they tend to share the financial burden of the wedding and establishment of their households.

Marriage in ancient Greece was the defining fact of a man's and woman's life, marking the passage to adulthood, and was celebrated over the course of two or three days. The tradition of musical wedding processions dates from ancient Athenian society. Unlike Jewish practice, the Greek father retained the freedom to terminate his daughter's marriage until after she bore her husband a child. Vows did not make marriage permanent; childbirth did.

During the early Roman republic, between the fifth and second century before Christ, marriage followed the Greek model. But by the late republic and empire a more egalitarian sense of wedlock developed in which marriage became a true partnership. The tradition of an engagement ring worn on the third finger of the fiancée's left hand dates from this time. Unlike the Greek practice of winter weddings, the Romans favored June nuptials, which took place in the bride's home. Spouses joined their right hands and kissed. In Rome the witnessing of marriage vows was considered so serious that guests were *obliged* to honor an invitation to attend. No excuses.

Mutual affection was considered desirable in Roman society even in arranged marriages, to the extent of joint suicides of spouses. But public displays of affection were frowned upon. Plutarch deemed it "disgraceful . . . to kiss and embrace in the presence of others."[14] But he praised "mutual trust and love" and "loving friendship" between married couples, affirming that "sexual relations are a foundation of affection, a communion, as it were, in a great mystery."[15]

Despite these romantic ideals, Marilyn Yalom reminds us, "Marriage throughout the ancient world was largely a family affair arranged for economic, social, or political reasons. No one expected the bride and groom to be 'in love.'"[16] Still, as couples have attested throughout history, an initial absence of infatuation and romance need not deter a couple from growing in affection for each other. In memorials to their deceased wives, medieval widowers remembered them as "sweetest" and "most delightful partner," and spoke of "fondness." "I loved her more than seemed possible," wrote one widower in Bologna, "because I don't believe there is or has ever been a woman better than she."[17]

MARRIAGE IN THE AGE OF FAITH

Beginning in the mid-twelfth century, the Catholic Church began to regulate marriage, discouraging private ceremonies like that of Shakespeare's Romeo and Juliet. A valid marriage began to insist on the presence of witnesses, including a priest to perform the ceremony, preferably in a church. The church also required that a couple's intention to marry be announced publicly for three weeks before the ceremony to ensure there were no objections that would nullify the union.

At the same time, however, the church downplayed the ancient requirement for parental consent, focusing instead on the mutual will of the spouses. Once physically consummated, the marriage was considered binding.

From the eighth century, marriage was celebrated as a sacrament—an occasion of grace. Since God was invoked as a party to the vows, holy wedlock was considered indissoluble. Heretofore, nearly all divorces had been initiated by men, so the church's solemnization of marriage overwhelmingly benefited women. In practice, however, men were confirmed as masters of their spouses both religiously and legally. The legality of wife beating persisted in some parts of Europe into the nineteenth century.

Jews only gradually absorbed Christian customs regarding marriage. By the year 1000 Ashkenazi Jews in Eastern and Western Europe were monogamous, but Sephardic Jews in Moorish Spain and the Near East maintained the right to polygamy, although it was infrequently invoked. A total ban on polygamy among Jews was effected with the formation of the State of Israel in 1948.[18]

Although marital affection was common from ancient times, *romantic* love was introduced by the French in the twelfth century. Ironically, its model was the chivalrous knight and unavailable lady, typically a young woman already married to a king. Because in practice it precluded marriage, romantic love was considered "pure," evoking noble sentiments and refined speech, with rewards more spiritual than sensual. In effect, romantic love altered the relationship of the sexes, granting the woman an emotional power over the man, bidding him to serve her. But such refined sentiments were largely restricted to aristocrats and poets, and unshared by common couples.

The practice of presenting the groom with a dowry continued from ancient times into the age of faith, signifying the worth placed by the bride's family on her and her intended. The dowry was intended to pay for the household needs of the newlyweds and was often paid in installments over years. If the husband died before his wife, the tradition throughout Europe was that she would inherit one-third of the total estate.

By the fourteenth and fifteenth centuries, wedding expenses and dowries had become so inflated that a family with many daughters was reduced to placing one or more of them in a convent, which also demanded a dowry for her maintenance, but typically only half as large as that expected by a groom.

MARRIAGE IN THE REFORMATION

The character of marriage was bound to be affected by the Protestant Reformation. Its leading figure, Martin Luther, had been a celibate Augustinian monk, but married Katherina von Bora in 1525. The new Mrs. Luther, herself, had been a celibate nun.

In England, King Henry VIII took six wives in succession in his effort to produce a male heir.

Luther argued that celibacy was nowhere required by scripture. Peter, the apostle and first pope, had been married, and St. Paul expressly allowed priests to wed.[19] In his 1520 "Open Letter to the Christian Nobility of the German Nation," the reformer argued that "not every priest can do without a woman, not only on account of the weakness of the flesh, much more because of the necessities of the household."

Moreover, he noted, sex was a natural function: "The pope has as little power to command this, as he has to forbid eating, drinking, the natural movement of the bowels, or growing fat."

Finally, Luther declared, "The commandment of God, which demands that no man shall put man and wife asunder, takes precedence of the law of the pope." At the same time, the reformer declined to include matrimony among the sacraments, because marriage was not mentioned in the Bible as necessary for salvation.[20] But, following St. Paul, Luther insisted that the mutual love of husband and wife was God's command. A true Christian vocation, he claimed, included conjugal and religious duties.[21]

When he took a former bride of Christ as his own earthly bride, "what began as a match of convenience for both of them eventually turned into a marriage of love."[22] "In domestic affairs," Luther said, "I defer to Katie. Otherwise I am led by the Holy Ghost."[23] The couple produced six children.

Following the practice of reformers on the Continent, the Church of England dropped marriage from the sacraments but went out of its way to preach that "marriage is a thing that pleaseth God" and promoted "nuptial love," with a new emphasis on "mutual society, help, and comfort" in the marriage ceremony.[24]

With the virtual elimination of monastic life in Britain and northern Europe there was now no longer an institutional alternative lifestyle for the unmarried. Historian Eric Carlson dates the primacy of love in Christian marriage to this period.[25] In England, parental consent was no longer a prerequisite for marriage. Marriages among aristocrats continued to be arranged, but nine out of ten English couples married freely, and as many as one bride in three arrived at the altar pregnant.[26]

PURITAN MARRIAGE IN COLONIAL AMERICA

Contrary to the popular image of the Puritans as dour and averse to life's pleasures, they welcomed regular sexual intercourse as integral to a lasting marriage: "Hand in hand, two Christian souls were encouraged to share the pleasures and duties of this earth as they simultaneously made their way, step by step, to eternal life."[27]

Nor was the Puritan wife expected to be sexually submissive to her husband, but to be equally expressive, indulging her power over him. In his book, *The Bride Bush* (1623), William Whately encouraged "mutual dalliances for pleasure's sake."[28] Anne Bradstreet (c. 1612–1672), the first American poet, was among the founders of the Massachusetts Bay Colony. She freely expressed her ardor. Fearing she might die in childbirth, she wrote her husband:

> How soon, my Dear, death may my steps attend,
> How soon't may be to thy Lot to lose my friend,

We both are ignorant, yet love bids me
These farewell lines to recommend to thee,
That when that knot's unty'd that made us one,
I may seem thine, who in effect am none.
If ever two were one, then surely we.
If ever man were lov'd by wife, then thee;
If ever wife was happy in a man,
Compare with me ye women if you can.

Once temporarily separated from her husband, Anne wrote:

Flesh of thy flesh, bone of thy bone,
I here, thou there, yet both are one.[29]

Typically, the Puritan husband took possession of his wife's property, but some women insisted on prenuptial agreements that specified what was theirs. Widows of the time were legally entitled to one-third of their husbands' estate, but in practice many insisted on a more substantial legacy.

At her Virginia wedding in 1687, although Sarah Harrison refused to take a vow of obedience to her husband, the marriage was considered legal nonetheless. Over time, mutual love became the cornerstone of marriage in colonial America. Still, as historian Edmund Morgan notes, companionship was not to be confused with romantic passion or to rival the Puritans' love of God. Rather, "if husband and wife failed to love each other above all the world, they not only wronged each other, they disobeyed God."[30]

COMPANIONATE MARRIAGE

At the time John Adams was helping to draft the Declaration of Independence, his wife Abigail urged him to "remember the ladies," by reforming marriage so husbands might "willingly give up the harsh title of Master for the more tender and endearing one of Friend." Speaking for her sex, she proposed: "Regard us then as Beings placed by providence under your protection and in imitation of the Supreme Being make use of that power only for our happiness."

The response of the future president of the United States to his wife was dismissive: "As to your extraordinary Code of Laws, I cannot but laugh."[31] Nevertheless, Adams "was indeed more 'friend' than 'master' in their private relationship. Abigail consistently addressed him as 'Dearest Friend' in the thousands of letters written during the years of his absence from Massachusetts."[32]

In fact, the American Revolution, with its emphasis on independence, fairness, and democracy, fostered what came to be known as companionate marriage, challenging the prevailing patriarchal relationship. Increasingly, men and women equally asserted the right to choose their life's mate in the name of love. Affection and friendship, as well as shared interests and values, marked marriage in the early republic, and couples, once married, asserted a growing independence from their parents.

During the half century following the American Revolution "love became the most celebrated criterion for choosing a spouse, even if property, family, and social status continued to weigh heavily in the decision."[33] The young American Eliza Chaplin assured a friend, "Never could I give my hand unaccompanied by my heart."[34]

The Victorian Age in Great Britain is popularly characterized as sexually repressed, but it was also a sentimental age, when the love letter became the instrument of courtship. For the Victorians love was not only ideal but was valued as a high moral virtue that possessed the power to improve the character of men and women alike. To love was to be a better person. The poet Elizabeth Barrett Browning condemned marriages entered for any motive less than love as merely "legal prostitution."[35]

To be sure, the Victorians' sentimental ideal did not completely translate into reality. Parish records of the time reveal that as many as 40 percent of first pregnancies were conceived before the wedding day. Moreover, marriage altogether eluded one in eight Victorians.[36] John Ruskin pronounced this paradox: "A true wife, in her husband's house, is his servant; it is in his heart that she is queen."[37]

One unfortunate consequence of the Victorian male's inclination to regard his wife as an angel was to expect her to be sexually submissive, with no desires of her own, and it drove many a husband to prostitutes. Fully half of all surgical outpatients at London's venerable St. Bartholomew's Hospital suffered from venereal disease, most of them afflicted with syphilis.[38]

STRAINS ON MARRIAGE

Just as the Victorians were establishing sentiment as the foundation of companionate marriage, the Latter-Day Saints in America were restoring Old Testament patriarchal polygamy. Mormons believed that "the more wives a man had, and the more children a woman had, the more they would be rewarded in heaven."[39]

In fact, not more than one in five early Mormon marriages was polygamous, and, of these families, two-thirds contained just two wives.[40] The practice of plural marriage continued as a fundamental tenet of the Latter-Day Saints from 1852 until 1890, when the church reluctantly agreed to abide by U.S. antipolygamy laws in the successful attempt to achieve statehood.

Love, let alone romance, played no great part in Mormon marriages. Primary value was set on family compatibility, financial responsibility, and service to the community.

Mormon households were far from harems. Those Mormon wives who found themselves in intolerable marriages actually had freer access to divorce than other American women of the time. Mormon wives were also encouraged to enter the professions and community service.

Plural marriage probably thrived as long as it did because frontier conditions favored larger households to handle the chores and because the Mormon wife had rather low expectations of affection and mutual devotion in wedlock. Still, Mormon wives in both exclusive and plural marriages enjoyed a high fertility rate, each averaging seven to eight children.[41]

Polygamy proved to be no threat to the Victorian ideal of companionate marriage, but the growing independence of women did. By the final two decades of the nineteenth century "the New Woman was recognizable by her education, her independence, her tendency to flaunt traditional family values and blur the boundaries between male and female behavior." An essay published by the feminist Mona Caird in the August 1888 *Westminster Review* reviled marriage as an institution that kept women in permanent bondage to their husbands.

Within two months her essay attracted 27,000 letters to Britain's *Daily Telegraph* alone, the vast majority of them from middle-class women. Disgruntled wives predominated in the correspondence. Happy wives were those less demanding of marriage, accepting that they were expected to be tolerant of their husbands' weaknesses. They acknowledged their dedication to making their homes a marital sanctuary, keeping their husbands sexually faithful and financially responsible, and devoting themselves to being partners, mothers, and homemakers.

A workman's wife from Plymouth admitted of her marriage, "My dowry was the love I had to give." A wife from Swaffham revealed, "Before many years we hope to celebrate our golden wedding, please God, and we are not tired of one another yet. . . . I know how to manage my husband now, and have learned to double his pleasures, which are not many, by sharing in them."[42]

ROMANCE, SEXUALITY, AND THE WORKING WIFE

As women became more independent, they increased their emotional expectations of marriage. Rather than accept the role of Victorian "angels," they opted for romance and sexuality. Dr. Clelia Mosher followed the lives of forty-five American wives between 1892 and 1920. Most were middle class and college educated. Their revelations presaged the Kinsey Report of 1953.

Most of Dr. Mosher's respondents reported having intercourse on a weekly basis, three-fourths of them usually enjoying orgasm. All but four of them employed some form of birth control, typically douches and diaphragms, or insisted that their husbands use condoms or practice withdrawal. While most of the women agreed that childbearing was the principal purpose of sexual intercourse, they concurred that sex is an expression of love that creates a spiritual bond between spouses. As early as 1893 one woman could affirm:

> The desire of both husband and wife for this expression of their union seems to me the first and highest reason for intercourse. . . . My husband and I believe in intercourse for its own sake—we wish it for ourselves and spiritually miss it, rather than physically, when it does not occur, because it is the highest, most sacred expression of oneness.[43]

During the course of the last century, romance and mutually satisfying sexuality became integral ingredients of marriage in America. But the character of marriage was further altered as married women were increasingly drawn from the home into the workforce. During World War II one in four American wives worked outside the home, outnumbering single women in the workforce for the first time.[44]

The working wife became the norm during the final half of the century, more often from financial necessity than personal inclination, leading to smaller families. Americans now marry later than at any time in the nation's history, and cohabitation before marriage is increasingly the norm. Indeed 40 percent of first babies are born outside of wedlock.[45]

Divorce now destroys about half of marriages in America. Choosing to be realistic and inclusive, nearly all of the mainstream Protestant churches have reluctantly accommodated serial marriages. Even the Catholic Church takes pains to find legitimate causes for annulling the marriages of incompatible couples.

As early as 1960 the University of Michigan asked 900 wives to list the benefits of marriage. They listed (in order of importance): companionship, the opportunity to have children, understanding and emotional support, love and affection, and better finances. Note that "love and affection" rated only fourth among benefits of married life.[46]

Still, hope springs eternal. At the turn of the millennium the *New York Times* asked newlyweds to rate the strength of their marriages. Some 86 percent insisted that their marriages were "for keeps" and would last till death did them part.[47]

Author's Note and Acknowledgments

$\mathscr{I}$ undertook this book in defense of marriage as a tribute to more than three decades of wedded life with Becky. Mark Twain was prescient when he proposed that "no man or woman really knows what perfect love is until they have been married a quarter of a century." Wedlock is an adventure.

Ours is the second marriage for each of us, so we can sympathize with others who got it wrong the first time. But finding the right person and inviting him or her to enter into a permanent partnership is just the beginning of a lifetime's work. Growing in intimacy and building a life together are infinitely more difficult than falling in love and celebrating a wedding. Marriages are made on Earth, not in heaven, and by mere mortals. Still, God can be trusted to be the silent partner in every loving marriage.

There are no prizes awarded for good marriages except for the gift of self that spouses make to each other. When wedded life is approached as a contest for advantage, there are no winners, only losers. The great advantage of the mutual vow of "till death do us part" is that love can endure and grow despite unpredictable and inevitable setbacks. The hurts that spouses inflict on each other, callously or inadvertently, are not easily forgotten, but they can be forgiven.

In an earlier book, *Celebrating the Rest of Your Life*, I confronted the inevitability of aging and argued that no person need drift in later life if he or she is willing to take vows to live with integrity. In the course of writing that book I remarked that the marriage vows in the *Book of Common Prayer* serve admirably not only for wedlock but for one's entire approach to life. But their original and essential intent was to define the union of man and wife.

In recent times couples have taken to rewriting the marriage ceremony. Brides today, for example, seldom promise to *obey* their husbands, but the remainder of the traditional vows remain essential to the health and permanence of wedlock. Couples must love and cherish each other, forsaking all others—for better or worse, in sickness and in health, from this day forward. Otherwise, it is only cohabitation, and not just the spouses, but their children and our society are the losers.

The bibliography that follows is only partial. I relied on much more, from newspaper clippings to the counsel of friends. I leaned most heavily on G. K. Chesterton's *Brave New Marriage*, Judith Viorst's *Grown-Up Marriage*, Marilyn Yalom's *A History of the Wife*, Nancy F. Cott's *Public Vows*, Andrew M. Greeley's *Faithful Attraction*, and Hendrick Hartog's *Man and Wife in America*, and I express my gratitude to those authors.

Thanks, too, to my editor, Sarah Stanton, who believed in the book, persuaded my publisher to take it on, then guided it through production.

My greatest resource is the woman whose life I am privileged to share. Becky encouraged me to attempt a book about marriage, drawing on the lessons we have learned through our years together. You will understand why, on occasions when I am asked to identify myself to a new audience, I am proud to introduce myself as "Becky Yount's husband."

David Yount answers reader mail at
P.O. Box 2758, Woodbridge, VA 22195
and
dyount31@verizon.net

Dr. Yount maintains a limited speaking schedule on the subjects of his books and columns and leads retreats and quiet days. If your local newspaper does not carry his Scripps Howard column, Amazing Grace, ask your editor to consider it.

Notes

INTRODUCTION

1. Robert Byrne, *The 2,548 Best Things Anyone Ever Said* (New York: Fireside, 1990), 2417.

2. Byrne, *The 2,548 Best Things*, 575.

3. Byrne, *The 2,548 Best Things*, 408.

4. John W. Wright, ed., *The New York Times Almanac 2008* (New York: Penguin), 291.

5. Wright, *The New York Times Almanac*, 292.

6. Wright, *The New York Times Almanac*, 291.

7. Wright, *The New York Times Almanac*.

8. Melanie Phillips, "Sex without Commitment," *Observer* (London), September 7, 2003, 23.

9. George Seldes, ed., *The Great Thoughts* (New York: Ballantine, 1996), 222.

10. Bergen Evans, ed., *Dictionary of Quotations* (New York: Wings Books, 1969), 432.

11. Evans, *Dictionary of Quotations*, 404.

12. Evans, *Dictionary of Quotations*, 412.

13. Evans, *Dictionary of Quotations*, 407.

14. Evans, *Dictionary of Quotations*, 402.

15. Charlton Heston, *The Actor's Life* (New York: Dutton, 1978), xvi.

16. Byrne, *The 2,548 Best Things*, 2016.

17. David Blankenhorn, *The Future of Marriage* (New York: Encounter Books, 2007), 14.

18. Jura Koncius, "Tossing the Bouquet," *Washington Post*, June 5, 2003, H-1.

19. Koncius, "Tossing the Bouquet."

CHAPTER 1

1. Andrew M. Greeley, *Faithful Attraction: Discovering Intimacy, Love, and Fidelity in American Marriage* (New York: Tor, 1992), 136.
2. Greeley, *Faithful Attraction*, 139.
3. David Popenoe, *The Future of Marriage in America* (Piscataway, NJ: National Marriage Project, 2007), 3.
4. Greeley, *Faithful Attraction*, 171.
5. Greeley, *Faithful Attraction*, 173.
6. Popenoe, *The Future of Marriage*, 19.
7. Greeley, *Faithful Attraction*, 150–51.
8. Greeley, *Faithful Attraction*, 152.
9. Greeley, *Faithful Attraction*, 152.
10. Popenoe, *The Future of Marriage*, 19.
11. Greeley, *Faithful Attraction*, 163.
12. Greeley, *Faithful Attraction*, 163.
13. Greeley, *Faithful Attraction*, 157.
14. Greeley, *Faithful Attraction*, 228.
15. Greeley, *Faithful Attraction*, 229–30.
16. Popenoe, *The Future of Marriage*, 19.
17. Greeley, *Faithful Attraction*, 41.
18. Popenoe, *The Future of Marriage*, 18.
19. Greeley, *Faithful Attraction*, 74–75.
20. Popenoe, *The Future of Marriage*, 27, 31.
21. Greeley, *Faithful Attraction*, 82–83.
22. Greeley, *Faithful Attraction*, 207–8.
23. Greeley, *Faithful Attraction*, 208.
24. Popenoe, *The Future of Marriage*, 7.
25. Greeley, *Faithful Attraction*, 111.
26. Greeley, *Faithful Attraction*, 119.
27. Popenoe, *The Future of Marriage*, 14.
28. Greeley, *Faithful Attraction*, 267–68.
29. Greeley, *Faithful Attraction*, 82.
30. Popenoe, *The Future of Marriage*, 21, 27.
31. Popenoe, *The Future of Marriage*, 18.
32. Greeley, *Faithful Attraction*, 283.
33. David Yount, "The High Cost of Hooking Up," Amazing Grace, Scripps Howard News Service (Washington, DC: June 2, 2004).
34. Popenoe, *The Future of Marriage*, 8.

CHAPTER 2

1. Quoted by Jonathan Yardley, *Washington Post*, November 11, 2003, C-9.
2. David Brooks, "Love, Internet Style," *New York Times*, November 8, 2003, 32.

3. Jennifer Egan, "Love in the Time of No Time," *New York Times Magazine*, November 23, 2000, 23.

4. Egan, "Love in the Time of No Time."

5. Rachel Greenwald, *Find a Husband after 35 Using What I Learned at Harvard Business School* (New York: Ballantine, 2000), 58.

6. Rebecca Mead, "Love for Sale," *New Yorker*, August 11, 2003, 105.

7. Mead, "Love for Sale," 104–5.

8. Ellen Fein and Sherrie Schneider, *The Rules for Marriage: Time-Tested Secrets for Making Your Marriage Work* (New York: Warner, 2001), 58.

9. Helge Rubinstein, ed., *The Oxford Book of Marriage* (New York: Oxford University Press), 9–10.

10. Rubinstein, *Oxford Book of Marriage*, 10–11.

11. Rubinstein, *Oxford Book of Marriage*, 3.

12. Rubinstein, *Oxford Book of Marriage*, 25.

13. Rubinstein, *Oxford Book of Marriage*, 5.

14. Rubinstein, *Oxford Book of Marriage*, 6.

15. Erica Jong, "From Fear of Flying to No Fear of Tying the Knot," *Sunday Times* (London), November 9, 2003, 5–7.

16. Rubinstein, *Oxford Book of Marriage*, 11.

17. Jong, "From Fear of Flying," 7.

18. Rubinstein, *Oxford Book of Marriage*, 16.

19. Rubinstein, *Oxford Book of Marriage*, 16.

20. Rubinstein, *Oxford Book of Marriage*, 16–17.

21. Rubinstein, *Oxford Book of Marriage*, 18–19.

22. Rubinstein, *Oxford Book of Marriage*, 27.

23. Rubinstein, *Oxford Book of Marriage*, 61.

24. Rubinstein, *Oxford Book of Marriage*, 46.

25. Rubinstein, *Oxford Book of Marriage*, 80.

26. *A Quaker Marriage* (Philadelphia: Philadelphia Yearly Meeting, n.d.), 1.

27. *A Quaker Marriage*, 1–2.

CHAPTER 3

1. Quoted in Elmore Leonard, *When the Women Come Out to Dance* (New York: William Morrow, 2002), 116.

2. Roger Dobson, "What Price Sex? About 30,000 Pounds," *Sunday Times* (London), April 11, 2004, 1–4.

3. Dobson, "What Price Sex?"

4. To be sure, annulments can be abused to cover up bad behavior.

5. Quoted in Phillip Kennicott, "Black Sheep of the Family," *Washington Post*, April 11, 2004, D6.

6. Kennicott, "Black Sheep."

7. Kennicott, "Black Sheep."

8. "I Get a Kick Out of You," *Economist*, February 14, 2004, 73.

9. "I Get a Kick Out of You," 73.
10. "I Get a Kick Out of You," 74.
11. "I Get a Kick Out of You," 75.
12. Marilyn Vos Savant, "Ask Marilyn," *Parade*, April 18, 2004, 17.
13. Clarence Day, "To My Wife," quoted in Rubinstein, *Oxford Book of Marriage*, 306.
14. Minette Marrin, "St. Valentine's Ghosts Wail in the Chains of a Myth," *Sunday Times* (London), February 15, 2004, 1–19.
15. Peter Perl, "Tough Love," *Washington Post Magazine*, February 8, 2004, 20ff.
16. David Brooks, "Sex and the Cities," *New York Times*, May 1, 2004, A25.
17. Quoted in Brooks, "Sex and the Cities."
18. Brooks, "Sex and the Cities."
19. Matthew 10:37.
20. Julia Bourland, *Hitched* (New York: Atria Books, 2003), 137.
21. Bourland, *Hitched*, 172–73.
22. Judith Viorst, *Grown-Up Marriage* (New York: Simon and Schuster, 2003), 48.
23. Viorst, *Grown-Up Marriage*, 49.
24. Viorst, *Grown-Up Marriage*, 51.
25. Quoted in Viorst, *Grown-Up Marriage*, 51.
26. Viorst, *Grown-Up Marriage*, 55.
27. Viorst, *Grown-Up Marriage*, 62.
28. Quoted in Viorst, *Grown-Up Marriage*, 65.
29. Sean Elder, "Why My Wife Won't Sleep with Me," *Sunday Times* (London), April 18, 2004, 23.
30. Elder, "Why My Wife Won't Sleep with Me," 23
31. Elder, "Why My Wife Won't Sleep with Me," 24.
32. Elder, "Why My Wife Won't Sleep with Me," 24
33. Laurie Wagner, Stephanie Rausser, and David Collier, *Living Happily Ever After* (San Francisco: Chronicle Books, 1996), 29.
34. Wagner, Rausser, and Collier, *Living Happily Ever After*, 84ff.
35. Gene Weingarten, "The Battle of All Mothers," *Washington Post Magazine*, May 9, 2004, 11.

CHAPTER 4

1. Quoted in Viorst, *Grown-Up Marriage*, 164.
2. Viorst, *Grown-Up Marriage*, 247.
3. Viorst, *Grown-Up Marriage*, 165.
4. Harriet Lerner, *The Dance of Intimacy* (New York: Harper & Row, 1989), 67–68.
5. Laura Sessions Stepp, "Score Card," *Washington Post*, May 22, 2004, C1.
6. Stepp, "Score Card," C1

7. Stepp, "Score Card," C2.

8. Stepp, "Score Card," C2.

9. Quoted in David Yount, *Celebrating the Single Life: Keys to Successful Living on Your Own* (Westport, CT: Praeger, 2009), 16.

10. Gloria Steinem, *Revolution from Within: A Book of Self-Esteem* (Boston: Little, Brown, 1993), 325.

11. William Shakespeare, *Hamlet, Prince of Denmark*, act 2, scene 2.

CHAPTER 5

1. Bourland, *Hitched*, 137.

2. Andrew Tobias, *The Only Investment Guide You'll Ever Need* (New York: Harcourt, 2002), 3ff.

3. Tom Mullen, *A Very Good Marriage* (Richmond, IN: Friends United Press, 2001), 68.

4. Mullen, *A Very Good Marriage*, 68.

5. Mullen, *A Very Good Marriage*, 75–76.

6. Matthew 6:25–26.

CHAPTER 6

1. Statistics from Phillip Longman, "The Limits of Medicine," *Washington Post*, March 31, 2004, A25.

2. Mullen, *A Very Good Marriage*, 89–90.

3. Mullen, *A Very Good Marriage*, 97.

4. Mullen, *A Very Good Marriage*, 86.

5. Quoted in Bernie Siegel, *Love, Medicine, and Miracles* (New York: Harper & Row, 1986), 15.

6. John Knowles, *Peace Breaks Out* (New York: Holt, Rinehart & Winston, 1981), 5.

7. Quoted in Gerald Tomlinson, ed., *Treasury of Religious Quotations* (Englewood Cliffs, NJ: Prentice Hall, 1991), 207.

8. Wagner, Rausser, and Collier, *Living Happily Ever After*, 66.

9. Wagner, Rausser, and Collier, *Living Happily Ever After*, 90.

10. Wagner, Rausser, and Collier, *Living Happily Ever After*, 99.

11. Wagner, Rausser, and Collier, *Living Happily Ever After*, 109.

12. Wagner, Rausser, and Collier, *Living Happily Ever After*, 138.

13. Wagner, Rausser, and Collier, *Living Happily Ever After*, 142–43.

14. Wagner, Rausser, and Collier, *Living Happily Ever After*, 146–47.

CHAPTER 7

1. From a plaque at Gunston Hall, Mason's home.

2. 1 Corinthians 13:1, 4–8, 13.

3. Shane Wilson, "The Truth about Being Single," *Sunday Times* (London), April 25, 2004, 12.

4. Wilson, "The Truth about Being Single," 15.

5. Wilson, "The Truth about Being Single," 16.

6. Popenoe, *The Future of Marriage*, 16.

7. Carolyn Hax, "Carolyn Hax," *Washington Post*, June 7, 2007, C6.

8. Arthur Levine, "Report on Student Relationships," Columbia University Teachers College, Winter 2006.

9. Abbreviated and paraphrased from Barbara de Angelis, *The Real Rules: How to Find the Right Man for the Real You* (New York: Dell, 1997), 111.

10. Abbreviated and paraphrased from Lee Reilly, *Women Living Single: 30 Women Share Their Stories of Navigating through a Married World* (London: Faber & Faber, 1996), 203.

CHAPTER 8

1. Quoted in Rubinstein, *Oxford Book of Marriage*, 171.

2. Viorst, *Grown-Up Marriage*, 71.

3. David Yount, *Faith Under Fire* (Pittsburg, PA: SterlingHouse, 2004), 64.

4. Yount, *Faith Under Fire*, 81.

5. Yount, *Faith Under Fire*, 81.

6. Yount, *Faith Under Fire*, 65.

7. *Washington Post*, March 16, 2004, A9.

8. Quoted in Yount, *Faith Under Fire*, 109–10.

9. David Yount, "Needed: More Babies," Scripps Howard News Service, January 3, 2001.

10. Sandra Hardin Gookin, *Parenting for Dummies* (Indianapolis: IDG Books, 1995), 9.

11. Kate Figes and Jean Zimmerman, *Life after Birth* (New York: St. Martin's Press, 1998), 175.

12. Figes and Zimmerman, *Life after Birth*, 176.

13. Yount, *Faith Under Fire*, 91–92.

14. Quoted in Marilu Henner, *I Refuse to Raise a Brat* (New York: ReganBooks, 1999), 15.

15. Laura Schlessinger, *Parenthood by Proxy: Don't Have Them If You Won't Raise Them* (New York: Cliff Street Books, 2000), 177.

16. Schlessinger, *Parenthood by Proxy*, 177.

17. Schlessinger, *Parenthood by Proxy*, 177.

18. Schlessinger, *Parenthood by Proxy*, 197.

19. Fred Rogers, *The Mister Rogers Parenting Book* (Philadelphia: Running Press, 2002), 38.

20. Linda Mason, *The Working Mother's Guide to Life* (New York: Three Rivers Press, 2002), 49–50.

21. Gookin, *Parenting for Dummies*, 207.

22. Marguerite Kelly, "The Age of the Tantrum," *Washington Post*, March 19, 2004, C8.

23. Kelly, "The Age of the Tantrum."

24. Gookin, *Parenting for Dummies*, 60.

25. Gookin, *Parenting for Dummies*, 276.

26. Gookin, *Parenting for Dummies*, 279.

27. Peter Perl, "Raising Austin," *Washington Post Magazine*, March 21, 2004, 15.

28. Perl, "Raising Austin," 32.

29. Quoted by Jennifer Frey, "Baby, Just Look at You Now," *Washington Post*, March 23, 2004, C1.

30. Frey, "Baby, Just Look at You Now," C10.

31. Quoted in Senay Boztas, "Welcome to the New Divide," *Sunday Times* (London), March 7, 2004, 1–16.

32. Boztas, "Welcome to the New Divide."

CHAPTER 9

1. Quoted by Maria McErlane, *Sunday Times* (London), January 4, 2004, 37.

2. Rubinstein, *Oxford Book of Marriage*, 146.

3. G. K. Chesterton, *Brave New Family* (San Francisco: Ignatius, 1990), 187.

4. Viorst, *Grown-Up Marriage*, 139.

5. Bourland, *Hitched*, 115.

6. Bourland, *Hitched*, 116.

7. Bourland, *Hitched*, 119.

8. David Yount, *Spiritual Simplicity* (New York: Simon and Schuster, 1997), 115.

9. Erica Jong, "Can Sensuality, Tantric Sex Take the Mind off Bad Prose?" *New York Observer*, April 23, 2001, 15.

10. Viorst, *Grown-Up Marriage*, 140.

11. Frank Pittman, *Private Lies* (New York: W.W. Norton, 1989), 34.

12. Philip Blumstein and Pepper Schwartz, *American Couples* (New York: William Morrow, 1983), 272–74.

13. Henry V. Dicks, *Marital Tensions* (New York: Karnac Books, 1967), 168.

14. Annette Lawson, *Adultery* (New York: Basic Books, 1988), 235.

15. Adam Phillips, *Monogamy* (New York: Pantheon Books, 1996), 98.

16. Yount, *Faith Under Fire*, 112.

17. Judith S. Wallerstein and Sandra Blakeslee, *The Good Marriage* (Boston: Houghton Mifflin, 1995), 10ff.

18. Wallerstein and Blakeslee, *The Good Marriage*, 331.

19. Wallerstein and Blakeslee, *The Good Marriage*, 332–33.

20. Quoted in David Yount, *The Future of Christian Faith in America* (Minneapolis, MN: Augsburg, 2004), 58.

21. Yount, *The Future of Christian Faith*, 66.

22. Yount, *The Future of Christian Faith*, 66.

23. Quoted in John Mortimer, *Where There's a Will* (New York: Viking, 2003), 23.

24. Quoted in Tyler Currie, "Can This Marriage Be Braved?" *Washington Post Magazine*, February 29, 2004, 18.

25. Currie, "Can This Marriage Be Braved?" 18

26. Currie, "Can This Marriage Be Braved?" 17.

27. Currie, "Can This Marriage Be Braved?" 18.

28. Matt McMillen, "Split Forecast," *Washington Post*, February 24, 2004, F2.

29. Currie, "Can This Marriage Be Braved?" 14ff.

30. John Donne, *Selected Poems* (New York: Penguin, 2007), 84, 177.

CHAPTER 10

1. Quoted by Godfrey Smith, "Do You Really Want to Go to University?" *Sunday Times* (London), December 7, 2003, 4–9.

2. Chesterton, *Brave New Family*, 226.

3. Quoted in Rubinstein, *Oxford Book of Marriage*, 301.

4. Leo Tolstoy, *Anna Karenina* (New York: Signet, 1961), 17.

5. *National Enquirer*, November 11, 2003, 21.

6. *National Enquirer*, August 5, 2003, 18.

7. *Sunday Times* (London), October 26, 2003, 1–14.

8. *Sunday Times*, October 26, 2003.

9. Catherine Hazard, "Cheating for Dummies," *National Enquirer*, November 4, 2003, 70.

10. Robert Winston, "Basic Instincts," *Sunday Telegraph Review* (London), September 15, 2002, 1–2.

11. Winston, "Basic Instincts," 2.

12. John Carey, *Sunday Times* (London), September 14, 2003, 31.

13. Shankar Vedantam, "Does a Ring Bring Happiness, or Vice Versa?" *Washington Post*, April 21, 2003, A9.

14. Vedantam, "Does a Ring Bring Happiness."

15. Viv Groskup, "Free and Uneasy," *Observer Review* (London), September 21, 2000, 4.

16. Groskup, "Free and Uneasy."

17. Groskup, "Free and Uneasy."

18. Groskup, "Free and Uneasy."

19. Groskup, "Free and Uneasy."

20. Bob Geldof, "The Father Love That Dare Not Speak Its Name," *Sunday Times* (London), September 7, 2003, A3.

21. Fein and Schneider, *The Rules for Marriage*, 211.

22. Fein and Schneider, *The Rules for Marriage*, 208.

23. Viorst, *Grown-Up Marriage*, 191.

24. Viorst, *Grown-Up Marriage*, 191.

25. Viorst, *Grown-Up Marriage*, 194.

26. Viorst, *Grown-Up Marriage*, 197.

27. Viorst, *Grown-Up Marriage*, 196.

28. Viorst, *Grown-Up Marriage*, 200–201.

29. Matthew 5:31–32.

30. *Catechism of the Catholic Church* (Liguori, MO: Liguori Publications, 1994), 406.

31. Blaine Harden, "Bible Belt Couples 'Put Asunder' More, Despite New Efforts," *New York Times*, May 21, 2001, A1, A14.

32. Viorst, *Grown-Up Marriage*, 196.

33. C. S. Lewis, *The Four Loves* (New York: Harcourt Brace, 1960), 115.

34. Viorst, *Grown-Up Marriage*, 203.

35. Matthew 19:6

36. Matthew 19:8

37. Ephesians 5:25, 28, 31–32.

38. Sarah Baxter, "U.S. Divorcees Take Flight the Birdnest Way," *Sunday Times* (London), September 28, 2003, 27.

39. Baxter, "U.S. Divorcees Take Flight."

40. Baxter, "U.S. Divorcees Take Flight."

41. Baxter, "U.S. Divorcees Take Flight."

42. Baxter, "U.S. Divorcees Take Flight."

43. Baxter, "U.S. Divorcees Take Flight."

44. Wagner, Rausser, and Collier, *Living Happily Ever After*, 29.

45. Wagner, Rausser, and Collier, *Living Happily Ever After*, 30

46. Wagner, Rausser, and Collier, *Living Happily Ever After*, 31.

47. Mortimer, *Where There's a Will*, 115–16.

48. Judith Viorst, *Necessary Losses* (New York: Fawcett Gold Medal, 1987), 309.

49. Quoted in Viorst, *Necessary Losses*, 310.

50. Viorst, *Necessary Losses*, 289–90.

51. Yount, *Faith Under Fire*, 62–64.

52. Quoted in Rubinstein, *Oxford Book of Marriage*, 302.

53. Rubinstein, *Oxford Book of Marriage*, 294–95.

54. Rubinstein, *Oxford Book of Marriage*, 283.

55. Rubinstein, *Oxford Book of Marriage*, 284.

CHAPTER 11

1. Nancy F. Cott, *Public Vows* (Cambridge, MA: Harvard University Press, 2000), 201.

2. Cott, *Public Vows*, 201.

3. Mary Ann Glendon, *The Transformation of Family Law* (Chicago: University of Chicago Press, 1989), 144–45.

4. U.S. Census Bureau, *Statistical Abstract of the United States* (Washington, DC: U.S. Census Bureau, 1995–1999).

5. Stephen D. Sugarman and Herma Hill Kay, eds., *Divorce Reform at the Crossroads* (New Haven, CT: Yale University Press, 1990), 136.

6. *Barelli v. Brusseau*, 12 Cal. App. 4th 667, 16 Cal. Rptr. 2d 16 (1993).

7. *People v. Liberta*, 474 NY 2d 567 (1984).

8. Cott, *Public Vows*, 211.

9. Cott, *Public Vows*, 212.

10. Timothy Egan, "The Persistence of Polygamy," *New York Times Magazine*, February 28, 1999, 51–55.

11. Cott, *Public Vows*, 214.

12. Tom W. Smith, "The Emerging Twenty-First Century American Family," *General Social Survey Social Change Report* no. 42, National Opinion Research Center, University of Chicago, November 24, 1999.

13. Pew Center, *Evenly Divided and Increasingly Polarized* (Washington, DC: The Pew Research Center for the People and the Press, 2003), 69.

14. Quoted in Cott, *Public Vows*, 216.

15. Cott, *Public Vows*, 219.

16. "Vermont Gives Final Approval to Same-Sex Unions," *New York Times*, April 26, 2000, A14.

17. Cott, *Public Vows*, 224.

18. Don Browning and Elizabeth Marquardt, "A Marriage Made in History?" *New York Times*, March 9, 2004, 29.

19. Quoted in Adam Haslett, "Love Supreme," *New Yorker*, May 31, 2004, 76.

20. Haslett, "Love Supreme," 80.

21. Haslett, "Love Supreme," 80.

22. Browning and Marquardt, "A Marriage Made in History?" 29.

23. Browning and Marquardt, "A Marriage Made in History?" 29.

CHAPTER 12

1. Minette Marin, "Adultery Is Inevitable, but Divorce Is Not," *Sunday Times* (London), April 23, 2006, I-18.

APPENDIX

1. Marilyn Yalom, *A History of the Wife* (New York: HarperCollins, 2001), xvii.

2. Yalom, *A History of the Wife*, 3.

3. Yalom, *A History of the Wife*, 4.

4. Deuteronomy 25:9–10.

5. Genesis 23:2.

6. Genesis 24:58–59.

7. Genesis 24:67.

8. Proverbs 31:1–28.

9. Mark 12:25.

10. Mark 10:9.

11. Mark 10:11.

12. 1 Corinthians 7:32–34.

13. Mark 10:6–9; 1 Corinthians 7:3–5.

14. Plutarch, "Advice on Marriage," in *Selected Essays and Dialogues* (New York: Oxford University Press, 1993), 286.

15. Plutarch, "Advice on Marriage," 249–50, 279, 281.

16. Yalom, *A History of the Wife*, 43.

17. James S. Grubb, *Provincial Families of the Renaissance* (Baltimore: Johns Hopkins University Press, 1996), 20–21.

18. Yalom, *A History of the Wife*, 43.

19. 1 Timothy 3:2; Titus 1:6.

20. Martin Luther, "An Open Letter to the Christian Nobility," in *Three Treatises* (Philadelphia: Fortress, 1960), 68–69.

21. *Dr. Martin's Small Catechism* (Concordia, MO: Concordia Press, 1971), 28, 72.

22. Yalom, *A History of the Wife*, 102.

23. Roland Bainton, *Women of the Reformation in Germany and Italy* (Minneapolis, MN: Augsburg, 1971), 27.

24. Eric Jose Carlson, *Marriage and the English Reformation* (Oxford: Blackwell, 1994), 42.

25. Carlson, *Marriage and the English Reformation*, 114.

26. Merry E. Wiesner, *Women and Gender in Early Modern Europe* (New York: Cambridge University Press, 1993), 49.

27. Yalom, *A History of the Wife*, 122.

28. William Whately, *The Bride Bush* (London: W. J. Johnson, 1975).

29. Joseph R. McElrath and Allan P. Robb, eds., *The Complete Works of Anne Bradstreet* (Philadelphia: Twayne Publishers, 1981), 179–81.

30. Edmund S. Morgan, *The Puritan Family* (Harper & Row, 1966), 47.

31. L. H. Butterfield, Marc Friedlaender, and Mary-Jo Kline, eds., *The Book of Abigail and John: Selected Letters of the Adams Family 1762–1784* (Cambridge, MA: Harvard University Press, 1975), 121.

32. Yalom, *A History of the Wife*, 154.

33. Yalom, *A History of the Wife*, 175–76.

34. Mary Beth Norton, *Liberty's Daughters: The Revolutionary Experience of American Women 1750–1800* (Boston: Little, Brown, 1980), 117–24.

35. Yalom, *A History of the Wife*, 357ff.

36. Norton, *Liberty's Daughters*, 21.

37. Julia Cherry Spruill, *Life and Work in the Southern Colonies* (Chapel Hill: University of North Carolina Press, 1938), 182.

38. A. N. Wilson, *The Victorians* (London: Arrow, 2002), 308.

39. Yalom, *A History of the Wife*, 253.

40. Stanley Snow Ivins, "Notes on Mormon Polygamy," *Western Humanities Review* 10 (1956), 229–39.

41. Yalom, *A History of the Wife*, 268.

42. Yalom, *A History of the Wife*, 274–75.

43. Yalom, *A History of the Wife*, 298.

44. William Chafe, *The Paradox of Change: American Women in the 20th Century* (New York: Oxford University Press, 1991), 130–31.

45. Chafe, *The Paradox of Change*, 353.

46. John D'Emilio and Estelle Freedman, *Intimate Matters: A History of Sexuality in America* (Chicago: University of Chicago Press, 1997), 172.

47. *New York Times Magazine*, May 7, 2000, 27.

Selected Bibliography

Anderson, Katherine, Don Browning, and Brian Boyer. *Marriage: Just a Piece of Paper?* Grand Rapids, MI: Eerdmans, 2002.

Arnold, Johann Christoph. *A Plea for Purity*. Harrisburg, PA: Plough, 1996.

Auden, W. H. *Tell Me the Truth about Love*. New York: Vintage, 1994.

Benne, Robert. *Ordinary Saints*. Minneapolis, MN: Fortress, 2003.

Blanchard, Kenneth, D. W. Edington, and Marjorie Blanchard. *The One-Minute Manager Gets Fit*. New York: William Morrow, 1986.

Chesterton, G. K. *Brave New Family*. San Francisco: Ignatius Press, 1990.

Conley, Dalton. *The Pecking Order: Which Siblings Succeed and Why*. New York: Pantheon, 2004.

Cosby, Bill. *Love and Marriage*. New York: Doubleday, 1989.

Cott, Nancy F. *Public Vows*. Cambridge, MA: Harvard University Press, 2000.

Fein, Ellen, and Sherrie Schneider. *The Rules for Marriage: Time-Tested Secrets for Making Your Marriage Work*. New York: Warner Books, 2001.

Figes, Kate, and Jean Zimmerman. *Life after Birth*. New York: St. Martin's Press, 2001.

Fulghum, Robert. *True Love*. New York: HarperCollins, 1997.

Gookin, Sandra Hardin. *Parenting for Dummies*. Indianapolis, IN: IDG Books, 1995.

Graff, E. J. *What Is Marriage For?* Boston: Beacon Press, 1999.

Groopman, Jerome. *The Anatomy of Hope*. New York: Random House, 2004.

Hartog, Hendrick. *Man and Wife in America*. Cambridge, MA: Harvard University Press, 2000.

Henner, Marilu, and Ruth Velikovsky. *I Refuse to Raise a Brat*. New York: ReganBooks, 1999.

Houghton, Alanson B. *Partners in Love*. New York: Walker, 1988.

Jacobs, Michael B. *Taking Care: Self-Care for 100 Common Symptoms and 20 Long-Term Ailments*. New York: Random House, 1997.

Koman, Aleta, and Edward Myers. *The Parenting Survival Kit*. New York: Perigee, 2000.

L'Engle, Madeleine. *Two-Part Invention: The Story of a Marriage*. New York: Harper & Row, 1988.

Mason, Linda. *The Working Mother's Guide to Life*. New York: Three Rivers Press, 2002.

Minirth, Frank, Mary Alice Minirth, Brian Newman, Deborah Newman, Robert Hemfelt, and Susan Hemfelt. *Passages of Marriage*. Nashville, TN: Thomas Nelson, 1991.

Mullen, Tom. *A Very Good Marriage*. Richmond, IN: Friends United Press, 2001.

Porter, Valerie. *The Guinness Book of Marriage*. London: Guinness, 1991.

Rogers, Fred. *The Mister Rogers Parenting Book*. Philadelphia: Running Press, 2002.

Schlessinger, Laura. *Parenthood by Proxy: Don't Have Them If You Won't Raise Them*. New York: Cliff Street Books, 2000.

Schlosberg, Suzanne, and Liz Neporent. *Fitness for Dummies*. Indianapolis, IN: IDG Books, 2000.

Siegel, Bernie S. *How to Live Between Office Visits*. New York: HarperCollins, 1993.

———. *Love, Medicine and Miracles*. New York: Harper & Row, 1986.

———. *Peace, Love and Healing*. New York: Harper & Row, 1989.

Smalley, Gary. *Making Love Last Forever*. Nashville, TN: Word, 1996.

Smith, Sidney J. *Before Saying Yes to Marriage*. New York: Sidney James, 2000.

Stoop, David, and Jan Stoop. *The Complete Marriage Book*. Grand Rapids, MI: Fleming H. Revell, 2002.

Swanson, David W. *Mayo Clinic on Chronic Pain*. Rochester, MN: Mayo Clinic, 1999.

Taylor, Maurice, and Seana McGee. *The New Couple*. San Francisco: HarperSanFrancisco, 2000.

Tobias, Andrew. *The Only Investment Guide You'll Ever Need*. New York: Harcourt, 2002.

Viorst, Judith. *Grown-Up Marriage*. New York: Free Press, 2003.

———. *Necessary Losses*. New York: Ballantine, 1987.

———. *Yes, Married*. New York: Fawcett, 1973.

Wagner, Laurie, Stephanie Rausser, and David Collier. *Living Happily Ever After*. San Francisco: Chronicle Books, 1996.

Wallerstein, Judith S., and Sandra Blakeslee, *The Good Marriage*. Boston: Houghton Mifflin, 1995.

Wright, Norman. *Quiet Times for Couples*. San Diego: Harvest House, 1990.

Yalom, Marilyn. *A History of the Wife*. New York: HarperCollins, 2001.

Index

About the Author

David Yount is the author of thirteen books on faith, spirituality, and confident living. His internationally syndicated column, Amazing Grace, appears weekly in newspapers with a combined readership of 25 million. He also hosts a weekly prime-time cable TV program over Comcast.

Dr. Yount has counseled hundreds of married couples and men and women contemplating marriage. In a long career he has been a college dean, seminary chairman, foundation president, and an award-winning newspaper editor.

He and his wife live on a lake in Virginia with two cats and a Scottish terrier. The Younts have three adult daughters and two granddaughters.